'*Heart of a Game Ranger* reveals the stark reality of the ranger's life in a time of crisis brought on by rhino poaching. For rangers, their beloved bush has become a killing field and they reluctant soldiers. But amid this unfolding drama, veteran ranger Mario Cesare also offers the reader wonderfully uplifting stories of the bushveld.'

– Karen Trendler, Working Wild

N
W E
S

Phalaborwa

Olifants North
Olifants River
KRUGER PARK

Sedumoni

Barrage

OLIFANTS
River Game Reserve

Goedehoop

Ingwelala

BALULE
Nature Reserve

UMBABAT
Nature Reserve

Olifants River

Brakspruit

KLASERIE
Nature Reserve

Klaserie

TIMBAVATI
Nature Reserve

• Hoedspruit

KAPAMA
Game Reserve

Hermansburg

KRUGER PARK

Blyde Dam

Hans Hoheisen

Orpen

• Ohrigstad

• Pilgrims Rest

• Acornhoek

• Lydenburg

• Bushbuckridge

SOUTH AFRICA

SABI SANDS
Game Reserve

Mala Mala

• Hazyview

• Whiteriver

HEART OF A
GAME RANGER

Stories from a Wild Life

MARIO CESARE

Jonathan Ball Publishers
Johannesburg and Cape Town

To Benjamin Osmers (Bennie)

Originally published in South Africa in 2017 by
JONATHAN BALL PUBLISHERS
A division of Media24 (Pty) Ltd
PO Box 33977
Jeppestown
2043

Reprinted twice in 2017 and once in 2018

This limited edition printed twice in 2021

ISBN 978-1-86842-752-9
Ebook ISBN 978-1-86842-753-6

*Every effort has been made to trace the copyright holders and to obtain
their permission for the use of copyright material. The publishers apologise
for any errors or omissions and would be grateful to be notified of any
corrections that should be incorporated in future editions of this book.*

Twitter: www.twitter.com/JonathanBallPub
Facebook: www.facebook.com/JonathanBallPublishers
Blog: http://jonathanball.bookslive.co.za

Cover design by publicide
Design and typesetting by Triple M Design
Printed and bound by CTP Cape Town
Set in 10.5 pt/15 pt Bauer Bodoni

CONTENTS

FOREWORD

It has been a privilege to know Mario and Meagan Cesare and their wonderful family for well over a decade. They are a charming and handsome couple but their bonhomie conceals a formidable and dedicated team engaged in combating one of the most challenging and reprehensible scourges of modern Africa.

For those raised here or attracted from abroad, there has always been an undeniable mystique attached to the Dark Continent. It was originally captured in the remarkable exploits of pioneers such as Frederick Courteney Selous, Colonel James Stevenson-Hamilton, Harry Wolhuter and Sir Percy FitzPatrick, to name but a few. These extraordinary characters faced drought, famine, flood and political turmoil with epic determination and resolution. Thankfully they preserved their experiences in their compelling writings, creating a genre of exciting and fascinating African literature.

The distant pioneering days have sadly returned with a dreadful twist. Political turmoil is now coupled with hi-tech criminals. Drought and flood recur with tenacious and devastating regularity, and armed conflict has taken on a new bizarre face with deviously innovative, greedy, mostly Asian and Middle Eastern so-called 'businessmen' exploiting impoverished locals for the widespread slaughter of irreplaceable national assets. The stakes are high, the returns irresistible, and the consequences tragic.

The men, and women, combating this curse are epitomised by modern heroes like the Cesare family, their illustrious canine Saba and a small core of loyal anti-poaching rangers. In the great tradition of their famous historic predecessors, they are worth their weight in gold, but are working more for love than for money, exposed to long hours, characterised by associated frustration and ever-present danger, the prime goal being to protect a continent's diminishing irreplaceable resources.

This book is a compelling, hard-hitting revelation of the perils and problems faced by the conservationists of this world written with direct and disarming candour in characteristic riveting style. It describes instances and circumstances that would make a Hollywood scriptwriter drool, but they are all too grippingly real.

In microcosm Mario Cesare vividly captures the ambience and magic of a magnificent private game reserve, but the story of that community located in its comparatively small paradise reflects the dilemmas and tragedy of the entire African continent and other parts of our world too. As humanity penetrates the solar system and moves beyond to the stars, perhaps it is worth reflecting on what it will take to protect our own precious planet, before we embark on pursuing more universal exploration.

This is a fascinating story narrated by an expert, a consummate officer and gentleman, but also a tough, relentless and thoroughly committed professional who, in the great tradition of the fabled Mounties, almost always gets his man and is not hesitant to tell it exactly like it is!

Douglas McClure

INTRODUCTION

In my first book, *Man-eaters, Mambas and Marula Madness*, I focused on sharing my passion for the African wilderness and its myriad life forms by taking the reader into the bush with me. From my earliest youthful recollections I tell of a passionate journey as an aspirant young ranger through to my experiences as warden of Olifants River Game Reserve, where my feet are now firmly planted. In my second, *The Man with the Black Dog*, I tell of the extraordinary relationship between me and my dog Shilo, and our lives and adventures in the bush together. *Heart of a Game Ranger* continues in a similar vein with an added sense of profundity. I also like to believe that a growing maturity cuts through some of the blinkered infatuation with life in the bush and delves into the depths of some of the challenging circumstances facing nature conservation today; a precursor to the focus that has inexorably shifted, shaping the broader mind-set of the modern-day game ranger.

Although this book can be picked up and opened at any chapter, or read through in sequence, essentially there are three gently interwoven – yet broadly defined – parts. My experiences on Olifants have provided unique conservation challenges in a rich life full of situations that have been anything but routine. There are stories of general interest as well as those I have selected from the numerous unpredictable situations that involve other wildlife in conservation-related situations. This is the nature of my work in Big Five country and is what makes it so worthwhile being a game ranger. Essentially it's all about beautiful

OLIFANTS RIVER GAME RESERVE

State land

Olifants North

Olifants River

Notorious
Bridge

Kudu Pan •   Flood Plains

Sedumoni River   Driftwood Drive   DINIDZA

SPEAKERS CNR   OFFICE M+M   Olifants River
Game Reserve

Phansi link   Pride Rock

Idube Dam   Nyosi Pan •   Tau Kopje

Serengeti   Jackal Plains

Bridge   *Pels Loop*

Warthog Wallow   • *Hide Dam*

River Drive   *Double Dam* •

Warthog Pan •   • *Sand Dam*

Mariepskop View   • *Nkonkoni Dam*

Figtree grove   *Big Dam* •

Olifants River   Nature's Valley

Palm Loop   Buffalo Plains

UKHOZI   • Wild dog Pan   KLASERIE
GAME
RESERVE

• Lion Pan

Brakspruit River   Tau 2   The Wallows

• Rhino Pan

Sable Plains

Hyena Lair

Rhino Pens   • *Sable Dam*

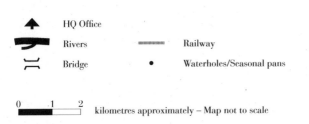

▲ HQ Office

▬ Rivers   ⊪⊪⊪⊪ Railway

⊐⊏ Bridge   • Waterholes/Seasonal pans

0   1   2
▬▬▭▭ kilometres approximately – Map not to scale

Reserve HQ co-ordinates: 24° 07' 12. 23'S 31° 01' 50.43'E

days that end in exhausted satisfaction and achievement, balanced by those that inexorably leave us in utter despair and frustration.

Being part of a huge open system that includes the greater Kruger National Park, we face the same threats to our wildlife as the rest of our country's national parks – particularly as regards rhino poaching. There is no clear-cut definition: rhino do not live and die in isolation; they share the stage with numerous other wildlife, including a number of lesser-known but equally threatened species.

Much has already been written that delves into the detail of the criminality, the nameless middlemen, syndicates and end users, even conjecture of high-level political involvement in rhino poaching. There is also the ongoing debate around the pros and cons of trade versus no trade. My intention is not to regurgitate the plethora of facts already out there, but rather to give the reader a deeper insight, a personal take on the situation as a conservationist, seen through my eyes and spoken from the heart.

My aim is to take you along as we get up close and personal, recounting some hair-raising incidents and the personalities involved at the core of the fray, in day-to-day life on the front line, to show what we are up against and our endeavours to tackle the specific poaching problem on our reserve.

Delving deeper into the realities, you will concur that Queensberry Rules simply have to take a backseat at times: combating rhino poachers is an adaptive style of brawling born of necessity. To this end I have become a street fighter in order to effectively mix it with brutal killers spawned in the gutters of humanity. It's an ugly conflict, a deadly game of hit and run played out on some of the most beautiful battlefields in Africa. Invariably these incidents comprise small forays, most of which we lose, losses that are made endurable by those times we put poachers to flight using both hi-tech and lo-tech methods followed by disruptive action. I will also attempt to share with you the heartbreak and sense of utter helplessness when we lose a rhino – and the euphoria of success when we save one. Of course there are also the rarer, bittersweet occasions that culminate in the apprehension and arrest of poachers, so be prepared for a roller-coaster ride through some emotional ups and downs and surprising twists of excitement.

It also needs to be said that conservation is losing more than rhino. In the wake of this scourge, we are losing valuable men and women as it becomes increasingly apparent that its consequences are deeper rooted than a simple scenario of good guys versus bad guys. I hope to paint the reader a picture of the poignant effect this has had, and is having, on the psyche of the wardens and their families engaged in this desperate struggle to preserve the rhino from extinction.

To combat rhino poaching on the reserve, we rely on a small but effective unit of trained field rangers employed by Olifants River Game Reserve. However, from time to time we make use of outsourced security on an ad-hoc basis, a combination that has worked well at limiting the number of rhino killed in our region. Despite the relentless onslaught, our dedicated rangers have kept the wolf from the door for long periods at a time.

Relating to the incredible variety of innovative thought that has gone into combating rhino poaching, this book would be incomplete without a brief mention of the unique all-women anti-poaching team known as the Black Mambas, to whom I have dedicated a chapter.

In addition to and among the countless tactics and techniques deployed against rhino poachers recently, one of the most effective is proving to be the deployment of trained canine units. So much so that I have devoted a portion of this book to the acquisition, life and training of a Belgian Malinois named Saba. She is one of the finest anti-poaching dogs in the field today and, I am proud to say, has been the precursor to the adoption of countless Malinois and other breeds that are now being trained for anti-poaching work countrywide.

BASIC INSTINCT

The buffalo cow's rasping tongue and wet nose were her newborn calf's first tactile impressions of the world outside. In stark contrast to the comfortable darkness of her womb, his big brown eyes now blinked in the brassy sunlight, its warmth complementing his mother's loving attention. It felt good. Suddenly she stopped licking, lifted her head and let out a harsh snort. The next thing the tiny buffalo felt was an approaching rumble, which shook the ground of his strange new world. Confusion and terror caused him instinctively to lie flat. And not a moment too soon as the hooves and horns of a hundred tons of African buffalo merged into a grinding mass. Like a black cloud in a red sandstorm, a thousand hooves thundered past kicking up clouds of fine dust, which hung in the air long after the reverberations had faded. Black on red blended, now dark brown; the little buffalo's coat, which his mother had meticulously groomed only moments before, was one with its surrounds. Then, slowly lifting his head, the calf blinked the dust from his eyeballs and looked around: he was alone.

A successful breeding season in South Africa's big game country, like that in any wilderness area, is reflected in the sights and sounds of newborn animals. Vulnerable and wide-eyed with bewilderment, they begin the most testing time of their lives, a necessary process for any baby and its mother. And it is the outcome of this ability to cope as a unit that determines the status of the species as a whole.

As self-appointed guardians of wildlife, conservationists are aware of these processes. However, recent events on the reserve have seen an increased level of 'intervention' in the natural order of things. Call it what you will, essentially well-meaning actions are often viewed as interference by man in the natural balance of an open system. Pundits, under the guise of science, argue against and criticise these undertakings, labelling those who advocate them as being 'bunny huggers' or professionally irresponsible. Others are moved by Gandhi's words: 'The greatness of a nation and its moral progress can be judged by the way its animals are treated.' Here's my take on this.

Our knowledge of ecology and the complex processes that drive natural systems is continually improving. We learn, even from our armchairs, that similar scenes to those being witnessed on our reserve at any point in time are being played out in the wilder parts of the world in various forms every day, and that the science behind nature's success is by definition a dispassionate sequence of events. Strictly speaking, human emotions – particularly feelings of empathy, pity and compassion – need to be taken out of the equation, or, at the very least, put into context. However, though we are constantly reminded that 'nature should be allowed to take its course', there is *nowhere* on earth that can be defined as 'pristine'; nowhere has the hand of man not had some influence on the environment in one way or another. So it's a question of what we define as natural, which in turn is determined by the degree of effect we have had on the environment. Needless to say, there will be a constant need to modify, manipulate and update this definition.

Most people on their first safari to Africa's Big Game country want to see a kill more than anything else, preferably a lion kill. On the other hand, seasoned visitors to the bush are less driven to witness the process in minute detail. As our attention shifts, the brutal reality of predator–prey relationships – the ongoing struggle for survival, to eat or be eaten – gradually ceases to be an all-encompassing focus. Indeed some of us find we never really harden or get complacent about it. Most move on to discover myriad other facets that make up countless nuances and experiences the bush has on offer. Over time, the fervour to get in among the blood and gore of these often dramatic scenes wanes. Instead we immerse ourselves in the deeper layers of Africa's fascinating wilderness, absorbing more of its complex intricacies with each experience.

Of course there will always be those with a more macabre bent for whom the hunting process becomes a fascinating study in itself: the more gruesome and dramatic the kill is, the higher on the scale their viewing experience is rated. However, it has been my experience throughout my career as a game ranger, having dealt with people from all over the world, that the vast majority who fall in love with Africa never lose their fascination with its super-predators. I suspect this sentiment has more than a little to do with the fact that lions and leopards, for example, are well equipped for the task and generally kill quickly. But not all predators are as well built for the kill as these huge cats are; there are vastly varying degrees and ever-changing circumstances. So it comes as no surprise that over-confident lions, as well as lesser predators, will occasionally bite off more than they can chew ... or at least attempt to.

As game rangers, this complex subject is further complicated by our individual personas; there cannot be too many grey areas of intervention open to interpretation in our jobs. For example, do we turn a blind eye to an impala with a broken leg, and 'leave it to nature', but immobilise a limping rhino to remove a splinter from its foot? Do we leave a lion to die slowly from wounds sustained when it is mauled by others in a territorial battle, while we treat another injured by the train? Or is it acceptable to abandon an elephant with a broken foot knowing how poor the prognosis is? ... I believe not.

I advocate human intervention wherever and whenever it can prevent or alleviate unnecessary suffering, particularly where actions by man, deliberate or accidental, can be shown to have been directly responsible, and where it can be carried out with zero or minimal disturbance to the natural process being played out. So I believe we should try and do what we can, whenever we can. Even if this means having to put a suffering animal out of its misery, as in the example of the impala with a broken leg ... or, for that matter, any wild animal where there is no alternative but for it to be left in the bush to die in agony with little or no hope of survival. However, going out to place a band-aid on every Bambi's bleeding buttock is not going to happen, nor will we be rescuing all the apparently orphaned animals we come across. Having said that, there will be occasions when we are faced with a decision that threatens to send this marriage of emotions off for some serious counselling.

Predictability and certainty are two words you won't find in the bushveld dictionary. In the wild, survival depends on evolutionary attributes that have been honed through the millennia, characteristics that include a strong territorial imperative, adaptive strategy and opportunism, to name but a few. In human beings many of these primal instincts have been lost altogether, but there are a few basic traits we all share and I suspect will always share, notably those that enable us to form relationships. Associations born of mutual dependence and friendship occur throughout the natural world in symbiotic relationships between different species, right down to those dispassionately fixed to survival, such as lichen. But there is another – one that irrevocably stirs a deep primal passion and knows no boundaries. Even science has been known to take a backseat in the face of this powerful force; indeed, most species living today owe their survival to it. I refer specifically to that of any mother's love for her young ... which brings me back to the baby buffalo.

Ever intrusive, often necessary, but occasionally entertaining, the two-way radio crackled, breaking the mid-morning lull with a tentative but familiar 'Mario, Mario, please come in'.

Although I could detect a lilt of urgency in the caller's tone, it lacked the usual irritation that most of the reserve's shareholders try to control but often find hard to hide, particularly when their gas has run out or their game-viewing vehicle has broken down. I immediately recognised the voice as that of Olifants' director Louise Cleary, and depressed the button on the microphone to answer.

'Hi Louise, I'm reading you. Go ahead. Over.'

A tentative 'umm' followed by the tailing click of the repeater as the microphone button was released to an empty silence. This was unusual for Louise, whose legal background instilled in her an authoritative confidence most of the time, like when on more than one occasion I have seen contentious issues and boiling testosterone reduced to a simmer while she held the floor and sagely put things in perspective at our board meetings.

'Umm ... we're at Sable Dam ... and there's a tiny buffalo calf being harassed by three black-backed jackals.'

Another, longer, pause.

And then, her voice even softer now, 'Is there anything we can do to help the poor thing?'

Having learned over the years that predators and scavengers do an excellent job of taking care of the weak, sick or injured in Big Five country such as Olifants, I replied in a matter-of-fact manner, glibly mumbling something about the jackals also needing to eat. But before waiting for a response, I quickly qualified what may have sounded callous, adding that the calf had probably been abandoned for reasons that may not be immediately obvious to us but were to its mother. Of course I had no idea of the drama that was unfolding in front of the people there, nor could I know that Louise's ecological awareness meant her decision to call me in the first place had taken nearly an hour of soul-searching. And despite the predicament she knew I was being put in, her primal instinct was kicking in and involuntarily overriding all else. There was no question: Louise could not escape the fact that first and foremost she was a mother.

As I said earlier, to further complicate these already complex matters there is mankind's consciousness, the basic instincts that have gelled into our make-up as human beings (scientists included, of course). So, like it or not, certain emotions are highly developed and ingrained in our genes, not least the primal power of motherly instinct, which is one we share with almost every other animal species on the planet. Whether you're a cantankerous buffalo cow protecting your calf (of which I have first-hand experience and the scars to prove it) or a human mother, the involuntary urge to protect your young, and sometimes even those of another species, is stronger than reason: it overrides logic and common sense. So it is understandable that this resignation to the inevitable, in this instance by a mother witnessing the drama unfold, would be thickly clouded with emotion. But as no two situations are ever identical in Africa's bushveld, I knew I needed to go out to the scene and assess things for myself.

Knowing what call to make under these circumstances can be very difficult. More often than not it has to be made on the spur of the moment ... and, as we know, there's no antidote for a bullet once it has left the barrel. Also, technically speaking, shooting a buffalo without a permit is against the law. But game rangers are tuned to run their best on a cocktail of practical science, emotion and circumstance ... a blended fuel, if you like. Vivid mental images of the buffalo calf being eaten by three determined but relatively small, hungry mouths was not painting a pretty picture in my mind. I knew the calf would take an agonisingly long time to die while bleating plaintively until its last breath. The least I could do was assist the process with a quicker, less painful death, I thought.

'I'll be there in 15 minutes,' I replied. Picking up my keys, I turned and walked over to the strongroom. I hardly heard the metallic clang of the lock on the huge door as I opened the gun safe, walked in and grabbed my .22 rifle. My mind was focused elsewhere in preparation and acceptance; for the rest it was mechanical. This would be the second time in as many days that the little weapon was going to be needed for humane work.

Arriving at Sable Dam, I saw three jackals standing in the open. Normally cautious and furtive, these little coyotes of Africa were quite unperturbed by my sudden approach. Apparently they had eaten the buffalo's afterbirth earlier, and clearly the taste of what could constitute the main course had their full attention. The jackals were now focused on what was going to prove a huge task for them; apparently they'd already been up to the calf, almost muzzle to muzzle, testing it ... sizing it up. Growing bolder, they were clearly determined to take it on, but were also cunning enough to know they would need help. One of them howled repeatedly: its high-pitched call for reinforcements would carry a good distance across the bushveld; soon there would be more jackals arriving. Then, with their strict territorial imperative temporarily put on hold, they'd band as one, attack as a pack, kill and feed as a pack ... There'd be plenty to go around.

I was relieved to see the killing had not yet begun. Louise tried to look composed as I approached her vehicle. She was trying unsuccessfully to hide the tears welling up behind her sunglasses, which now looked like a pair of badly fitting scuba goggles, a picture of utter sadness. I drove up alongside to find her teenage daughter Jennifer and son Tim leaning across to my side. Gesturing to the base of an African wattle tree, they pointed out the shape of an apparently terrified buffalo calf that had taken refuge in the shade. Hmmm ... 'terrified', I mused ... not an adjective I'd normally use when referring to this species.

As I approached the buffalo calf, which had been lying in the cool, dark recesses of the tree's lower branches, it lurched to its feet. Standing up on little hooves that were only starting to harden in the dry air, it teetered on legs that until a few hours ago had been cloistered in the warm comfort and protection of its mother's belly. Then it slowly moved out into the sunlight, steadying itself on splayed legs. I could now clearly see the bloody remnant of its umbilical cord. The calf was no more than a few hours old, eight at the most. Even so, at some point in its infantile reckoning it must have realised its life was being threatened by the jackals and instinctively sought the thickest bush it could find to back into. In this case, the wattle tree with its soft green foliage had created a soft shroud that seemingly provided enough protection for the time being.

Despite being so young, and with absolutely no life experience to draw on, this tiny buffalo was born with an inherent never-say-die attitude, a trait indelibly etched on its genes, one this species is well known for the world over. However, as courageous as its defence was, deep down I knew resistance on this scale was futile and would only postpone the inevitable: the jackals would attack it relentlessly until,

7

weakened by lack of nourishment, the calf would no longer be able to stand – then the killing would begin.

As hard as this was to accept, there was also something about this little buffalo's determination and will to live that made me look at this situation differently. This calf was no runt; it appeared perfectly normal in every respect, and its coat had been lovingly licked clean; despite the dusty hue, it glistened in the sunlight as if recently shampooed. From the circumstantial evidence I was able to glean, I strongly suspected this calf had not been deliberately abandoned. So, acting purely on gut feel, I made a judgement call and decided there was 'reasonable doubt' in this case. Somehow we had to try and reunite the calf with its biological mother, fully aware that if we failed there'd be no option of adoption or 'rehab': we would then have to abandon the brave little calf to its fate – or, as the Spanish say, *Que sera, sera* ...

Calling out across the clearing to Louise, I asked her where the rest of the herd had moved to. From her explanation it was apparent they'd been seen more than a kilometre to the west of the water hole, relatively far away yet close enough to be worth a try, I thought. To compound our dilemma, baby buffalo don't wear name tags, nor do buffalo cows file missing calf reports, so how the hell were we going to find its mom among 50 others without getting severely gored or worse in the process? But there was no time to debate the issue; we needed to act quickly.

Confident that the herd, but more importantly the calf's mother, was far enough away to pose no danger to us, I climbed down from the Land Cruiser and, with my hand outstretched, slowly approached the little buffalo. The calf looked straight at me with its huge, confused eyes and then, still teetering on unsteady legs, moved cautiously towards me. Man, this was serious lump-in-the-throat stuff. Ever tentatively, the little buffalo came closer and closer, until it was within a few centimetres of my hand.

Ears flat and craning its neck now, the calf's broad, glistening nostrils flared as it audibly drew in the air around me. The smell of human sweat, mingled with a hint of the Paco Rabanne my kids got me for

Christmas, filled its infantile nasal receptors, causing it to retreat instantly. Incredibly, having no way of knowing other than instinct, and at only eight hours old, it already knew that the smell of man, however well masked, meant danger. The calf turned, trying to escape back to its refuge, but I had anticipated this move. Reflexively, my hand shot out and grabbed hold of one of its back legs. I called over my shoulder for Tim and his dad, Chris, to help me load the now-bellowing calf into my Land Cruiser. This done, we followed Louise's vehicle as she led the way to where the main herd of buffalo was last seen. We drove with purpose, and it wasn't long before we'd located the herd moving slowly through the bush on the edge of a seep-line.

Things needed to happen quickly; even so, it couldn't be a case of 'chuck and chance it'. There were a few important considerations to take into account: though I'd never done this before, at least I knew we needed to be downwind from the herd, then to drop the calf at precisely the right moment and distance from the herd, for this to have even a remote chance of working. Very importantly, the calf needed to bleat; to this end, it had to be literally 'dumped' out of the back. If its mother was within earshot, she would recognise her calf's call and come for her baby; at this point she'd be unstoppable, and I knew that. However, if even one buffalo in the herd saw anyone climb out of the Cruiser to try and gently offload the calf, it would cause the rest to stampede. With the herd spooked, we'd have to risk recapturing the calf and trying again once they had settled, and who knows how long that might take. There was no question: we were only going to get one shot at this.

The buffalo were moving slowly, grazing peacefully on the lush grass, totally unaware of what we had bundled up in the back of my pick-up. I slowly drove into the bush, getting in front of the herd; then, manoeuvring the vehicle in reverse, I managed to back up to within 30 metres of them. Unfortunately, it wasn't all going our way ... as luck would have it, two huge bulls were on the perimeter of the herd closest to us, and they lifted their heads curiously at our approach. Buffalo hunters will tell you that when you're looking for big bulls they're usually to be found tailing the herd or surrounded by sharp-eyed, radar-eared cows.

9

But Murphy had decided *this* was how it was going to go down today.

Undaunted, I was confident that somewhere among them was one particular buffalo who was feeling a little different from the rest. One who felt an uncomfortable ache from her swollen udder, an unexplained emptiness where only hours before was the fullness of a growing weight she had carried for months. Something was still raw and incomplete, and as the mother of a new baby, her hormones were ill at ease. I was reasonably sure this would be enough to keep her just that little bit more aware than the rest. She would be alert and on edge; I was banking on that.

African buffalo are extremely resilient, so don't get me wrong: within a few days or so, I believe she would have forgotten about the birth and the loss of her calf as she focused on survival. But right now I knew she was more than simply one of the most dangerous animals in Africa with a strong herding instinct: she was also the mother of a newborn baby.

Chris leaned over the tailgate of the Land Cruiser and, without showing too much of himself, managed to drop the calf onto the grass. Perfect, I thought, driving away as quickly as the terrain would allow; unfortunately it wasn't fast enough to leave the calf behind. Having now bonded with its 'captors', and not wanting to be deserted again, the little calf hobbled after us bleating pathetically. Thankfully, it didn't get far, stumbling headlong into some thick undergrowth and a small bushwillow, where it tripped and fell, halting its progress, but thankfully not the bleating.

The big buffalo bulls closest to us had hardly started to move in our direction when, from within the main body of the herd, a buffalo cow came charging in, followed closely by a young heifer. The cow, obviously the calf's mother, went straight in to rescue the baby buffalo from the tangle of undergrowth. Once done she gave the tiny calf a quick reassuring lick-cum-nuzzle, further proof that she had not deserted this calf of her own volition, then she spun around to face us. The look she gave us didn't say 'thank you for saving my baby' – far from it – it was more a look that said 'Bring it on!' Knowing them as I do, I would not have expected anything less from a buffalo.

African buffalo are neither endangered nor vulnerable; they don't need our 'help'. Truth be told, in relation to the available resources in our reserves, there are simply too many of them. So why bother saving one more, you may well ask ... Why not allow nature to take its course? Dispassionately speaking, if this had been shown to be a totally natural situation, where man's hand had no part or influence in what had occurred, then sure, we could have turned away coldly and allowed the fittest to survive. However, I can argue, with some conviction, that the predicament this calf found itself in was more likely to have been precipitated by man, to some degree, than by an entirely natural sequence of events.

Prey species such as buffalo are always a little edgy in the vicinity of water holes. These focal points create perfect ambush settings; they are relatively small areas of mass congregation that can sometimes lead to confusion or panic, and predators know this. A buffalo cow giving birth or having just given birth is at her most vulnerable. So, being in the proximity of a water hole exacerbates the problem, and this is all the more reason for not only her but the whole herd to be jittery; it is at this time that even the smallest scare could cause a stampede.

Once I'd seen the calf up close, it was clear in my mind that this apparently healthy animal had not simply been abandoned. This was later confirmed by the mother's reaction when reunited with her calf. Yet still the question remained, why was it on its own? Were the buffalo ambushed when they came down to drink? Or could the predator's strategy have been to coldly calculate and wait for the calf to be born, licked clean and up onto its feet before they attacked? These were just some of the questions that raised doubts about the predator hypothesis. It was highly unlikely that predators lying in ambush would exercise this degree of patience, and even if they had the calf or its mother, or indeed both, would have been taken shortly afterwards, while both were at their most vulnerable.

I believe that there is a more probable scenario. Given that there were an unusually high number of visitors traversing the reserve at the time, there is every chance the already nervous herd could inadvertently have been stampeded by a game viewer. Whatever it was, there can be no doubt that pandemonium ensued when the buffalo herd stampeded. The resulting cloud of dust, kicked up by hundreds of thundering hooves, would have been enough to disorientate the newborn calf, causing separation from its mother in the confusion. According to RD Estes' *The Behavior Guide to African Mammals*, buffalo mothers can be pulled in both directions, shuffling between the newborn calf and the herd. But sometimes the pull of the herd is stronger and young calves are abandoned.

Folklore tells of the slave Androcles who removes a thorn from a wild lion's paw. Years later he comes face to face with the same lion in a Roman arena; the lion recognises him immediately and instead of tearing him to pieces in front of the crowd, licks his hand. Needless to say, the Emperor spares both their lives ...

So maybe this was kismet ... Maybe one day when I am charged by a buffalo and my rifle misfires, when certain death is imminent ... Maybe out of the thick bush off to one side a huge buffalo bull will emerge, knocking the charging buffalo out of the way, saving my life ... Maybe the bull will turn around, look at me over its huge glistening nostrils, give me a wink and bellow ... 'Now we're even.' ... Maybe?

... Yeah, right!

WHAT'S IN A NAME?

Fig Tree Grove: a rather innocuous sounding name. One that conjures up thoughts of a niche drenched in a kaleidoscope of dappled shade dancing a *pas de deux* with whatever rays of sunlight penetrate through the leaves. Or perhaps a peaceful glade tucked away in a secluded corner of a garden in some eastern Mediterranean country. Not quite the spot one would expect to find on the banks of a crocodile-infested river in a Big Five game reserve in southern Africa. But this is where shareholders of the reserve are able to park their game viewer in the shade of a grove of huge sycamore fig trees, so it makes perfect sense. Those so inclined can alight in relative safety, stretch their legs and amble down to the river's edge a short distance away or simply enjoy a peaceful picnic off the beaten track.

People are naturally drawn to water, so were it not for the danger from the omnipresent crocodiles and hippo a short distance away, most would kick off their shoes and wander around in the relatively cool shallows of the river. In light of these risks, wading the shallows gives way to simply strolling on the sandy floodplain, which nonetheless is pleasant respite from having endured the robust suspension of a game viewer for hours.

Olifants River Game Reserve had received good rains that season, and although the bankside vegetation was particularly luxuriant, the receding river had left a narrow, ripple-lined stretch of tempting beach sand to walk on. None of the people alighting from the vehicle that day were under the age of 70; nevertheless, it was an easy walk and soon they were all making their way down the gentle slope to the stretch of sand.

They'd only stepped out a few metres from the vehicle when a snort and the sound of what they initially thought was a hippo came from the luxuriant undergrowth. Thick green reeds and lush cocklebur bushes gave way, flattened in a swathe, as the broad boss and wide horns of a huge buffalo bull scythed through the vegetation. Bearing down on the front of the group, the buffalo homed in on the leader, who had the presence of mind to dive into the thick stand of cocklebur and escape. With its intended victim now out of sight, the buffalo chose someone else, turning on a slightly built lady who had never played scrum half in her life and so couldn't dive out of its way with quite as much alacrity. Instead she stumbled in the soft sand and fell headlong into a narrow erosion gully, a fall that undoubtedly saved her life.

Those who witnessed the sequence of events unfold a few metres in front of them vividly remember being horrified at the buffalo's determination to get at the elderly lady lying in the ditch. It seemed to be fixated on her and no one else, sweeping its huge horns from side to side, trying to impale her. Fortunately, the bull's horns being wider in spread than the ditch's opening meant it couldn't get the viciously pointed curves in deep enough. Luckily it did not try this lengthwise along the ditch, but instead went down onto its knees trying to pound down on her with its huge boss, also to no avail. All the while the buffalo completely ignored the desperate shouts and screams from the rest of the group. Eventually, after what seemed like long minutes, the now apparently exhausted animal gave up and slowly moved off.

I was phoned shortly after the incident by shareholder Colin Mason who was evidently still in shock. Apart from the injured ribs sustained when he took the dive into the bush, Colin was unharmed and was able to relay the gist of the incident to me, the minutiae of which faded into grey noise. Expecting to hear the worst, all I could focus on was the good news that nobody had suffered any serious injury. Having narrowly escaped with my life after being attacked by a wounded buffalo 10 years previously, I knew how serious an attack from one of these powerful animals could be. African buffalo are arguably the most dangerous of Africa's Big Five, and when one of them makes up its mind to charge you, nothing but its death or yours will stop it.

Slowly I began to focus on what else Colin had to say. He went on to describe this particular buffalo to me in some detail. Admittedly, much of it could fit a number of cantankerous old buffalo known colloquially as 'dagga boys'. These are invariably old buffalo bulls that form small bachelor groups or sometimes prefer their own company. All of them have one penchant in common: they enjoy wallowing in mud wallows, primarily for the cooling effect, but also for the clay-like consistency, which serves to encrust ectoparasites such as ticks that become embedded in their thick hides. Many of these are rubbed off later along with the dried mud, usually against boulders or tree trunks. These features are well chosen, for being the right height and shape, and with regular use become highly polished rubbing posts over time. However, when Colin mentioned that this particular buffalo had a huge swelling on its front left leg, I immediately recognised the individual he was referring to.

This had been the third report of this buffalo's belligerent behaviour in the last two months, but nothing to date had indicated this level of determined aggression. It had chased my road maintenance team, who were fortunate enough to have a tractor and trailer to climb onto and escape. Two weeks later one of our security staff escaped from this bull by climbing a tree; he then called in on his two-way radio and was summarily rescued. In neither instance did the buffalo hang around after the initial charge.

There was no time to waste on doubtful speculation; I knew what needed to be done. Having made a quick call to the conservation authorities, whom I briefed on the situation and my probable intentions, I gathered all the gear I would need and drove straight to Fig Tree Grove. I was quickly able to verify the accuracy of Colin's story by the scuff marks, footprints and tracks left in the soft sand. Then I picked up a single set of buffalo tracks and followed them up a gully into some really thick bush leading away from the river bank. As there were no other tracks, I was certain this was the bull in question.

Although it is well known that buffalo, particularly old lone bulls, can be aggressive and are to be avoided at the best of times, unexpectedly walking into one happens to even the most cautious among us. Fortunately, in this scenario they are often as surprised as we are and run away most of the time. Unless wounded and relentlessly pursued, a buffalo will usually shy away from confrontation with humans. So for this buffalo to charge with dire intent, and for no apparent reason, when there were ample other options each time it came across people, was indeed unusual behaviour that needed to be investigated.

The distinctive 'natural growth' on this particular buffalo's left front knee was a result of brucellosis, a disease caused by the bacterium *Brucella abortus*. It had managed to live with this affliction for many years and, until recently, appeared unhindered by the swollen joint. However, I suspect that as the buffalo got older and infection began to set in, its aging system was finding it increasingly difficult to cope with sustained bacteria build-up. The buffalo began to lose condition, and the relentless pain it was suffering must have caused it to become aggressive, to the point where this animal now posed a serious threat to human life.

The buffalo's deterioration over the last few months was noticeable to the point where we were all expecting the lions to take it at any time, which although a natural end for old bulls like this, would have been a slow and painful death. But owing to this latest incident, given its propensity to attack without provocation, this buffalo could not be left to kill or injure anyone, nor indeed be allowed to suffer any more than he already had. Therefore I believed that the old bull should be taken out quickly and painlessly.

Although my analysis culminating in this decisive action had taken some time, my strategy as usual was to get it over with as soon as possible. There was no one to call in for backup at such short notice; so, for the second time in my life, I would be hunting a buffalo on my own, without a second gun. A fleeting thought did prick my conscience: was I being impatient and arrogant, or plain stupid? If I was seriously injured or killed it would be hours before anyone came to look for me.

However, in my mind, given the state the buffalo was in, I felt I had the advantage ... I felt it was a calculated risk.

It was long past midday now; the fig trees shielded the blazing sun overhead and drenched the grove in relatively cool shade. Yet I was sharply focused: this was no time to entertain any thoughts of a siesta to stave off the inevitable for the cooler part of the day. The sandy beach beyond the shady glade glared back in contrast, as if every tiny grain's facets were reflecting the sunlight, creating a scene that belied the near tragedy there only a couple of hours ago. Reflexively, I slid a round into the chamber of my .416 Rigby rifle and moved out into the sunlight.

It was easy to follow the old bull's tracks, which headed up a steep-sided gulley away from the river. Besides being the only set of tracks, confirmation that I was on the right spoor was revealed every now and then by droplets of foul smelling pus left on the sand. What little movement of air there was drifted down onto me. This was comforting: being on my own without any backup, I did not need him to get wind of me and run – or worse, come charging at me out of the thicket.

Having followed the tracks into the gully for a couple of hundred metres, I reached a point where the movement of air was minimal and the smell seemed to hang thick in the air. The buffalo was close; it was very close. And although I could smell the old bull, I still couldn't see him or hear him. Climbing up and out of the steep-sided gully I was able to gain the advantage by looking down into it. Having gone about 25 metres, I saw the back of a buffalo sticking out of some thick bush: his head was down as if the weight of those huge horns was just too much to keep up, his breathing laboured and deep; I knew it was him. He was facing away from me, totally unaware that I was right behind him. Reaching down I found a small stone, which I tossed onto his rump. He spun around in an instant, as if stung by a wasp, and glared straight up at me, his glistening nostrils flared. I took aim and squeezed the trigger. In the next instant the old bull was no longer in any pain.

Closer examination of the buffalo's foreleg showed that a gangrenous growth had developed around the cyst, which had burst in places and spewed pus each time he moved or tried to bend his leg. As the growth grew larger and larger it must have reached the point where he could no longer tolerate the pain. Little wonder he had such a dangerously short temper.

I took a couple of photos for the record, then using my knife, I opened the carcass where it lay. This would enable larger scavengers and myriad other organisms to utilise it and gain maximum benefit from its death.

BIG CATS OF OLIFANTS

'Spectacular' best describes the view from Sunset Plains: it never fails to impress. Today's scene at the most popular sundowner venue on the reserve was a veritable slice out of the Ngorongoro Crater cake. Oblivious of our presence, herds of wildebeest kicked up clouds of fine grey dust as they sandbathed in the flattened remains of ancient termite mounds. Zebra, impala and giraffe completed the mosaic that spread out before us. Stretching across the width of the plains and all the way to the horizon, their individual markings faded against a burnt-orange backdrop as the sun dipped behind the mountains, unmistakable forms that became familiar silhouettes. Two black-backed jackals scampered across in front of us without a sideways glance, clearly on a mission. I remember wondering where they were off to in such a hurry. All around us there was a hub of activity; everything was playing its part in preparation, in readiness for nightfall. It was awesome in every sense of the word.

We felt accepted as part of the scene, privileged to be in their company, which was clearly of the highest calibre. Come to think of it, the shareholders who had gathered around to share sundowners with us weren't too shabby either. For some, there is little to beat the crispness and promise of early dawn; for others, the bush at night exposes an exciting new dimension; for me, late afternoon to sundown has always been my favourite time of the day. But all good things come to an end, so with the onset of darkness we reluctantly packed up our respective coolers, said our goodbyes and headed home.

Meagan and I took the less-travelled route under the pylons, easing the Land Cruiser into third gear, driving slowly so as not to stir up too much dust for those following in open vehicles. We hadn't driven more than a few hundred metres when the radio crackled. Those shareholders who had taken the other route had come across a pride of 13 lions moving in to where we had stood sipping gin and tonics minutes before. Patient and well mannered, the lions had possibly waited for us to move off before homing in on the bounty milling about only a couple of hundred metres away. Only the jackals I'd seen earlier had an inkling of their proximity. For a jackal, knowing where the lions were often meant the prospect of leftovers from a possible kill. It was just one of their cunning survival strategies; lions amid so much prey meant there was an excellent chance something would go down that night.

What a thrilling end to the day!

There is little that excites a visitor to Africa more than a pride of lions on the hunt. And though this is undoubtedly a scenario that takes some beating, there have been times when being impressed didn't revolve around seeing lions. In fact, our reserve's very existence owes much to another big cat. Somewhat more elusive and enigmatic than lions, leopards nevertheless occur here in good numbers, but, owing to their solitary habits, are not seen nearly so frequently.

Back in the late eighties the developers of Olifants River Game Reserve needed more than delusional optimism to realise their dream. As pragmatists they knew that vision alone was not going to do it. They had to convince the local bank manager of the reserve's potential in order to facilitate the substantial bank loan needed to get the development ball rolling. However, the timing could not have been worse for their sales spiel – not only was the bush wearing its winter coat, which caused the railway and power lines to stand out like pimples on a pasty face, but most of the roads were in desperate need of repair and a succession of low rainfall years had taken its toll on wildlife numbers. Needless to say, the game drive was unconvincing, yielding very little for the hours spent bumbling around in the heat that morning. In a desperate last-ditch effort, it was decided to have one last look at a small water hole en route to returning for a late brunch.

At first they must have thought their eyes were playing tricks on them. That perhaps, like the illusion of water created by a heat mirage in the desert to a thirsty person, here was an image of something just as desperately needed. Only this was no shimmering mirage. As the dust settled, everything sharpened into focus, emphasising its reality. Against the far earth wall, in the dappled shade of an overhanging bush, lay a huge male leopard. Although nobody had told the bank manager what a privilege it was to see one, or how infrequently one comes across these elusive cats, he must have known. Later he admitted that seeing that leopard, which appeared so utterly at home and content, was what swung him round.

To reiterate that leopard sightings are a rarity to be cherished, a prominent founder shareholder of the reserve had to wait 15 years before spotting his first leopard. Not that they were particularly scarce during those early years, rather I suspect it took a while for these wary felines to realise that approaching game viewers meant them no harm, and that there was no need to hide or slink away whenever they saw or heard one approach, which was something these shy cats invariably did, particularly when a second vehicle approached the sighting.

I am often asked how many leopards I think occur on Olifants ... Well, here's my answer – though I must add, it is not given without a good measure of extrapolation and thought, taking scientific population censuses from studies done in areas with similar habitats and prey densities into account. Personal observations and recorded sightings by shareholders over the last 23 years were tallied, as well as unofficial reports from our field rangers and farm hands. Based on a judicious compilation of the above, and personal gut feel, my conservative estimate is that that there are somewhere between 18 and 24 leopards on Olifants – or broadly speaking, for the Balule Reserve, one leopard for every 500 hectares. Taking the overlapping nature of male leopards' territories into account would increase the number a little. I would err on the high side, as I believe there are usually more leopards about than we suspect, as the following study illustrates.

Owing to an upsurge of incidents involving leopards in the staff village of Skukuza, the Kruger National Park's largest camp, an in-depth scientific study of the status of leopards in the area was called for. Results from collaring and subsequent monitoring revealed there were many more leopards than anyone had previously thought. In fact, the study revealed that over 30 leopards called this camp and its immediate environs home! Not surprising when one understands a little more about the predator–prey relationship in this scenario. The dense acacia bushveld and lush riparian habitat around Skukuza supports high numbers of impala, the primary prey species of leopards in the Lowveld. However, there can be no doubt that these already ideal conditions were boosted by resident staff, whose domestic pets, refuse dumps and leafy gardens created additional prey and more hunting opportunities.

'Adaptable' has to be this species' middle name. As the Skukuza study discovered, many leopards can live in a relatively small area provided there is a plethora of prey. This was revealed when rangers at Mala Mala Game Reserve, well known for its abundant game, recorded a simultaneous viewing of eight different leopards at different localities across the reserve! Studies in the Lowveld area have also revealed that male leopards weighing over 75 kilograms are not uncommon and specimens approaching 85 kilograms have been recorded, with an exceptional brute weighing over 90 kilograms recorded in the Gravelotte area. It is clear, then, that if a system can provide a leopard's needs, they will thrive – not only in numbers but in size.

On the other extreme, leopards found in the Middle East – eking out an existence in the highlands of Iran and Pakistan – are small: an average adult male only weighs around 25 kilograms. Owing to the scarcity of prey and persecution by stock farmers, population studies of these mountain-dwelling leopards also reveal a much lower density-to-area ratio than that of their bushveld–savanna cousins. Apparently those in the Western Cape fare a little better: although life is tough, they appear to be coping well and adult males can weigh up to 40 kilograms. And how fantastically adapted to its environment is my personal favourite, the snow leopard?

Without really trying, but by virtue of their perfect design and stealthy demeanour, leopards blend naturally into the bushveld background. When a leopard decides it doesn't want to be seen, it simply disappears, effortlessly merging with the surroundings and melting into the bush. Besides owning the night, leopards are loners – naturally secretive and relatively quiet – so their position and movements are far less predictable than those of lions, for example; as a result, they're not as frequently seen on game drives. Despite this, it has become apparent that the 'world view' among the leopard population on Olifants Game Reserve is changing, and an increasing number of people are seeing leopards each time they visit the reserve. Most importantly, more and more leopards are being reported behaving as naturally as can be expected. Sightings are more often than not of a reasonable duration, and game viewers filled with wide-eyed people look on in awe as kills are made, or mating leopards go about it without embarrassment. There are also reports of leopards relaxed enough to doze off in close proximity to the vehicles ... Wow!

Lions, on the other hand, are not only more visible, they're also social and vocal, and therefore more predictable. One is able to locate them by homing in on their roars and, more frequently, by tracking their spoor. For example, it is much easier to track a pride of noisy lions leaving a couple of dozen paw prints than it is to pick up evidence of a single stealthy leopard. A leopard's print is much smaller and, being a considerably lighter animal, its pad impressions are fainter. Also leopards don't advertise their kills to airborne scavengers, as lions inadvertently do (usually a dead giveaway as to their whereabouts).

Unlike leopards, when lions are displaced by incoming males the shifts can be quite disruptive. Invariably there is noticeable drama, usually followed by the death of any cubs and younger lions that get in the way of the new males. When three interloper males moved in from the Klaserie Nature Reserve, they stamped their authority by killing one of the males and a dominant female of the resident Olifants pride. (As it happens, this pride had never quite gelled as a family unit. Not only was its cohesive structure plagued by a suspected cub killer within its ranks, but earlier that year one of the coalition males was killed by a speeding train.) Outnumbered three to one, the remaining male led the rest of the pride's breeding females and subadults away from their territory to where they hoped to find refuge. A few crossed the causeway onto Olifants North, and yet others moved from the frying pan into the fire by leaving the reserve and crossing the Olifants River onto state-owned land known as Doreen, where they were at the mercy of trophy hunters and poachers.

Knowing such violent takeovers to be a natural part of lion ecology, we all hoped that the new males, already dubbed 'The Three Musketeers', would woo the females and establish a pride once the dust had settled. Alas, due to their relative youth and inexperience, this did not materialise. Vocal as they were in victory, their defiant roars soon fell silent, and the deep spoor they left in the soft sand blew away in the wind, not to be seen again on Olifants for a long time.

Shareholders on Olifants build up an intimate rapport with the lions on the reserve, and those lions they had become accustomed to, and that had become accustomed to them, were now gone. It goes without saying they were missed, and besides those that settled on Olifants North, which were seen regularly, there were only sporadic sightings of lions south of the river. But this is the social ecology of lions, which adds to the aura of these magnificent big cats.

So, how many lions are there on Olifants at the moment? Until recently we'd pinned our hopes on the two mothers and their eight cubs in the Palm Loop as the nucleus of a new pride. However, since then we have confirmed there are at least 21 lions on the reserve. Recently, two prides totalling 19 lions were seen on a drive. The 'Lisbon Pride' was seen at one of the main water holes in the east of the reserve. An hour later, some six or seven kilometres away, the 'Palm Loop Pride' was located at the reserve's largest water hole, Hide Dam, by the same vehicle. Hold that thought ...

Minus one! As I pen this chapter, my field rangers have just called in on the two-way radio to say they have found a large male lion that has been killed by other lions. The unfortunate interloper was caught in an area on the Palm Loop not too far from where most of the reserve's cubs are born. He could not have chosen a more likely spot to get challenged by territorial males. Driving through to the scene, I came across the two huge males in a stand of wild sage bush close by. These were undoubtedly the pride males that had killed him.

Fortunately, being part of an open system means we're able to absorb the dynamism of pride reshuffling. I had a feeling the situation wouldn't last too long, and I'm pleased to say stability has been restored as predicted. Regular sightings of lions frequenting their old haunts have been reported. Both the lions and the reserve's shareholders appear content. For the moment, that is.

Cheetah sightings are becoming a rare event on the reserve. And I suspect for a host of environmental factors, not least the high number of lions and leopards resident in the area. Admittedly, although I have never known these nomadic predators to be plentiful on the reserve, it has been my general observation in the Lowveld that when lions are around, cheetahs make themselves scarce. Even though the ample clearings and abundant impala in our area make for both ideal prey and perfect hunting conditions, Olifants has never been known to have cheetah stay for any length of time. Records of cheetah being killed by leopards and lions on Olifants over the years seem to support my suspicions.

Notwithstanding the scarcity of cheetah, and as if in ironic defiance of their past status on the reserve, there have been two confirmed sightings of the rare mutation known as 'king' cheetah in the last 15 years. The first one seen on Olifants was spotted by one of our directors at the time, Dr Melvyn Greenberg, in 1994. The second was photographed by a shareholder, Andrew Ochse, in 2004. However, it was later revealed that this particular individual was lured through our southern fence onto a neighbouring property. At the time this game farm had a tame female cheetah, which I suspect was used to entice the wild king cheetah. It was then promptly captured and sold on.

King cheetah have unique markings, like fingerprints – as do all other spotted cats. A simple photo of any side can positively identify and distinguish an individual, as indeed we were able to do with the second king. However, once through a fence onto someone else's land, unless microchipped, legal ownership can no longer be claimed. I believe the unfortunate animal spent the rest of its life in an enclosure at a well-known local game ranch in Hoedspruit as part of their 'cheetah breeding programme'. According to researchers and staff at the centre, which I visited recently, there are no known king cheetah in the wild. I wonder why …

Taking into account feedback from wardens in the neighbouring regions of Balule, as well as records of known individuals seen on Olifants, I guess there are probably fewer than 10 cheetah in the greater area of Balule Nature Reserve. Considering the size of the reserve, these are relatively low numbers (which do fluctuate from time to time), and from my observations, their population has remained unimproved – or rather, should I say, marginal – for the last 23 years. Cheetah are great wanderers, capable of covering huge areas, so it will always remain an unexpected and memorable privilege when we do see them from time to time, as I recently did. Usually the visits are fleeting and these beautiful animals move on before you really get to know them.

Understandably, the following story would fall into the category of 'highly improbable' and were it not for the witness present at the time, and subsequent confirmation by a number of shareholders on the reserve, I would have been more circumspect about sharing it with you.

As one of my duties as reserve manager, I am occasionally called upon to shoot an impala or two to supplement staff rations. When I do so, I am extremely selective and will not harvest an animal from a breeding herd or when there are other species in the vicinity. To this end I prefer to shoot lone rams or select from small bachelor groups of a few individuals. That way, in my crazy reckoning, there's 'nobody' left or, at worst, only a couple of witnesses left to tell any other impala of the murderous man and his rifle.

To help me spot and load on this day, I took one of my field rangers, Adam Ngobeni, along with me. It was already mid-morning by the time we'd sighted-in the rifle and headed out. This is one time that I focus on getting all the detail right; there's no rush when I take on this unenviable task. Being methodical and deliberate minimises the chance of a mistake or wounding an animal. With Adam standing on the back, I drove slowly, making my way to the relatively open plains area of the reserve known to be frequented by impala.

It was beginning to get warm and most of the plains game had already moved off the clearings into the shade. But it wasn't long before a tap on the cab indicated Adam had spotted some impala. He pointed to a couple of rams about a hundred metres off to our left. They were slowly walking away from us through the open grassland towards the thick bush on the edge of the clearing. I turned in and stopped the vehicle. In the time it took me to set up for a shot, the first ram had already disappeared from view into thick bush. I quickly shifted my focus to the second ram, the crosshairs of the telescopic sight settling on him as he stopped momentarily on the edge of the bush. The impala collapsed dead at the shot.

I started the vehicle and drove in carefully through the thick grass. Adam jumped off as I stopped to turn the vehicle around and facilitate loading the carcass. Looking behind as I began to reverse, I could see he'd already opened the tailgate and a moment later was standing on the back of the vehicle holding the impala carcass by its horns waiting for me to come around and help him lift it into the back, as was our routine method.

Leaving the engine running, I opened my door and climbed out, only to find myself face-to-face with a huge male cheetah standing next to the vehicle! Neither of us moved. We stood there looking at each other, the door open and my left hand still on the steering wheel. At that point the cheetah was less than two metres away from the side of the vehicle.

Remarkably, the cheetah didn't utter a sound: there was no spitting, no growling, nothing! Instead its gaze shifted to the load body of
the Land Cruiser, where it appeared to be totally focused on the dead
impala Adam was clutching. Naturally I pulled myself back into the
driver's cab, at which point the cheetah slowly moved around to the
open tailgate. And although its tail was curled tightly between its legs
there were no other outward signs of stress … It had still not uttered a
sound!

I craned my neck around through the sliding cab window and could
see Adam was just as bemused as I was. 'I think he is very hungry,'
Adam said.

The cheetah stood there craning its neck, almost touching the impala's rear end with its nose, its big brown eyes fixed on Adam holding the
horns. 'OK, drop it for him; we can get another,' I said.

With that, Adam let go of the impala, which was immediately seized
by the cheetah as it hit the ground. An impala ram can weigh upwards
of 75 kilograms, so it was all the cheetah could do to drag it the short
distance into the shade of the bush close by. Besides the thump as the
carcass fell to the ground, there was nothing heard; the cheetah had
still not made a sound!

As we drove away, I made a general announcement on the two-way
radio that there was a 'cheetah on a kill' and gave the location. Needless
to say, the response to my white lie was overwhelming, and the viewing
much enjoyed. One of our directors, Glen Forsdyke, was the first on
the scene. It was only later, in private conversation, that I was able to
explain to him exactly what had happened. The story has since become
general knowledge among the staff and shareholders alike. However, I
suspect there are some who will remain dubious and think that Adam
and I may have spent a little too much time in the sun. Yet others have
even asked to sample some of the 'stuff' they are convinced we must
have been smoking at the time!

I am sceptical of giving human attributes to animals, particularly
wild animals. So my immediate suspicion was that this cheetah was an

escapee from a safari park or 'breeding project' or, at the very least, a research subject that had somehow thrown its tracking collar and wandered into our reserve. I was convinced this was a cheetah that had somehow lost its instinctive fear of man, a cheetah that had been fed by man at some stage, possibly even off the back of a vehicle. A suspicion not based on conjecture.

Rewinding nearly 38 years brought back vivid recollections of when I was a young ranger working at Thornybush Game Reserve. I was placed in charge of the care and regular feeding of 12 cheetah, which the reserve housed in a 100-hectare enclosure at the time. Originally from Namibia, they'd been captured in the domestic stock farming areas, where they were classified as stock-damaging wild animals, vermin doomed to be destroyed or relocated to private safari parks or game reserves.

Having spent a year with these cheetah I naturally got to know each one individually and in turn they got to know me, becoming more and more tolerant of my presence. After a while most of them would allow you to watch from a safe distance while they fed. However, despite this taciturn acceptance, they never let me forget they were wild animals; there were invariably the accompanying spitting, snarling, threatening displays and hunched-back prancing from a few at the outset until they settled down. Most of them would allow you closer as time passed, but you could not get away without at least being snarled at. I remember one female in particular, named Pumani. This cheetah remained as skittish as the day she arrived and never allowed me or anyone else to get close. She never fed in anyone's presence and she never 'tamed down'.

Numerous phone calls and intensive investigation followed this extremely unusual scenario that Adam and I were witness to. However, no one could throw any light on the cheetah, and nobody claimed to have had a similar experience either. Given my rudimentary knowledge of the animal, gleaned from having worked closely with a dozen wild cheetah in a captive situation, I was puzzled by this one's behaviour, to say the least. I have since given this unusual interaction some thought, and the following is my layman's hypothesis.

Cheetah don't reach this size and age in the wild unless they know how to survive, so clearly this animal was an experienced hunter. Also, there was no faint smoothness or indentation on his neck hair that would have revealed he had worn a collar that had been recently thrown. This was not an escaped, domestic or a semi-habituated cheetah. So I suspect he had been lining up these two impala earlier and was preparing to attack when we happened on the scene. Then he must have watched in utter despair as the two rams, unaware of his strategic stalk, walked away from our vehicle's clumsy approach and headed for the relative safety of the bush. The cheetah saw as the front impala disappeared into the thicket and then, shortly after that, must have seen the second impala disappear into the grass as it fell to my bullet. However, the rifle is silenced so there was little to distract his attention from his fixation on the impala ... In his mind, that impala had tripped and collapsed, an opportunity not to be missed as a predator. But instead we unceremoniously helped ourselves to his impala! What a cheek, he must have thought, and then ambled in cautiously. I know little of the social behaviour and body language of cheetah, but it was apparent from his demeanour, particularly the way he held his tail tucked between his legs, an attitude that showed he was gutsy, that there was no aggressive intent. This was not a contest; he wanted no fight. He simply came in to quietly and calmly claim what was rightfully his.

For a few weeks after our surreal encounter, reports of regular sightings of this cheetah were received. As I'd surmised, all indications were he was indeed an excellent hunter, as he was seen by shareholders making a number of kills, including a yearling wildebeest calf. The latest reports of this cheetah indicate he's still around and has moved on to the west of Balule ... possibly in search of female companionship.

STICK-TAILED JACKALS

Most wild animals infected with sarcoptic mange, *Sarcoptes scabiei*, will eventually succumb to the indirect effects of this parasitic skin mite. In our area it is the black-backed jackal, *Canis mesomelas*, that appears to be the most susceptible species – particularly those that frequent, or have territories near, areas of human habitation. An example being the situation immediately across the river, where we find a relatively high human density and associated high numbers of domestic animals, such as dogs and cats, that may be responsible – albeit inadvertently, as vectors.

Without the certainty of in-hand examination and microscopic analysis of the mites, the first obvious sign of sarcoptic mange on jackals is tail hair loss. Their normally bushy tail, also known as a 'brush' in fox-speak, loses both hair and flexibility, giving it a stiffish, 'stick-like' appearance. This hair loss then quickly spreads over the entire skin surface. Eventually the skin resembles parchment, sometimes cracking in the folds and giving rise to suppurating sores. Bad as this is, the condition is made worse by the animal constantly scratching itself in order to relieve the incessant itching. Consequently, the creature succumbs to a slow deterioration in physical condition. Unable to hunt properly, it slowly starves; eventually too weak to even scratch, it dies. This has to be one of the most horrible ways to die.

Despite the negative prognosis for wild jackals infected with mange, animals that are able to be brought to hand are easily treated and cured. Apparently there is an effective cure for sarcoptic mange, the

most widely applied treatment being regular shampooing with a recommended ectoparasiticide. Another tried and trusted *boere* (farmer's)
remedy uses sulphur and Vaseline, though any detergent containing
borax is also effective. These applications are all fine if your pooch or
moggy contracts mange, but it would simply be impractical to apply
this method of treatment to a wild animal, particularly the highly
strung, sensitive jackal. The stress of capture and the darting of an
already stressed animal may very well do more harm than good. And
jackals are smart ... you'll only trap them once.

Having had to put down half a dozen black-backed jackals in an
advanced stage of this disease over the years, I knew I couldn't carry on
like this. The last straw was when I had to destroy a jackal less than 50
metres from my house. Every day for weeks I'd watch as this jackal's
condition slowly deteriorated, and as I'd become somewhat familiar
with her it made what I knew I had to do even harder. Most significant
was that this particular jackal had unwittingly shown me an aspect of
their behaviour that, to those unaware of the situation, went largely
unobserved.

For the most part, black-backed jackals are nocturnal hunters and
scavengers. And where they are not persecuted by stock farmers, as
in game reserves such as ours, they lie in the open shade during the
day. However, where they *are* hunted, jackals remain hidden from view
in thick bush, down burrows or tucked away in forms. Consequently,
there is little chance to witness the full effect and extent of this disease
and how the animals try and cope with its symptoms. At best we get
fleeting glimpses of them scratching themselves, and see the bare, raw
skin between patches of lacklustre fur. We cannot begin to imagine the
pain and misery they endure, sometimes for months on end, before
finally curling up nose to tail and dying ... As I have found them.

Each morning on my way to work I'd see the mangy jackal. She
would scrape herself a small hollow in the softer sand on the side of the
road, and there she'd lie in the dusty, sun-baked soil for hours. I also
noticed she would still be there in the heat of the day, preferring to lie
in full sunlight. At first this puzzled me: I couldn't work out why, when

everything was seeking shade from the relentless African sun, she chose to lie in it ... Then the penny dropped: apparently skin mites don't do well in direct sunlight; they're less active and don't burrow as much; this would be the only relief she'd get from the maddening agony of scratching an incessant itch. The jackal had obviously found that the burning heat of the direct sun gave some relief and was relatively tolerable ... Possibly it was the only time she could get some rest.

It was nearly 40 degrees in the shade the day I found her lying on a pile of dried elephant dung. Fortuitously, dung beetles, tree squirrels and ground birds had broken up the dung and spread it out in their search for finer material and undigested seeds, making a soft, spongy bed in the middle of the road. The jackal appeared comfortable lying there. As I got closer, she lifted her hairless head, and wearily squinted in the bright sunlight, looked straight at me, blinked slowly and then put her head down again. I couldn't watch this poor creature suffer a moment longer. As had been done with others suffering the same fate, she was quickly and painlessly put out of her misery.

I walked up to the jackal and looked at the tiny, wasted body that had endured so much for so long, and I wondered what purpose this amount of suffering could possibly serve. Gazing up into the cloudless sky, my thoughts were momentarily interrupted by the vapour trail of a jetliner returning from somewhere in the east. Looking far beyond the streaks of white that trailed behind the silver speck (77 tons of metal kept airborne by man's ingenuity), while at my feet this little jackal lay dead ... I questioned God.

There had to be something that could be done, I thought. To stand by and watch helplessly as these beautiful animals died of something so terrible yet so treatable was frustrating to say the least. There had to be another way, so I contacted veterinarian Dr Pete Rogers with the problem. I asked him if there was anything we could give the jackals that would work through ingestion, via the bloodstream. He said yes: provided we could get the jackal to take minced meat; we could then lace the food with Ivermectin (usually injected intramuscularly). The other good news was that one treatment may be all that would be required. I needed a subject for the experiment, and not surprisingly, it didn't take long to find one. But wild jackals don't make for good subjects.

Less than a week after putting the jackal out of its misery, I came across another mangy jackal. Although also in an advanced stage of the infection, she still had a fair amount of hair on her skin. I'd see this little waif fairly regularly on those afternoons when I went on a jog around the river floodplain near my house. Again, as with the usual symptoms, the jackal was always lying on soft sand in the direct afternoon sun when I came upon her. She was a young animal and was always on her own – a veritable little runt, as if somehow she had been abruptly cut off from adequate nutrition at puberty. I couldn't help thinking that perhaps the jackal I'd shot lying in the sun on the blanket of elephant dung had been her mother, and suddenly a great sense of guilt overwhelmed me. Had I inadvertently handicapped this pitiful little creature even further? If so, she had made it on her own from a very early age. Her sheer will to survive in spite of all the odds made me more determined than ever to find a solution to this problem. I also somehow felt I owed this particular jackal a fair chance at life.

With the fable of Hansel and Gretel in mind, I managed to bring the jackal in along a trail of 'crumbs'. Instead of breadcrumbs I used dog cubes spaced at roughly one-metre intervals, until the jackal was lured to where the controlled feeding was to take place. This process took a few days – and to complicate matters, there were beady eyes and sharp noses everywhere: opportunists like warthogs, monkeys, baboons and civets, and of course other jackals would be quick to capitalise on the handout. And given the little jackal's physical condition, she was in no shape to compete for the food, so any contact or competition with these other animals had to be avoided if this was going to work.

It took some careful timing to ensure that only this specific jackal would get the food, but I persisted and it worked. Within a week the little jackal was coming to my call, which comprised a series of short, high-pitched barks imitating that of a black-backed jackal. She began to anticipate my arrival and come loping in with little hesitation, eating the dog cubes and one or two small mince balls I'd leave for her.

At no point did I let her associate me with the food, which was always placed on the ground while I was still in the Land Cruiser. If she had seen anything of me, it would have been my lower arm as I leaned out. Despite knowing the food was there, and as desperately hungry as she was, typical of the species she remained wary and would never eat while I was nearby.

After 10 days of feeding the jackal, it was apparent she trusted the food completely. It was as good a time as any. I laced four small mince balls with a dose of Ivermectin and dropped them out as I always did. Then from a distance I watched through my binoculars, anticipating that her sharp sense of smell would pick up the medicine and reject the meat. Instead, to my relief, she ate the lot! The conditioning over the last 10 days had paid off.

I continued with the supplementary feeding in order to monitor her progress; I needed to see how effective the treatment was proving to be. Within two weeks the little runt had put on some condition, developed a coat that almost identified her as a black-backed jackal, and she had a shiny black nose. Most importantly, I noticed she didn't scratch nearly as much as before. Dr Rogers suggested another follow-up treatment two weeks hence, which was also carried out successfully.

We had effectively treated the symptoms, and I was really proud of the results. Now the possible causes needed to be identified, if possible. What a pity it would be if, after all this effort, the jackal simply got reinfected and slid down the same slippery slope again. Well, I'm not going there at this stage; suffice it to say that I will remain optimistic that we are able to keep ahead of things until a solution can be found, which hopefully won't be too long.

There is no doubt in my mind that there is more than one source for this infectious mite and numerous pathways for it to take hold. Possibly compounding the issue is a primate rehabilitation centre across the river from our reserve, where hundreds of baboons are confined to wire cages and live in close proximity to one another, from where no successfully rehabilitated troops have been known to emanate ... But where else does one place unwanted primates? They too need a place in the sun; somebody has to take care of them.

Although not susceptible to sarcoptic mange infection, baboons and monkeys are known to act as vectors for the mange parasite, carrying and spreading the mites for days, which, in itself, is perfectly natural. However, coincidence and circumstantial evidence concerning the unnaturally high numbers as a significant contributing factor cannot be ignored, therefore potential carriers, perpetuating the virulence of this particular epidemic, warrant further investigation. There is growing concern that this may be why the majority of jackals with mange appear to have become infected in this relatively small section of the reserve, mainly the riparian habitat along the Olifants River, within sight of this centre.

Confined on a few hectares, the over 700 caged primates interact with wild free-roaming troops, even to the point where feeding and sexual intercourse between captive and free-roaming individuals has been observed to occur through the wire mesh. Of equal concern – however irrelevant it may be to this story in terms of mange infection – is that no one knows what effect high concentrations of captive primates may have on the spread of other diseases into the wild populations of the surrounding nature reserve. This level of contact cannot be healthy: is it purely coincidence that the jackals on the floodplain, only a few hundred metres from the caged primates, have a noticeably higher incidence of mange infection than anywhere on the reserve?

This also brings to mind another almost forgotten episode in this rampant scourge's history, which is, of course, the devastating loss of significant numbers of the lesser-known and uncommon side-striped jackal, *Canis adustus*, which was virtually wiped out on Olifants by mange in the early 1990s. Sadly, since then they have been out of sight, out of mind ... well, until now, that is.

Although slightly larger than their more carnivorous cousins, side-striped jackals do not compete with black-backs for food: they are primarily omnivorous, preferring insects, small rodents, carrion and fruit (particularly the fruit of trees such as jackalberry, brown ivory and sycamore fig), so cross-infection between the two jackal species at this juncture would be less likely. In fact, the last side-striped jackal infected with sarcoptic mange died under the large brown ivory tree at our clubhouse in 1994. Since then, only two sightings have been recorded. Although relatively common in the miombo woodlands of Zimbabwe and mopane veld of Northern Kruger, we fear that the side-striped jackal may now be virtually extinct from our reserve. And yet the incidence of mange infection among the black-backed jackal population is on the increase.

Interestingly, chacma baboons and side-striped jackals have a very similar diet, therefore it would be safe to assume that they would have come into contact with each other from time to time feeding under the same fruit trees. And, as I said earlier, although baboons do not suffer any detrimental effects from the mite that causes this mange, I suspect they may very well act as temporary intermediate hosts of the parasite. So, captive primates that are closely associated with domestic animals could very well become virulent vectors, and inadvertently pass these mites on to their free-roaming counterparts, in turn infecting the most susceptible host, in this case jackals. This is only now beginning to make sense, and goes some way to provide answers to the question of how the mange spreads so rapidly among the side-striped jackals in the region, and then to black-backed jackals.

Under normal circumstances the two jackal species would not interact. For the most part, geographically speaking, their ranges rarely overlap. However, there are places where this does occur, like Olifants, where the smell from the decaying carcass of a side-striped jackal would most certainly have attracted scavengers, not least black-backed jackals and hyenas. Even a curious sniff, or any contact with this highly contagious mite, would result in infection.

Over the years we have been able to ascertain that this particular infection, unlike most other parasitic diseases among wildlife, is not triggered by poor environmental conditions, overpopulation or poor nutrition. Possibly a combination of complex factors, including those above, may exacerbate this condition, as I have observed that even the healthiest jackals, in peak condition, will suddenly contract this awful disease, and eventually die from it a few months later. So what causes these outbreaks from time to time on our reserve remains a mystery.

The cornucopia of suspected sources is daunting, but I for one will not give up trying to find a way to minimise the spread of this ghastly parasite. As for the jackal I treated, which has since been named Jacqueline, I am pleased to say she has recovered completely and is now so pretty that a handsome mate has moved in, and the two of them have set up a territory on the river floodplain. Their distinctive calls now complement the other sounds that fill the night air of the same area her mother used to call home.

KING LEO

Lions are arguably the kings of wildlife. And, except for a handful of Asiatic lions that still eke out an existence in the Gir National Park of Gujarat, India, they are quintessentially African. No other creature epitomises this continent's wilderness quite like these huge felines do.

When a lion roars, the world stops to listen. There's no need to put a finger to your lips and shush anyone. Those in close proximity will automatically sit in silence, open-mouthed in awe. The volume and resonance of the sound defines primeval wildness. Teetering on the fine line between enjoyment and fear, it is a privilege to be in the presence of such awesome power without having to endure the gut-wrenching terror this would have instilled in our primitive ancestors. As if his voice is not attention grabbing enough, there is no other animal on earth quite as regal looking as a full-maned lion, of this there is no question. However, that said, his appearance and status denote anything but an underlying arrogance: if truth be told, this facade belies a fear that constantly simmers in the pit of his stomach.

There can be no complacency or moment of weakness, a pride male knows he cannot drop his guard – or even appear to drop his guard – for a minute. The next time you are in close proximity to an apparently inattentive male lion, take a little piece of cellophane and crush it in your hand. This will produce a sound not unlike dry grass being trampled underfoot or under paw. A lion will usually tolerate the noisy jabber, popping of beer cans, the clicking of camera shutters or the squeal of the camera's motor drive, but nothing will make him sit bolt upright quicker than the sound of crunchy plastic wrapping. He is constantly tuned to what this sound could mean; he knows that subtle crunching sound will one day signal his nemesis.

A male lion's rise to power is rarely through passive succession. He knows that the same brutal force he used to get to his 'throne' will sooner or later be employed against him, or worse. So the next time you see a pride male tuck in first at a kill invariably made by the females, spare a thought, because although he is perfectly capable of hunting for himself, it's a small repayment, the very least they can do for his protection and imminent sacrifice. It is paramount that he is well fed, as the pride's well-being – particularly that of the cubs – depends on his strength and fitness.

Essentially all lions, but particularly male lions, have a really tough childhood, so those that reach adulthood deserve all the respect and admiration bestowed upon them, particularly those mature specimens that have made it to pride male status. Statistics vary from region to region, and although I have seen two litters where there was 100 per cent cub survival rate on Olifants, these were exceptional phenomena, definitely not the rule. Depending on a myriad of environmental factors, it would be safe to say a male cub born on our reserve has a less than 30 per cent chance of making it beyond its third year. Becoming a pride male reduces this factor by even more, to the point where less than 20 per cent of male cubs will ever sit on the throne. Even so, it's only once incoming pride males establish themselves that their work begins. There will be cubs to kill, others to sire, lionesses to protect and a territory to defend ... And he will live like a king, until the crunch comes.

Harsh as it may seem, it's easier to accept when a pride male is ousted in the autumn of his life, having lived a little, fought a little and loved a little, than to watch a healthy young male, not much more than two years old, sentenced to a slow, painful death – even if this is as nature, in its pristine process, decrees.

As if the neighbourhood wasn't tough enough, Olifants River Game Reserve is subject to a number of unnatural factors that affect our lions, and that in turn influence our decisions on the management of injuries they suffer as a result from time to time. For example, the trains that use the line running through our reserve have accounted for dozens of lion fatalities and injuries over the last 20 years. Not to mention our notorious neighbours north of the Olifants River who actively hunt lions and have on more than one occasion gutlessly left wounded individuals to die. And then of course there is wire snare meat and muti poaching as well as the escalating incidents of poisoning that plague every reserve in the country.

Lions, leopards and hyenas often fall foul as ancillary targets when they're drawn by curiosity to the stench of death and investigate abandoned carcasses caught in snares. Invariably, there are other snares close by that are activated and in which the predators inadvertently get ensnared themselves. Of greater concern is the increasing evidence to suggest lions and hyenas are being specifically targeted by poachers. Our field rangers have recently come across snares that have been purposely set around a carcass to ensnare predators. Tiger numbers are dwindling in the wild, and as a result the bones that were supplied by illegal hunting of these big cats have become increasingly scarce. Poachers have now turned to lions, killing them for their bones, which, needless to say, like rhino horn and ivory, are destined for the insatiable Chinese and Vietnamese markets, which are more than content with the substitute. A lion carcass can fetch $500 for its bones alone! Of some concern, but much less of a threat, is lion fat, which is highly prized by our traditional medicine practitioners, who cater for a relatively small market.

So when it was reported that a lion had been seen with what appeared to be a broken leg and was unable to move except by dragging its hindquarters, I dropped everything and rushed to the scene. Situations such as this always require urgent assessment as a matter of course in order to rule out poisoning, snaring or other unnatural causes.

As it happened, a number of shareholders out on a game drive along the popular river road known as Pel's Loop had watched the dramatic scene unfold in front of them. Apparently the lion was not a victim of foul play at the hand of man, rather it appeared he was the unfortunate casualty of the rite of passage: he'd run the gauntlet as laid down in lion law, one that all young male lions have to run. Being young and inexperienced, the lion must have found himself in the wrong place at the wrong time. As a consequence he suffered serious injury from his own kind and only closer examination would reveal to what extent.

Having called the sighting in, all that those at the scene could do was watch helplessly as the injured lion, clearly in great discomfort, appeared to seek respite from his pain by lying down in the cool wet sand and shallow water of the river bed. At this time of the day the shadows cast from the larger riparian trees had lengthened and the shallow section where the lion lay was in partial shade. Supplemented by the Blyderivierpoort Dam's colder mountain water, the Olifants was running relatively cool and clear. Under the circumstances, these conditions must have provided a modicum of relief. The rest of the pride lay around close to him and otherwise all appeared rather peaceful, until one of the lionesses pricked up her ears and looked towards the bank where a large breeding herd of elephant came into view. Suddenly all the lions were now alert. In anticipation of the cool water and having fed in the adjacent dry woodland, the elephant came lumbering down, impatiently focused, as they do when approaching water after a long hot day.

Intent on using the same spot to drink, splash around and cool off, they made straight to where the lions lay. At that point the injured lion was still able to move, albeit with difficulty. However, having been slowed down by the injury, he couldn't get out of the lead elephant's way as quickly as the rest of the pride did. The matriarch followed by a very young calf may have interpreted the lion's slow response as a threat to her calf. The enraged cow went straight in and attacked the injured lion, aggressively tossing the hapless animal into the air. Unlike the grace and sense of balance a cat always maintains by landing on its paws, the lion's limbs appeared awkward and gangly, like a badly

cared for teddy bear flung across the room by a spoiled child. It seems
that when the lion landed, he fell hard, collapsing in a limp, lumpy
heap. It was at this point, we suspect, that one of his already injured
legs was broken above the knee joint, rendering the lion crippled.

Upon arrival at the scene I saw a young male lion, which I estimated
to be about 30 months old. He was lying in the sand on his own, panting hard. The elephant herd had moved slightly downriver, so I edged
closer to the injured lion in order to make him react; I needed him to
try and get up so I could ascertain the extent of his predicament. He
responded as instinctively they do; it was a pathetic sight. In an effort
to get up he managed to lift only his forequarters; there was no support
from his back legs, so he simply collapsed again. I could clearly see that
not only was he paralysed, but at least one of his back legs appeared to
be broken. Besides the obviously serious injury, the animal was otherwise in excellent condition.

Using binoculars I tried to determine the cause and extent of this
lion's initial injuries. It was a little like trying to describe your symptoms to a doctor over the telephone and expecting an instant diagnosis
based on conjecture. However, one didn't need seven years of study at
Onderstepoort Veterinary College to see that the young lion's left back
leg was broken. I also knew that an apex predator, like a lion, with such
an injury in the wild was doomed.

Despite this observation and my layman's diagnosis, there was still
not enough evidence to make an informed decision as to what action
to take, if indeed any at all. In other words, I could not simply shoot
the animal as I would have done had it been lying on or near the railway line, thereby instantly ending its suffering. There was a protocol
to follow when injuries were deemed to have been sustained through
natural causes. This invariably meant the heart-wrenching, coldly scientific approach of allowing nature to take its course. And I feared that,
strictly speaking, it would need to be applied in this instance.

As the incident had occurred on Olifants property, the directors of
the reserve were briefed. Later, in consultation with our chairman,
a decision was made as to what course of action to take. We agreed

that Dr Pete Rogers would be called in to immobilise the injured lion. A detailed examination would then be made allowing Pete to give us his professional opinion upon which we could then make the correct humane decision. At this point the cause of the lion's original injury was only conjecture.

Earlier that morning the rough location of the lion had been established, and as I had an unavoidable board meeting on the reserve later the same day, a ranger was placed on standby to take Pete in when he arrived. However, as it turned out, a dog bitten by a venomous snake in Hoedspruit delayed Pete, and he was only able to come out an hour or so later than scheduled. So, fortuitously for me, this delay, coupled with the meeting ending earlier than expected, meant I'd be able to attend the immobilisation and assist with the subsequent evaluation and decision.

Locating the lion was easy enough. Having virtually no use of his back legs, he had hardly moved, so was duly darted and immobilised approximately 60 metres from where he was last seen the evening before. Upon closer examination, and contrary to what we initially thought, it was clear this young male had been bitten through the knee joint by another lion. However, despite the injury, he had been able to move some distance and to keep up with the rest of his pride.

Needing to confirm his diagnosis, Pete had us put on surgical gloves in order to probe the wound and feel the fractured bone. I remember how hot it felt, and tried to imagine how much pain the jagged bone on flesh must have caused with every movement. We all agreed there was no point in bringing the lion out of its immobilised state simply to have him wake up to agony and then be left to die. It was clear that there was absolutely no hope of survival and only a lingering, painful death awaited this lion if left in that condition and nature allowed to take its course. I looked at Pete, and even this hardened surgeon looked back at me with his vision blurred by watery eyes. So, with nothing but the slightest nod, the decision was taken and implemented.

Instead of the conventional euthanasia compound, potassium chloride was used to painlessly and swiftly end the lion's life. This particular chemical was administered so that the carcass could be left in the open to be consumed. From the largest scavengers to the smallest bacteria of decay, nature could safely process the carcass and return its nutrients back to the soil.

The dead lion was gently carried into a donga close by, as would have happened if nature had been left to take its course and he had crawled away to die. In his condition, he would have taken over two weeks to die of starvation or possibly organ failure due to infection – either way, suffering unnecessary agony.

I said goodbye to Pete and drove back alone, somewhat light-headed with the sense of relief that we were able to save this lion any further pointless suffering, but heavy-hearted at the loss of such a magnificent young animal. Admittedly there were tears in my eyes; perhaps I was getting too soft for this job. But nobody would ever know, as they'd dried up by the time I got home.

Strictly speaking I was still on duty, so I climbed into the shower and washed off the smell of suffering lion and any other residue of external melancholy that may have been evident. It was time to prepare for the traditional post-board meeting braai with the directors down at the clubhouse and I needed to put on my 'everything's under control' face.

MAN-MADE NEMESIS

Switch to any one of the wildlife channels on television and, more often than not, you will find programmes aimed at increasing the viewer's awareness of the plight of the planet's dwindling wildlife and their habitat. Some are concerned with broader conservation issues; others feature subject matter that is quite specific, often focusing on feel-good rescue missions in life-and-death situations. The drama usually unfolds with dedicated people frantically doing something to save an animal, or group of animals, from whatever it is that poses the threat. These authentic accounts are visually dramatic, and sometimes there's a warning – 'Not for sensitive viewers' – but thanks to clever editing the outcome is inevitably positive. Admittedly, the most popular of these tend to be veterinary-related rescues, which give off the impression that once the immediate problem has been solved, the animal scampers, swims or flies off back into 'the wild' and everyone lives happily ever after …

As conservationists it doesn't matter where on the planet we find ourselves, the very nature of our calling means we need to adapt to the ever-changing dynamics of the environment, so inevitably there will be hurdles to overcome and challenges to meet from time to time. With judicious management, most are tackled and resolved, yet some of the tribulations that 'come with the territory' are simply beyond our control, leaving even the most dedicated conservationist swathed in a sense of frustration and helplessness. It can slowly erode your resolve and wear you down, leading to moments of despondency in which you start believing the grass may be greener elsewhere. And we all know the moral of that adage.

Who among us has not fantasised about immersing ourselves in some wildlife utopia; who hasn't had a hankering to visit or work in those inaccessible and remote wilderness environments that appear to thrive completely free of human influence and intervention? How wonderful if there were indeed such places on the planet. The reality is that while there are oil tankers, offshore oil rigs, nuclear power plants and greenhouse gas emissions, coupled with a burgeoning human population, this will remain a fantasy. And those apparently pristine ecosystems cannot escape the fact that they will not be immune ... In truth, far from it.

Closer to home the undeserved nemesis of some of our reserve's wildlife is neither environmental nor socio-political, yet there are times when I feel it may as well fall into the same category as some uncontrollable natural phenomenon: no less powerful and beyond our control. We take every precaution within our capabilities to manage and limit the effects of this menace, but like those expert oarsmen in raging white water, using skilful dips of their paddles to keep the boat pointed in the general direction, we are compelled, as are they, to go with the flow most of the time. Every molecule of these massive, mechanical monsters has been moulded by man; and they are driven by men. They are in fact ... trains!

Despite train operator awareness and specially imposed speed restrictions through our reserve, the laws of physics simply don't allow thousands of tons of steel moving at 45 kilometres per hour (or more) to stop in time. Unavoidably, a number of wild animals are killed or injured in our area each year as a result. So it has become an integral facet of our job as conservators to minimise these incidents wherever and whenever we can, and when they do occur, implement damage control as best we can. We treat every incident as unacceptable; it never becomes simply a statistic. To this end, there are a number of procedures and protocols we have put in place that have reduced the incidents by more than 60 per cent over the years. However, despite this achievement, there are times when the law of averages catches up with the practicality of having trains running through a Big Five reserve, and when some tragedies will inevitably occur.

Bad news travels fast and it is no different in the bush. Late one night I received a call from Transnet's operations headquarters in Kaapmuiden to say an elephant had been hit by the train on the Palm Loop section of the line. Nothing focuses one more than this kind of bad news. Shock is followed by an overwhelming sense of helplessness and sorrow, which fades into doleful acceptance of inevitability and the process to follow.

China needs the magnetite for steel production and farmers need phosphates for fertiliser to grow maize to feed millions of people. So the death of a single elephant in a population of nearly 700 could be deemed collateral damage ... Right? Not in my book!

Reluctantly but routinely I checked my rifle, knowing these situations often involved having to put these huge animals out of their misery. As it was close to midnight, I decided to go out alone to assess the situation before waking the world. Protocol dictates we remove any carcass from the tracks as soon as possible. This is done so no scavengers attracted to the train-killed animal begin a feeding frenzy and, being focused on feeding, end up as casualties – secondary deaths – as well. To affect damage control and minimise any suffering, the latter always being a priority with me, means that getting to the scene as quickly as possible is of the essence. So, without wasting any time or rousing anyone else, I drove straight out, and arrived within 15 minutes of receiving the call.

This notoriously sharp bend in the line winds through the heart of the reserve's most popular lion nursery area, a relatively narrow seasonal river course that features hidden pools of water surrounded by soft sand and fringed with shady palm fronds throughout the year. Little wonder this is where nearly every lion born within our pride's territory takes its first breath. However, this beautiful section, known as Palm Loop, also runs close to the railway track and has an ugly reputation as a 'death bend' where trains have accounted for a number of animal casualties over the years.

I arrived at the precise reference given by the train driver, but could see nothing. An elephant lying on the tracks or nearby is not something I would easily miss, so I telephoned the depot to double-check. Again they confirmed I was indeed at the right spot. After parking the Land Cruiser, I climbed out and clambered up the slope onto the train tracks. Using a powerful handheld LED flashlight I began searching down the tracks on foot ... Nothing. Then, as I was about to turn around and check in the other direction, the beam's peripheral light caught something starkly pale against the dark grey of the granite gravel lying between the lines. Moving closer I saw it was the broken tip of an elephant's tusk, about half a metre long and as thick as a man's lower leg. Huge scuff marks and grooves gouged in the gravel close by indicated an elephant had been struck by the train at that point, evidently knocked down onto its face, breaking the tusk. Incredibly, the elephant's tracks revealed it had survived the impact and moved off out of sight and earshot. Despite finding small amounts of blood, it was impossible to tell how seriously the elephant was injured from this scant evidence. Alone, and with only a handheld torch and a rifle, I knew there was nothing more to be done until morning. I decided to return at first light with our master trackers and follow the elephant's tracks until we could locate it and assess its injuries.

As luck would have it, Big Game Heli had a Robinson R44 flying the area that morning, doing rhino work in the south of the reserve. They agreed to go up and have a quick look for the elephant, thereby saving both us and the elephant any unnecessary anguish. Needless to say, the bull was located in less than 30 minutes. Besides a broken left tusk and bloody, grazed knees, he appeared none the worse for the ordeal, which is more than I can say for the numerous other animals hit by trains on this infamous bend over the last 25 years.

Everyone in the area was made aware of the situation and told to monitor its progress. A week later, one of the rangers on a game drive with guests from a nearby lodge reported that the elephant was limping. Pete Rogers was called and, in less than an hour, the bull was darted and immobilised from the air. Although nothing life threatening, a thorough examination revealed an infection had set in on one of its leg wounds, which required treatment and long-acting antibiotics. The elephant has since made a full recovery.

As the throb of the helicopter's rotors faded into the distance, I poured a cup of coffee from my flask and reflected on two other incidents that had happened in virtually the same area on the line. One that didn't end well and one that did, both of which will remain etched in my memory forever.

Meagan and I were called out one sweltering morning to check on a lion that had reportedly been hit and injured by the train. Upon arrival, we found the entire Olifants pride lying in the sun on the opposite side of the tracks – 11 magnificent lions we knew well. Looking through my binoculars, they all appeared to be fine; except for the fact that they lay panting in the hot sun, instead of seeking shade at that time of the day, their behaviour appeared quite normal.

'How can you tell which one has been injured?' Meagan asked.

'You can't in this situation; I'll need to get them to move,' I replied.

Before any protest from Meagan could cause any indecision or delay, I slipped my rifle from its bag, climbed out of the vehicle and clambered up the steep gravel rail bed. Chunks of granite the size of a small child's fist clattered and crunched noisily underfoot, announcing my presence. Straightening up, I showed myself. This was too much for the lions: they would stay with a comrade in trouble, enduring the hot sun, but not when a man approached them. Needless to say, all but one of them grunted, then moved off quickly. I recognised her one tatty ear; it was one of the dominant lionesses of the pride. With her head lowered, ears flat and growling a deep guttural growl, she remained where she lay. I will never forget the look in her eyes: a mixture of pain, fear and confusion. There was no flicking of her tail from side to side, and given her level of rage at that point there should have been lots of that! This was my cue. I shouldered the rifle and, taking careful aim, placed a bullet between her eyes.

It was later revealed that the train had hit her in the lower back, snapping her spine. She'd been lying in agony, but comforted by the support of the rest of her pride, for five hours. The bullet was a mercifully swift end. Just months later another lion suffered severe trauma to its lower back and had to be destroyed. It is interesting to note that both lions were struck in same area of the lower back, indicating that they had almost made it as they tried to leap out of harm's way in a leaping–twisting dive.

Fortunately lions are extremely agile, like their smaller cousins, and the prospect of imminent collision with a train can sometimes conjure prodigies of athleticism. The following incident illustrates just how.

Even in the relatively warm Lowveld winter can get nippy, and the wind chill factor can make early mornings bitterly cold, particularly when you're out in an open game-viewing vehicle. Often it is so cold that you will be compelled to seek the warmth and comfort that only a good-quality down parka can offer. However, it has to be said that more often than not the rewards for braving these miserable conditions are well worth it. The discomfort endured for the short while it takes for the African sun to rise and warm things up is soon forgotten.

Shortly after sunrise, on just such a morning, a group of enthusiasts found themselves parked next to each other in their respective open game viewers. They sat quietly sharing some hot coffee while enjoying a special African moment together – watching a pride of lions, no less. Seeing a pride of 10 lions in the wild is not an everyday occurrence, and those there knew it. The lions had eaten well, having killed a zebra the previous evening, and now lay sprawled out in the clearing some 20 metres from the railway tracks, doing what lions do most of the time. After a while, one of the young males got up and stretched, his sagging belly nearly touching the ground. Composing himself, and without a backward glance, he nonchalantly headed straight towards the railway tracks in the direction of the two vehicles, probably on his way to have a drink of water at a nearby water hole.

The lion was apparently unaware of the train approaching from the north. With hardly a sound, the huge electric locomotive came into view, rounding the notoriously dangerous bend along the Palm Loop station siding. Though the lion could not see the train, it was now clearly visible to the people who were frantically waving and shouting at the train driver to slow down. In spite of their efforts and expressive gesticulating, the train came through and hit the lion. There was very little the driver could have done in such a short space of time; he also didn't see the lion until the last moment. Anyway, I can attest to the fact that a heavily loaded train can take up to half a kilometre to come to a stop. It's also possible that rather than focusing on the track ahead of the train itself, the driver may have been distracted by the two game-viewing vehicles and the wild gesticulations of their occupants. The lion, in turn, may have been wondering what the people were doing waving their arms about and lost focus as a result.

When they turn in a somersault, lions will usually land on all fours – and this lion was no exception. To the envy of any gymnast in the world, he did a full somersault and two half twists, almost landing on top of one of the vehicles, and then hit the ground running. The obviously shocked and dazed animal made off, quickly moving through the clearing and up towards the lookout on the eastern side of the railroad. According to one of the observers, Neil Hulett, who had bred cheetah when he farmed in Zululand (as it was known then), it was apparent from the way the lion ran off that no limbs had been broken.

Concerned that the lion may have sustained internal injuries, we spent the next couple of days monitoring him. To cut a long story short, he survived the ordeal unscathed, and has since been given the appropriate, albeit unimaginative, name of 'Train Basher'. But until he reappeared a few days later, there were some very concerned people trying to locate him.

In all fairness, the response from the railroad company, Transnet, was quick. Action was taken by their disciplinary board in the form of a written warning to the driver, citing the 'offence' as no attempt to slow down and failure to report the incident. The driver later confessed that he was afraid of what the people viewing the lion may have done to him had he stopped. Good point!

'Third strike and you're out.'

There was now overwhelming evidence that something needed to be done to minimise these collisions. We needed the technical assistance of Transnet's engineers, who committed themselves and came to the party. Since this incident, an automatic 24-hour speed monitoring device has been installed on the line at Warthog Pan. It records the speed of every train going through that point, and immediately sends the data through to their head office. The position for installation was selected under our guidance as we gave Transnet's environmental department the point on the line where the cell phone signal was strongest. It's not a hidden camera, and the train drivers know of its position, but it compels speeding trains to slow down as they approach the device. By the time the train picks up speed again, it is past the problem area. We were more confident that the most vulnerable area along the line was now being policed.

For a change, man didn't interfere with nature in this instance, man interfered with man for the good of nature – and it worked. Although the big cat lost one of his nine lives, the odds are now in his favour.

We can take much comfort from the fact that many of the train drivers are well aware of our reserve and its wildlife, and I must add that some are quite passionate about this part of their route. I was not convinced that the human factor had been explored enough, however, until the following incident planted a seed of hope in my mind. I now knew that there were faces belonging to those men behind the tinted windscreens at the controls of those massive machines – and most of them had good hearts.

What lions like about steel train lines, concrete sleepers and rough granite gravel beats me. I regularly chase them off the tracks when I come across them draped over the lines, particularly young cubs whose agility is not quite up to scratch yet, when they are relatively slow, gangly, all paws and curiosity. Small cubs appear to have a penchant for lying on the gravel bed, with their chins on the steel line, and dozing. At 2 am one morning I received the dreaded call, this time from a train driver I knew. He said he'd hit a lion cub and killed it, but would wait for me to arrive and make sure it was indeed dead.

I was still putting my boots on when the phone rang again. His voice thicker this time, he asked impatiently if I was still coming. When I arrived I found a three-month-old cub quite dead and a big burly train driver in tears.

CUB KILLER

Three days after the tragic loss of the cub on Palm Loop's 'death bend' we received a report that an adult male lion had been seen in the vicinity of Hide Dam, apparently limping very badly, with what appeared to be a broken back leg. The locality of the sighting, approximately one and a half kilometres from where the cub was killed by the train, was most significant. Naturally we began to put two and two together, concluding that the probability was high enough to link this to the incident less than 72 hours before. Although the evidence was largely circumstantial, it smacked of more than coincidence: the lion had to have been hit by the train, we thought. The prognosis of a broken leg on a wild lion is tantamount to a sentence to death by slow starvation, so I knew that if the train was the culprit, the injury would qualify as man-induced, allowing the lion to be destroyed. With a great deal of apprehension and uncertainty I decided to check things out for myself.

We found the lion lying in the shade of a thorny clusterleaf tree. The tree had grown into the shape of a gigantic green toadstool in response to selective browsing pressure from impala and giraffe, and now so shaped provided a dense shade umbrella. There was very little of the lion visible. However, as he lay there flat on his side with his back to me in the soft sand of the dry rivulet, I could see from the rapid rise and fall of his chest that he was panting heavily in an effort to keep cool. The shade offered the only respite from the heat, which was exacerbated by the lack of air movement. It must have been stifling.

As much as I didn't want to, I needed him to get up onto his feet and to walk, or at least try to, so I could assess the extent of his injury. In acknowledgement of my arrival he cocked his head lazily in my direction, then slowly looked away again. With the Land Cruiser in low range, I began inching closer to him; as I did so the tyres crunched the tinder-dry grass stubble, which immediately got his undivided attention. He lifted his forequarters and sat up, glaring at me over his shoulder.

Looking at him through my binoculars, I could see a few battle scars on his face, which is typical for an adult male; it was obvious he'd been through a couple of scraps recently, but what concerned me was his emaciated condition: this lion had apparently not eaten properly in weeks. Again I began moving slowly towards him, getting closer and closer until I was within 15 metres of him. At this point he lifted himself up on one back leg, almost falling over in the process, as he tried to move away from me to a place where he would feel less threatened.

The unfortunate animal was obviously in great pain, clearly unable to put any weight on his left back leg, yet there was no discernible outward sign of trauma nor any of the abnormal swelling usually associated with a fracture or serious injury. To my untrained eye, the source of the problem appeared to be high up on the leg, probably a dislocated hip joint. Nonetheless, as the British would say, there was no time for mucking about: here was an animal clearly in agony that desperately needed a decision from me either way. What I know about diagnosing orthopaedic problems leaves a lot to be desired, so, giving him the benefit of the doubt, I made the call.

A couple of hours later, long-time personal friend and veterinarian Dr Gerrit Scheepers and I were wading across the Olifants River. Between us we carried all the necessary kit needed to help immobilise and treat the lion. The antithesis of the muggy ambient heat, the river was running cool and clear, and except for a short section it was no more than knee deep for the most part of its hundred-odd metres' width. The curious crocodile we thought might try and bother us simply slunk away downriver, either sensing our urgency and purpose or having read up on the ballistics of the rifle I was carrying over my shoulder.

Earlier on, shortly after confirming that Gerrit could make it, I had used the time awaiting his arrival to shoot a couple of impala. These would be used as bait in case any other lions in the vicinity needed to be distracted. Having curious or protective lions hanging around can prove to be a problem when trying to isolate one of the pride. It is also rather disconcerting for the vet to concentrate on the injured animal while worrying about other lions wanting to crowd the 'operating table'. We hoped the impala carcasses would help ensure that the rest of the lions would be distracted for long enough to allow us to do the necessary work unimpeded.

A number of concerned shareholders who were at the scene kept an eye on the lion while we backed off to prepare the dart. Gerrit duly loaded the gun, whispering to me that he would set the air pressure for a range of 20 metres. Carefully manoeuvring the Land Cruiser, I managed to place him in the best position to shoot the dart. Unfortunately, possibly sensing something was not quite right or owing to his discomfort, the lion was now sitting on his haunches obscuring the prime target, so the alternative area, namely his shoulder muscle, was aimed for.

Phhhitt! The fluorescent-pink flight plume of the dart was clearly visible as it hit home high on the lion's shoulder, a perfect shot. On impact, the lion gave a grunt then slowly hobbled off on three legs in the direction of the dam, which was about 50 metres away. Zoletil, the immobilising drug of choice, takes approximately eight minutes to work; however, this lion was in relatively poor condition and, as we expected, began to show signs of the drug's effect more rapidly.

The lion stood for a minute or two, glanced back at us and again headed towards the dam. Slowing down now, his back legs began to sway and he stumbled a couple of times, but not before he'd managed to scramble up onto the earth wall where he hovered precipitously before tumbling down the steep slope to the water's edge. We were more than a little concerned about the situation: the last thing we needed after all our effort was to have him drown in front of us. Gerrit got to the lion first, grabbing him by the tail, and managed to prevent him from collapsing and falling into the water. As scrawny as he was, the lion was now a dead weight and proved difficult for Gerrit to move on his own, so we rushed in and helped to pull him away from the river.

In a semi-paralysed state, the lion glared at us through confused, fear-filled eyes. It seemed that he had some idea of what was happening. Then, as if warning us against becoming complacent, he confirmed our suspicions by uttering a low growl, lifting his lip to reveal a huge set of canines, the same formidable feline weaponry that on a good day could collapse a full-grown buffalo. Had the Zoletil been any slower in working its magic, we most certainly would not have held on too long before getting a little 'cut up' about the situation ourselves.

With the help of a couple of volunteers we loaded the lion onto the back of my vehicle, wrapped a towel over his head to cover his staring eyes, and drove him a safe distance from the water. In a shaded section of the small river bed, we gently laid him down. Once we were sure there were no other lions in the vicinity, Gerrit began with a thorough examination of the patient, talking me through each step as he usually did.

From the type of wounds, we could see he had been in a fight with another lion recently. However, other than the odd scratch and a couple of small bite marks on his face, there were not too many outward signs of anything abnormal. That was until Gerrit drew my attention to where the lion had taken a solid bite to the knee joint. The two puncture wounds on the inside of the leg were clean and bloodless, which explained why we had not seen them even through our binoculars. The upper canines of his adversary had penetrated deep into the joint – one had gone under the feline equivalent of the knee cap! It must have been excruciatingly painful and explained why the lion couldn't place any weight at all on this leg.

Long-acting anti-inflammatory drugs, antibiotics and a vitamin booster were administered to aid the healing process, reduce swelling and relieve pain. While he was sedated, and although it wasn't really necessary, we did the 'band-aid' thing and took the opportunity to treat all his war wounds and scratches. Antiseptic spray was applied to the cuts, some eye ointment rubbed into his eyes, and ectoparasite muti sprayed onto his ears and down his back. Finally we wet him down thoroughly to keep him cool while the effects of the immobilising drug wore off. This was the best medical attention we could offer under the circumstances.

Lastly, as we had not needed the impala carcasses to keep other lions away, we took advantage of the unique situation and decided to leave both with the sleeping lion. As Zoletil has no antidote, it would take a few hours for the lion's liver to metabolise the drug. Then he would wake to find he was sharing his shade with an impala carcass, not knowing how it got there. (This apparently trivial point may seem superfluous, but in fact it was crucial there be absolutely no association made between food and humans or food and vehicles.)

Imagine not having eaten anything for nearly two weeks, growing weaker every day while watching herds of plump game file past you to drink. The lion must have dreamed of juicy impala, wildebeest and fat, succulent zebra until his stomach ached and he salivated in his sleep. Then waking, he'd find nothing but the dry sand under his nose, relentless heat and the crippling pain in his knee, exacerbated each time he needed to move to the water's edge to quench his thirst. Today, however, it would be different: he'd wake to find much less pain in his knee, a juicy impala right under his chin – and it wouldn't be a dream. I left the other carcass about 25 metres downwind in the hope that if the other lions arrived while he was still dazed it would keep them occupied while he managed to get a mouthful or two – or indeed slipped quietly away to escape them.

Back across the river, Gerrit and I hurriedly shared a chocolate bar and drank some cold juice from the cooler. It was getting late, and he had to get back to his surgery to tidy things up before going home. The late afternoon sun had begun slipping behind the riverine trees; their longer shadows were now cast ominously over the river's deeper sections where the ever-present but well-hidden reptilian danger lurked. We still had to 'run the gauntlet' and wade through, then back again to my side; however, that time, on the return leg, I'd be on my own. Of course Gerrit waited until I'd returned safely to the opposite bank, then he waved goodbye and drove back to Phalaborwa. I never did see any scale or tail of the huge croc we'd spotted earlier. Seeing Gerrit standing there with his hands on his hips, it did cross my mind that maybe these 'flat dogs' were just as wary of vets in their trademark white gumboots and sleeveless overalls as most dogs and cats are.

Returning to where the lion lay, I noticed he began lifting his head every now and again, as the effect of the drug began to wear off and he slowly began to come around. As groggy as he was, his nostrils were filled with the tantalising, all-too-familiar smell of fresh impala, but frustratingly he just couldn't shake the fuzziness until half an hour later when, although not fully recovered, he was able to begin feeding. I imagine it must have been like trying to chew gum with your jaw numbed with novocaine. Fortunately, there was no sign of any other lions. Had they given him up for dead, I wondered.

The following morning at first light, I returned to where we'd left the lion, only to find he'd moved to where the second impala had been left. Having devoured the one we left under his nose, he now lay flat on his side, as bloated as a tick, right up against the second carcass, which he cuddled like a kid sleeping with a teddy bear, one of his huge forearms possessively draped over its neck. Although he couldn't fit another mouthful into his belly, he was going to guard it until he could … Nobody else was going to get any. Later that morning, when he went down to drink at the dam, I noticed he was able to move a lot easier: it was apparent that the anti-inflammatory drugs and antibiotics were working. Two days later, after devouring the second impala, he limped away into the bush an otherwise-healthy lion … It was also the first time I'd heard him roar since we'd treated him. Could it be that now, with his strength and confidence restored, he was on a mission to settle a score?

In what is generally regarded as a naturally functioning ecosystem, these meddlesome efforts raise the question of how much good such missions of mercy actually do in the context of their effects on the bigger picture. Sometime, instead of allowing our heads to rule, we give in to our hearts, where emotions take over and dominate the decision process. They inevitably compel us to micromanage and interfere, and as will be shown, this may not always be the right option.

During the weeks and months that followed this incident, Olifants' lion population began to take on some unusual and inexplicable characteristics. Mating lions were seen more frequently than we have ever experienced. Lionesses in the pride that fell pregnant would make an appearance with their young cubs and then disappear, not to be seen again until they returned a few weeks later minus their cubs and in oestrus again.

There were five male lions in the area, four of which were seen together fairly regularly, and although there was always a fifth lion around, he always appeared to hang back, often successfully hunting and making kills on his own. Towards vehicles, this lone male always appeared more aggressive than the other four, and although I couldn't be sure, there was something about his demeanour that left me with a strong suspicion that this was the injured lion we had recently treated.

Popular conjecture is that, as an interloper, unable to challenge the coalition of four, he had become a cub stalker and killer instead! In all likelihood his life-threatening injury was sustained when he was caught by the males of the coalition when he tried to intervene and mate with one of the females in oestrus or, indeed, while threatening cubs. Why they did not kill him or inflict more damage remains a mystery.

It is quite possible that in helping this lion what we actually did was aid and abet a killer – identified, sentenced and punished by those who knew better, and by those laws of nature we had no right interfering with. With our hearts ruling our heads, and with only the best intentions, we may have inadvertently unleashed a monster back into lion society. Much as I hoped we were wrong, there appeared to be no other logical explanation for the disappearance of three litters of cubs, or the fragmentation of the pride, since this lion was given another chance at life … Or was that merely coincidence?

A few months later Meagan and I were out on a game drive with Irving Stevenson and his family. Irving and I hadn't seen each other for decades and were celebrating this rather special reunion. The two of us went back a long, long way; in fact, it was Irving who had introduced me to the Lowveld over 40 years earlier. The sun had just set and we were sitting quietly on one of the high points on the reserve listening for lions. Although we'd heard no lions roaring, we did hear impala snorting in the distance. My ears pricked up immediately, as this was their high-pitched rasping alarm snort, not the blow and throaty rattle that we'd been hearing during the prevailing rutting season. These impala were definitely not happy about something, and I was reasonably sure this was in response to a predator of sorts, so we drove to where we thought they were. Irving was no stranger to the bush: a few minutes later his powerful spotlight beam picked up the reflection of hundreds of eyes ahead, reminiscent of the lights from a distant Karoo town, blinking back at us in the night.

Closer now, we could see the herd of over a hundred tightly packed impala standing there poised for flight, ears forward, necks craned like herons about to strike, and all looking in the same direction. Sure enough, it wasn't long before the sweep of the spotlight picked up the yellow reflection of a pair of eyes, low down in the grass on the edge of the runway some 50 metres away. Moving in closer, the powerful beam now revealed a male lion lying down in the grass: he casually looked at us, blinking in the light but otherwise apparently unconcerned by the intrusion. It was clear from his attitude that he wasn't hunting. Looking through my binoculars while Irving held the light on him, the scarred face was vaguely familiar, and then it dawned on me that this was the same male we had treated six months previously. We turned off the main headlights and spotlight, leaving only the soft glow of the park lights, which threw just enough light on the lion.

He lay there sphinx-like with his ears cocked forward, showing absolutely no interest in us or the herd of impala close by. The lion appeared to be preoccupied with something else, and although it was nothing I could put my finger on, his behaviour made me feel uneasy. Being on his own, I expected him to roar, communicating his position to the other lions. Lions don't like being alone, so we sat quietly waiting for him to call. After about 40 minutes, during which time he didn't utter a sound, we decided to head off down to a nearby water hole and then make our way home.

It was decidedly nippy that evening; in fact, it was damn cold. I took the shortest route home, which happened to be along the relatively wide firebreak road. We hadn't gone more than a couple of kilometres when the headlight beam picked out familiar shapes in the road some 50 metres or so in front of us. The lions were walking side by side; their shadows were caricature-like silhouettes, elongated renditions that stretched far ahead of them on the road.

I slowed the vehicle down to walking pace in order to keep up with the two lionesses and their three tiny cubs, which I guessed could not have been more than three or four weeks old. Although they were unhurriedly making their way along the road, the cubs were clearly unaccustomed to moving at this pace and occasionally stumbled. Not being used to the lights, they may have been startled and confused by their own shadows, so we hung back as far as we could. One of the lionesses, probably their mother, kept stopping every now and again, looking back over her shoulder and waiting for the cubs to catch up.

We stayed with the lions for another 20 minutes, the cold all but forgotten at the excitement of seeing the tiny cubs. Satisfied there was enough distance between them and the male, we left the happy wanderers walking along the road, turned the vehicle around and took a longer route home.

It was obvious that the big male had an inkling about the cubs; were they his, perhaps? Could this explain why he was so preoccupied, so intent on listening rather than advertising his presence and territorial tenure as a male lion normally does? Was he waiting for a clue that would inadvertently give away their whereabouts so he could meet up with them and rub noses?

... Or was he simply trying to locate these cubs in order to kill them?

TALL ANIMAL STORIES

Of all the larger animals that occur on our reserve, it is apparent that giraffe are among those most prone to mishap. The Afrikaans vernacular *kameelperd* is most apt in describing this species' unique locomotion. Directly translated into English, it means 'camel horse', and a more descriptive name would be hard to find, as this deceptively agile creature in fact walks like a camel and runs like a horse. When at a full gallop, giraffe are difficult for predators such as lions to stop. However, they're relatively easy to see and therefore become easier targets in the thickets, or wherever the terrain can assist the lions in tripping them up.

From time to time these enormous animals also suffer limb injuries, or worse, when they are caught in steep-sided railway cuttings, a common hazard throughout the reserve. Giraffe are tempted by the browse that sometimes grows along the inside edges of these cuttings and are drawn in, but they find it almost impossible to clamber out of the embankments in a hurry. Invariably they have to double back or continue on through to either end, and some of the cuttings are hundreds of metres long. Unfortunately, many are caught in the middle where they fall foul of oncoming trains in their panic to get out of the way. Trying to use their long limbs and high centre of gravity to clamber out usually results in them falling back in, and in front of oncoming trains.

Venturing out on a fairly sturdy limb here, it needs to be said that giraffe have one of the strongest bone structures in the animal world; actually it wouldn't surprise me if, proportionately speaking, they had the strongest bones of any large mammal. This is largely due to the ivory-like density and smaller marrow cavities of their bones, which give them the characteristic strength necessary to support the weight of an animal that has such a high centre of gravity compounded by its extraordinarily long neck and limbs. This basketball player of the animal kingdom may be up for the game and able to reach the tops of trees, but as with some tall ball players, there are compromises to being built out of proportion. Despite their strength and agility, giraffe do suffer lameness, swelling of the joints and sometimes broken limbs.

A mature giraffe bull can attain a height of over 5,5 metres. Try to picture three tall men standing on top of one another's heads ... *that's* how tall. Bull giraffe can weigh nearly 1 500 kilograms, which is almost as heavy as a 15-man Springbok rugby team. If you exclude the likes of Victor Matfield and Pierre Spies, that is. So understandably when giraffe are pursued by predators they're bound to end up with an injury sooner or later. A long-limbed animal of this mass running through the bush at speeds in excess of 50 kilometres per hour is an accident waiting to happen. However, these injuries are not common, and they're not always the result of running from predators, so whenever possible we try to assess the cause in order to rule out any unnatural wounds, such as those inflicted by hunters and poachers' snares or sustained in collisions with trains.

In some cases, as with humans, older giraffe simply feel and display the effects of old age – for example, stiff joints and lameness. And, as the following will show, not all the misfortune that befalls giraffe on our reserve can be attributed to their physiology.

Our field rangers returning from a routine anti-poaching patrol reported a giraffe bull, apparently in its prime, suffering from a badly swollen leg. As it was late in the day, I decided to go out first thing the following morning to assess the situation for myself. At first light I found the giraffe in much the same place as had been reported the previous day. This in itself didn't bode well; it was a strong indication of a debilitating injury.

The huge old bull allowed us to approach to within a few metres of him before moving off, and then only with great difficulty. It was a pathetic sight to watch as he hobbled away on three legs. The size of the swelling on the lower front leg, and the way he was limping, left me in no doubt as to the poor animal's predicament and the course of action to take. Under normal circumstances one should allow nature to take its course, but with so many giraffe being hit by the train we could not rule this possibility out. Our policy on the reserve is quite simple: man induced, man to rectify.

I telephoned Gerrit Scheepers, and an hour later he was on the scene with all the necessary veterinary paraphernalia he usually knew to bring along. The dart was prepared and a few milligrams of M99 duly loaded, then cautiously he stalked the animal to get within range. Using the latest state-of-the-art Dan Inject dart gun, he took aim. The fluorescent-pink plumed dart was easy to follow through the air on its curved trajectory all the way into the giraffe's rump. A few minutes later the giraffe began to stagger, lifting its feet in a high-stepping chopping action like a Lipizzaner in a show ring, then collapsing heavily onto its side. Less than 10 minutes had elapsed.

A thorough examination revealed that although the fetlock was badly swollen there was no fracture, so treatment included the administration of a long-acting antibiotic, cortisone and some potent anti-inflammatory drugs. For good measure we threw in a complimentary boost of vitamins, as we always did. A few minutes later, having reversed the M99 with M5050, the giraffe was up and on his feet, then simply walked slowly away. He stopped a couple of times and threw a casual glance back at us over his shoulder, not quite understanding what had happened, though he must have felt some relief from the effects of the treatment, as his limp had all but disappeared.

Once the effect of the anti-inflammatory drug wore off he may well have started limping again, until the injury healed completely. Nevertheless, we left him browsing on a knobthorn tree, his long blue tongue and glue-like saliva stripping the leaves from the stems in-between the vicious hooked thorns, and we headed home. This was one of those days when game rangers get back from the bush exhausted, dirty and hungry but with a sense of accomplishment, and for no other reward than simply success itself. Indeed, it is days like this that qualify as good at the office.

We all held thumbs that the giraffe would make it, and even though we knew the prognosis was good, we also knew the bush was not exactly an ideal convalescent home. Of particular concern, and what we were watching for, was that the hoof might fall off. If it did, he would have had no hope of survival in the wild. After 10 days there was nothing to report, and more often than not in these situations, no news is good news.

A few weeks later, a young giraffe cow was reportedly seen with a bad limp. The injury appeared to be high up on the left front leg. Fortunately, veterinarian Melvyn Greenberg, better known by his radio persona 'Dr Platzhund', was visiting the reserve at the time and was on hand to give his expert opinion on this injury. Regrettably, in this case the prognosis was not good. The poor animal had a badly broken upper leg, and to complicate matters further it was an open fracture with a massive infection. As there was nothing that could be done for her, no attempt was made to dart her. Melvyn suggested that she be put out of her pain immediately, a gut-wrenching, yet entirely compassionate decision. You win some; you lose some.

Although there was no obvious or direct evidence to indicate an unnatural cause, the fact that this animal was found less than 300 metres from the railway line raised our suspicions. In addition, this had happened in an area where three other giraffe had been killed by the train in the last 10 years. Furthermore, the height of the break was not consistent with the usual injuries and fractures we see, those known to be the result of running and stumbling. These fractures invariably involve the giraffe's lower limbs. Again, based on circumstantial evidence and gut feel, I had no choice but to judge the train as the culprit and return a verdict of guilty.

Trains are not the only abiotic threat facing the gentle giraffe in our area; there is another more sinister tool in man's hand – namely, steel wire and cable. Snares made from this material are indirectly responsible for the indiscriminate death and maiming of thousands of wild animals in Africa each year. And they need not be so wantonly destructive. Although not my hunting tool of choice, when selectively deployed and used with discretion, a snare can be an effective hunting tool.

Snaring animals for food is an archaic practice; even so, there are many fur trappers and hunters in countries like Scotland and Canada who legally employ this technique today, albeit on much smaller animals. However, their methods and ethics do not allow for the destruction of non-target species, therefore unnecessary suffering or maiming is largely avoided. These snares are monitored daily, often twice daily; more importantly, every snare is deactivated or removed when the hunter leaves the zone to try another area.

Poachers in Africa, on the other hand, will lay up to 50 snares in an area and then spend the absolute minimum time harvesting what they trap. In the well-patrolled reserves of the Lowveld, time is of the essence – it's a matter of hit and run – so when only a few of the snares laid are successful, the animals are quickly retrieved. The remaining snares are simply abandoned and left to lie in the bush, waiting like buried anti-personnel mines for unsuspecting animals in the weeks, months and even years to come. The result is that animals that are later caught often end up either rotting in the snare or breaking it off with the noose embedded in their flesh. Larger predators, particularly hyenas and lions, lured by the smell of the snared carcasses or the distress calls of trapped animals, move in to investigate and themselves become victims of this scourge.

As a result of the prevailing drought, grassless conditions around old settlement sites have exposed much detritus of humanity, the debris of those who occupied the area as long as a century ago. Needless to say, I love to scratch around and pick up relics of the early inhabitants of, and pioneers in, the area. One day I found an old saddle stirrup, a number of Martini-Henry bullet casings and some rusted belt buckles.

I also came across a rusted snare lying on the ground close by. This particular noose had been made from a type of steel fence wire known to have been used by farmers over 50 years ago. Although not set, and relatively innocuous, this rusted snare, which may well have been set nearly half a century ago, would be just as deadly if it was used today!

Thicker cables are retrieved from scrap heaps, or simply stolen, and then stripped down to make thinner, more manageable nooses of death; these are then strategically set to ensnare any unsuspecting animal. The thickness and deployment of the snare cable used will depend on the size of the animal being targeted. Usually, if those specific animals were to fall victim, death by strangulation would result; however, more often than not much larger animals get ensnared. The ensuing desperate struggle can last for hours or even days. Sometimes they manage to break the snare at its weakest point, which is usually at a knot either at the anchor point or at the base of the noose. However, by this time the cable or wire has pulled taut, cutting through flesh and tendons, sometimes to the bone. Breaking free at this juncture does not mean freedom for the animal; instead, it's the beginning of a nightmare of unspeakable agony. Were these unfortunate animals able to choose at the outset, then death by strangulation would have been a comparatively quick and painless option. Blood flow is cut off and massive infection begins to set in. Without intervention, the slow ordeal to an inevitable outcome begins. It is usually at this stage that we come across the victims by noticing a limp or typical swelling above the constriction and uncharacteristic social behaviour.

In areas of intensive subsistence poaching, many farmers have taught their dogs to sit and bark if they happen to get caught in a snare. This elementary training has saved many dogs' lives and alerted farmers to snare-infested areas. Unfortunately, most of the domestic animals that get caught in snares react as their wild cousins do and try to break free, which some manage to do, but others don't. If an animal trailing a snare is fortunate enough to get noticed, and if there is still enough time to remedy the situation, the outcome can be a fortunate one. But more often than not wild animals are found at the point where there is no hope of recovery, and these are destined for a merciful bullet. Those that can be saved with professional help are given every chance, and no expense is spared. In these situations on our reserve it is a question of judgement on my part, and in most cases once the decision to intervene is taken we act quickly. I believe in the old adage, 'If you need a pair of shoes, you don't go to the butcher', so in such circumstances there is no question in our minds: without hesitation we call on a veterinarian for assistance.

Giraffe are well designed to browse tree leaves up to a height of nearly six metres above the ground: their long, powerful necks and snakelike tongues make this entirely possible. However, this is as far as the advantage goes. Having a neck that long is a bit like carrying a stepladder around with you: it needs to be guided, steered through gaps in thick bush, brought down to negotiate overhanging branches and poked through openings … and therein lies the danger. Snares set for kudu, zebra and wildebeest would be set at roughly chest height for a giraffe, so only when the giraffe lowers its head and neck to that height to negotiate a gap would it get snared around the neck. Make no mistake, giraffe are also a favourite target of poachers; however, when they are targeted specifically, the snares are set higher and constructed out of at least eight millimetre cable! Not even the largest bull giraffe is able to escape from steel cable that thick.

Mid-morning, and the radio crackled – it was another urgent call from our field rangers. They reported seeing a giraffe with a snare around the base of its neck, drinking at one of our water holes. If it's able to drink, I thought, there may be a good chance of removing the snare and saving the giraffe, so on this assumption I telephoned Gerrit, who thankfully could hand over some of the morning's scheduled clinic appointments to his partner. In my mind's eye I could see Gerrit rubbing his hands with glee; he so much preferred working with wildlife.

A little over an hour later, his little Cessna touched down on the runway. We loaded the dart gun and other veterinary gear into the Land Cruiser and made our way to the water point known as Wild Dog Pan some three kilometres away, where rangers had been diligently monitoring the giraffe since earlier that morning.

It was one of those typically cool and windy August days in the Lowveld. Cooler conditions alleviate one of the dangers involved in immobilising animals in Africa; there is no need to worry about the increased risks associated with darting wildlife in high ambient temperatures. Studying the giraffe briefly, Gerrit was able to estimate its weight and condition in order to calculate the correct dose to load; we then drove out of its line of sight and prepared the dart. I grabbed a small pair of bolt cutters and pushed the one handle through my belt (ordinary side cutters are not nearly as effective). Once I had pulled the snare free of the giraffe's skin with my Leatherman tool, I would use the blunt-nosed bolt cutter to cut the exposed cable.

Gerrit couldn't have placed the dart better. (At nearly R1 000 per dose, not to mention the cost of the dart itself, a missed dart could be an expensive error.) Upon impact the giraffe took off at a run, and following immediately so did I. But not before shouting over my shoulder and indicating to Gerrit and the game scouts to follow me in the Land Cruiser. The portable radio and bolt cutters really weighed me down, but more than that they were really awkward to run with. If the drug hadn't begun to work, slowing the giraffe down, I would have lost sight of him. After running for nearly a kilometre he slowed down to a high-stepping gait, typical of the effects of M99, then began to stumble, then stopped struggling, and moments later, like a tall building being demolished by staged implosions, collapsed in a heap.

At this point I was completely out of breath, but I managed to radio my position to the rangers. Still puffing and panting, I rushed up to the back of the giraffe's neck, opened the handles on the bolt cutters and pushed the open jaws into the middle of the mushy tissue, where the small amount of pus that oozed out helped me to locate the buried cable. Fortunately I was spot-on and managed to cut through the snare in one squeeze of the handles.

The effort exerted by the giraffe in trying to break free had pulled the noose tighter around his neck, but the four-millimetre cable snare had only cut through his thick skin and buried itself in the softer muscle tissue of the neck before breaking. Within a minute Gerrit arrived and started working on the wound. Except for the giraffe's unexpectedly long run, everything had gone like clockwork ... so far.

I am forever amazed at the efficacy of M5050, used to reverse the effects of M99. It is not unlike a deeply hypnotised subject being brought out of a hypnotic state at the count of five, or a snap of the fingers; it is a dramatic, almost magical reaction. The antidote was routinely loaded and administered directly into a vein in the giraffe's ear. Within 30 seconds the giraffe made its first attempt at getting to its feet, then it tried for a second time and then a third, only to collapse each time with a lumpy sounding thud, as its head hit the ground. We stood by anxiously, utterly helpless; we all knew that only its own power would get it up onto its feet. Gerrit looked concerned, saying that the prognosis didn't look good at all, and that if the giraffe didn't get up now, it never would. When the giraffe tried again, I leapt in under its head to try and help support the weight of its upper neck and head on my back, not realising just how big and heavy a giraffe's head actually is; it crushed me to the ground so hard I grunted as the wind was knocked out of me. Despite every attempt by the four of us, there was nothing we could physically do to help the desperate animal. With a great sense of sadness and failure we decided the giraffe had to be destroyed.

Gerrit took it to heart and insisted on getting to the cause of the giraffe's inability to get up. With the aid of a front-end loader we placed the carcass onto the tractor's tip trailer and drove back to base camp where Gerrit conducted a rudimentary autopsy. Everything about the animal, particularly its condition, appeared normal. However, when the rumen was examined we found that it only contained a minimal amount of coarse leaf material; this was obviously abnormal and explained everything. The snare had been so tight on its neck that it had prevented the giraffe from regurgitating a bolus, so he had been unable to chew the cud and swallow solids, only water had been able to get through. He simply didn't have the energy and strength to get up. If only we had known this at the time, a simple glucose drip would have boosted his diminished blood sugar level and given him the boost necessary to get onto his feet until replenished by browse.

To this day, a drip and a vitamin booster are part and parcel of Gerrit's treatment in all remotely similar cases ... just in case the animal needs it.

The increase in rhino poaching incidents in the Lowveld has had far-reaching negative spin-offs for other wildlife on our reserve. We'd been compelled to take our eye off the ball and focus our attention and anti-poaching resources on measures to combat the threat of rhino poaching. Needless to say, the heightened vigilance in one sector has led to unscrupulous opportunists taking advantage of the situation and filling the vacuum in another. Subsequently, snare-laying activity in those areas our team routinely patrols in prevention of bushmeat poaching began to increase; much of this took place in the relatively thick Commiphora woodland found primarily in rocky, hilly terrain. This habitat is not favoured by the white rhino in our reserve, so all the more reason, we thought, to focus our anti-poaching resources in the hot spots. These measures appeared to be helping on the rhino front, and all things considered, we'd had some respite on the other front: almost three months had gone by without the dreaded report of some unfortunate animal carrying a snare on the reserve. However, I knew we were tempting fate.

Neil and Morag Hulett, two of our reserve's long-standing shareholders, were out on their routine morning drive one day when they reported a giraffe bull limping badly. It was the second animal that they'd called in in as many weeks. A week previously Neil had called in a wildebeest cow with a deep snare wound on its lower hindleg. Unfortunately the wire cable had cut through the tendons; the poor beast was doomed and she had to be destroyed. Naturally, I said a silent prayer that this giraffe wouldn't have the same prognosis.

According to Neil, the giraffe was unable to put any weight on its leg at all, and besides the enormous swelling, he couldn't see any sign of a snare or of constriction (which usually indicates a buried snare).

'Stay with him, Neil, I'll be along shortly,' I said, turning my Land Cruiser around and heading to his location.

'It doesn't look like he will go very far,' Neil replied.

I arrived about 15 minutes later and managed to drive closer to the giraffe than Neil was able to. Hauling out my 10 x binoculars, I focused on its swollen hoof. At first there was nothing suggesting a snare, then as it lifted its hoof slightly, I could just make it out: a small piece of steel cable jutting out above and behind the hoof, as thick as a matchstick but less than half as long. Had the grass been an inch longer, I would never have seen it. The next time my finger moved, it was pressing 'Call Gerrit' on my cell phone.

Everything went like clockwork; this time there was no drama, no running and no chasing. We simply trailed a long length of rope and moved in slowly, giving the animal a wide berth. Then as the M99 began to take effect, the giraffe's legs were bundled together, tripping it up and bringing it down. Gerrit dived in, cutting the snare off immediately, while the rest of us battled to keep the giraffe's head upright. Drugged though it was, we could not hold onto its head and with powerful sweeps of its neck, it threw us around like limp rag dolls. I knew as it was happening that I would be sore the next day, and my prediction was spot on!

The antidote was administered and within seconds the giraffe was able to support its own neck upright. With huge wide eyes it stared at us through eyelashes that would have left Liza Minnelli green with envy. Despite the unnatural events unfolding, I detected no fear in those eyes, only surprise and confusion that lasted mere moments. Then, in one effortless movement, it was up and on its feet. There it remained for a few moments, still staring down at us, until it began to walk slowly away, with a barely noticeable limp. Incredible! I thought. Gerrit looked at me and smiled: a good sugar boost had made all the difference. Two minutes later, not more than 25 metres away, the giraffe began browsing, totally unconcerned with us, or its now relatively painless leg.

ELEPHANT CONUNDRUM

Notwithstanding the fact that elephant are being poached out of existence in many parts of their former range in Africa, here at home, down south, it's a different scenario entirely. Given the status quo, we are fast approaching the Rubicon in terms of elephant population management in South Africa. Even so, there are indications that the focus of this is about to change, as already evidence of ivory poaching is reaching worrying levels in the Kruger National Park. However, for the time being the fact is that elephant in the Lowveld are evidently in desperate need of more *Lebensraum*, particularly in those private reserves adjoining the Kruger. When fences were removed between the Kruger and these private reserves to the west, elephant moved in and took advantage of the relative abundance and variety of feed in the new areas. Initially their numbers were easily absorbed, but it has now become apparent that they have reached saturation levels in many private reserves – in particular, those where elephant populations are not autonomously managed.

The total population of elephant in the Kruger National Park and associated private reserves to the west is fast approaching 25 000! When I started my career in conservation, the Kruger maintained their elephant population at around 8 000. These numbers were managed by means of regular lethal culling, a method of population control that has since become anathema in the wider world's opinion. At the time that culling was being implemented, the private reserves to the west were still fenced out and elephant were largely excluded. So the

Kruger was in fact managing the elephant population within its confines quite effectively. Even so, occasionally a handful of bulls would break through and visit the private reserves from time to time.

I recall guiding overseas clients back in the late 1970s, when we would only come across mature bulls, often on their own or in small herds of invariably fewer than seven individuals. The older an elephant gets, the more likely he or she is to develop recognisable external characteristics or distinguishing external features, for example, a noticeable tear on the outer edge of the ear or sometimes even a hole in the ear. Chipped or missing tusks are also common. One particular bull I remember had a huge smooth knob the size of a grapefruit on his upper trunk, a feature that made him instantly recognisable. Naturally we would come across the same bulls frequently and some of the guests suspected we were driving them around in circles. Admittedly, this aspersion dented the ego of this 23-year-old ranger a little, but what the hell, we lived through it OK. Elephant are one of the Big Five, and as far as most visitors were concerned, seeing one or two individuals was all they needed to tick their list. In my view, the African wilderness will never be complete without these magnificent animals. They denote a deep-seated primal wildness, and none more so than a breeding herd of elephant.

Although this recollection takes me back to 1979, I can remember that particular morning like it was yesterday. I was on my way from Mala Mala Game Reserve to Skukuza Airport to collect guests when I came across a small breeding herd of elephant in a dry river crossing known as Dudley Drift. I had never seen an elephant cow and calf in the wild before, and here in front of me, in the middle of Sabi Sands, was a herd of 17! Filled with excitement, I called the sighting in over the radio and every person on the reserve who could get there, did. Petty territorial feuds were unofficially put on temporary hold; there was a non-negotiable 'ceasefire' so all could come and witness such a rare spectacle.

A few years later, orphaned elephant, the residue of culling programmes in the Kruger, were brought into Sabi Sands in an effort to establish a viable breeding herd. Eleven young animals ranging in age from four to twelve years were released onto the reserve to fend for themselves. Although well meaning, this pilot project proved to be a disastrous introduction. Having no protection or guidance from adult elephant, some of the youngest were killed by lions, while others sought the companionship of buffalo herds. Over time, all but the oldest three elephant had disappeared by the time I'd left. Today, a mere 37 years later, by way of natural migration, fence removals and ideal habitat, well over a thousand elephant call Sabi Sands home!

After the culling programme was stopped, the elephant numbers in the Kruger National Park began to grow. Expanding the area into which elephant could move freely from the Kruger – namely, Mozambique to the east and the private game reserves to the west – brought temporary respite. However, there can be no denying the fact that the meta-population of elephant in the Lowveld has virtually tripled since the culling days. It is also becoming clear that, despite almost 30 per cent more area for the elephant to move in, they are still running out of living space and thereby being left with little option but to denude available forage areas. Their numbers are growing exponentially, and the land area available for them is shrinking. Particularly here on Olifants, where to see a herd of 60 elephant is the norm and hardly warrants a call on the two-way radio as there is likely to be another herd comprising similar numbers at the next water hole, especially in the winter months. This is no hyperbole, and it doesn't take a doctorate in ecology to predict that, given the available resources, these numbers and the potential growth are simply unsustainable.

We've all heard this before; there are numerous documentary films, heaps of scientific papers, books and magazine articles highlighting the plight facing elephant in the broader African context. With one or two exceptions, these deal primarily with the threat from increased levels of ivory poaching and emphasise less the problem of man's need or greed for the elephant's ever-shrinking wilderness. Livestock and agriculture are moving in and taking over former rangeland. The shrinking area elephant are left with means that the remaining habitats are persistently over-utilised without seasonal respite. There is little or no time for vegetative recovery, succession or recruitment of woody species. In terms of the perceived threat to biodiversity, conservationists are divided, but most believe that the environment simply cannot sustain the current levels of what is seen to be overzealous feeding behaviour. At this rate there is no doubt that other important species of wildlife will be negatively affected.

Elephant appear to be dammed if they do and damned if they don't: almost everywhere they find themselves, there is conflict of one sort or another. And paradoxically, their ultimate survival will depend on the very beings that they are in direct conflict with. We need greater insight, and as much information as we can collect, in order to better understand the problems facing these wonderful animals, so that practical management solutions of mutual benefit can be found and implemented. Quickly!

What better way to understand people and get to know them than by living in their homes, following them around as they go about their daily lives? Indeed, many researchers do just that when studying remote tribal cultures. Realistically speaking, though, it is simply not a practical option for humans to live with wild elephant 24 hours a day for months on end. Fortunately there is a less invasive solution. Using modern technology we can follow their real-time movements, collect data and learn about them without influencing their natural patterns of behaviour or intruding on their most intimate moments. This can be done by fitting a satellite-linked tracking device to an integral member of a subject herd – for example, the matriarch of a breeding herd would be ideal.

Since the mid-1990s, Dr Michelle Henley of Save the Elephants (STE) has placed monitoring collars on hundreds of elephant in the Timbavati, Klaserie and the Umbabat nature reserves. However, only five of these collared elephant were known to use the Balule Nature Reserve area from time to time. Now that more than 600 elephant resided in our area, it was high time Balule was invited to the collaring party.

The primary purpose of this collaring exercise was mainly to broaden the range of Dr Henley's research by including elephant from Balule, and to expand further research into the Associated Private Nature Reserves (APNR). Projects would aim to throw light on matters such as population dynamics and the movement of elephant within the APNR, their effect on tree species, the possible establishment of safe migration corridors from one reserve to another, and the monitoring of contraceptive population control subjects.

For the first recipient of a GPS collar, we sought an adult elephant cow, one that was part of a sizeable herd within the Balule Nature Reserve. However, at the time a suitable breeding herd could not be located within the specific region chosen, so I was tasked at very short notice with locating a herd in the Olifants region. To this end we scrambled all our resources, not the least being our shareholders, and the hunt was on. All went quiet on the radio waves until, less than an hour later, one of our shareholders broke the silence to say she had located a breeding herd moving north across our southern cutline.

Knowing the herd was heading to water, we knew this was our chance. The operation got underway as preparations were made to co-ordinate the helicopter, veterinarian, ground crew and the sponsors. All the while I kept tabs on the herd as they milled about feeding in the thick bush east of the water hole known as Sable Dam. Soon I could no longer see them but was happy enough to be able to hear them as they slowly moved deeper into the bush. At the present pace of their feeding I was comfortable they would not have got too far by the time the helicopter arrived. In the meantime many of the shareholders on the reserve at the time, as well as the organisers and the donors of the collar, began to rendezvous at Sable Dam.

The helicopter with the vet on board came in relatively high, located the herd, then circled the nervous animals a couple of times, which caused them to form the classic protective circle around the calves. Some elephant still remember the Kruger National Park's culling programme, which was carried out using helicopters. It is no wonder that this fear has been passed down through the generations since. Maintaining a non-threatening altitude, the helicopter hovered for a moment, positioned itself and then nosed straight in like a peregrine falcon swooping on a pigeon. The serious business had clearly begun. As the elephant milled about amid the dust and confusion, the selected cow was quickly singled out, separated from the herd and darted.

It was clear these guys had done this numerous times before. This was amply demonstrated by the skill and professionalism of Pete Rogers who perched precariously out on the skids of the chopper, taking aim with the dart gun, while Big Game Heli's pilot, the late Benjamin Osmers (Bennie), expertly positioned him for the best shot placement. This was always quite breathtaking to watch. Once the dart was in, some really awesome skill was revealed as Bennie and his machine became one, and the 'dancing' started. Bennie appeared to move the helicopter in time to music only he could hear. As he began to dance with the elephant, there were moments when they appeared to touch as he tried to position her point of fall and, more importantly, separate her from the rest of the herd. I'm convinced that skilled helicopter pilots, particularly those who capture game for a living, must have done classical ballet or at least ballroom dancing at some point in their lives, though I don't know one who will readily admit to it.

Despite skilful manoeuvring with the helicopter, the elephant went down in an awkward spot on the edge of a small drainage line, which partially obscured her from full view. Nevertheless, now that she was separated from the herd, we managed to move in with two vehicles and position ourselves some 15 metres away from the hub of activity surrounding her. This was a limitation for all of those parked on the periphery, but still it was an interesting deviation from a routine game drive.

The collar is an expensive piece of kit, at around R60 000. Then of course there are the helicopter costs, vet fees and so on. These costs are largely recovered by having people, mostly overseas guests, pay for the privilege of getting up close and being able to touch such a magnificent animal. This is not only a once in a lifetime experience for most of them, but entitles them to front row seats, as it were. So we watched from a distance as they touched and felt ... and touched again. As an added bonus they got to 'help' with the fitting of the collar and data collection, which includes all the necessary measurements, and the taking of blood and tissue samples.

Knowing the elephant was lying on a relatively uncomfortable rocky piece of sloping ground, and in order to minimise any risk of pressure injuries, she needed to be brought around and onto her feet as soon as possible. Understandably, in this instance less time than usual was spent on these formalities, and she was given the antidote. Within seconds the few milligrams of M5050 injected directly into her bloodstream completely reversed the immobilising effect of the M99. After a couple of ungainly attempts the elephant stood up, remaining still only for a few moments until she'd gathered her senses and her inbuilt compass needle was able to point her in the right direction.

Although I have seen the dramatic neutralising effect of M5050 on M99 in action hundreds of times, it never ceases to amaze me. It was as if the drama of the previous 20 minutes had never occurred: she shook her head at us indignantly, turned around and headed off to find the rest of the herd – no staggering, no disorientation ... nothing. Everything appeared perfectly normal as she ran through the bush. Only this time she was unknowingly carrying some hi-tech monitoring equipment with her.

I couldn't help thinking that mankind can be marvellous ... sometimes.

Elephant are fast becoming their own worst enemies, not for any other reason than their apparently destructive feeding habits. It appears, to our limited understanding, that they are effectively destroying the very vegetation and habitat that sustains them.

Despite the abundance and variety of herbaceous feed available on our reserve, no one appears to know why elephant continue to ring-bark trees, mainly knobthorn and marula, well into the summer months. Usually this rate of bark stripping is observed at the tail end of winter and during severe drought periods when the elephant utilise the bark, and I have seen starving impala, kudu and giraffe home in on the trees pushed over by elephant. Knobthorn in particular produces green nutritious leaves in the driest months of the year, which are eagerly browsed. So although to the eye this initially appears as wanton and wasteful, I keep telling myself there has to be a bigger scheme at play; there must be something that flies in the face of all conventional understanding of ecological processes, something we all have yet to understand. But most of us are not comfortable with change, especially such rapid change to biodiversity as is under way right now.

Watching as the landscape is dramatically altered by elephant in just a few decades gives rise to more than casual concern. By our very nature we constantly look for answers, seeking solutions that make us comfortable, or at least that can prepare us for, and justify, the actions we take in exercising control. If we don't find them, we tend to reach conclusions based on perceptions and on the interpretation of current scientific principles as we know them. Lateral thinking is desperately needed, but in what direction?

African elephant are huge animals that require large tracts of relatively unspoilt habitat in order to meet the nutritional needs of their ever-growing numbers. Deprived of sufficient range, they will soon denude what feed is available and be forced beyond the reserve's boundaries. Inevitably, this brings them onto the fringes of human settlement, where they soon develop a penchant for domestic crops, which places them in direct conflict with subsistence farmers and where they are destroyed by park rangers from time to time. Also of concern is that they are more exposed outside the sanctuary of national parks, thereby becoming more predictable and subsequently easier targets for poachers.

Enter Dr Lucy King, whose innovative solution to a centuries-old problem has all but eliminated the need to shoot *shamba*-raiding elephant in Kenya. Her award-winning study, for which she earned a

well-deserved doctorate, shows the power of lateral thinking and commitment to non-violent alternatives. When Dr King discovered that
bees are definitely not an elephant's favourite insect, she began finding
a way of using African honeybees as an effective deterrent. Her tests
were conclusive, resulting in strategically placed beehives solving the
problem of marauding elephant. However, not only did her idea culminate in effectively keeping elephant out of rural cropland, but it has
since developed into a substantial apiary industry, providing jobs and
meaningful income for the local communities. The production of deli-
cious organic honey, which is sold on the European market at premium
prices, far outweighs the benefits they received from the subsistence
crops they initially needed to protect ... Brilliant!

One of the biggest hurdles to overcome in applying this solution to
selected tree stands in Balule Nature Reserve is that we are situated
in a semi-arid region. We need to see if there are enough pollen-bear-
ing plants to support hives through the Lowveld's winter season, as
this is time of the year when the trees are most damaged by elephant.
As I write, research using African honeybees as a deterrent to protect
selected trees is underway. At the moment the focus is on the vulnerable and locally endangered marula trees in Balule.

Besides ring-barking, which in most cases kills the tree but does at
least yield some nutrition, elephant will sometimes push down, uproot
and damage trees, without utilising a single morsel of the organism.
Huge trees are simply pushed over and left: some specimens which
have been ring-dated were found to be well over two centuries old!
This raises the question whether elephant are totally non-selective
when it comes to the type of vegetation they use. I think not: I believe
they target trees for reasons known only to them at this stage. The why
of which we are yet to understand, but select they sure do, and the one
exception I know of proves the rule.

Shepherd's trees are relatively abundant and found throughout our
reserve in almost every soil and habitat type; they also occur in many
of the harshest environments in southern Africa. The evergreen foliage
is browsed on by all those herbivores able to access its leaves, including

man's domestic stock, yet elephant neither eat, damage nor destroy these trees. Nobody can tell me why this sought-after fodder tree is left untouched, while those species known to be far less palatable, or decidedly unpalatable, are targeted instead. I believe there's a PhD in this question for someone up for the challenge, but somehow I suspect that at the end of their study there may very well be more questions than answers.

We know that elephant are highly intelligent creatures. However, I don't believe they should be credited with reasoning or conscious perception of consequences, particularly of their feeding activities. This is the realm of man only. Essentially elephant are blameless of malice or that which is deemed to be pointless destruction, even though it doesn't make sense to our sense of logic to destroy what you depend on for sustenance ... So, again, why do they not utilise our ubiquitous shepherd's trees while utilising all others?

So, although I'm not a visionary, I cannot believe a creature this huge has evolved to be pointlessly destructive, to the point of self-destruction. Instead I suspect there are timeframes and cycles we do not comprehend yet: we have neither the lifespan nor the patience to see these cycles through. Most importantly, I know it is only humankind that wantonly destroys. In the meantime, while those minds far more analytical and adept than mine tackle this question and hopefully come up with answers, I will console myself with the knowledge that ecosystems are dynamic. At least I know that changes are occurring all the time on the planet: most are subtle, some not so, and there are myriads we aren't even aware of yet. I don't wish to contemplate how boring our lives would be if we knew the answers to everything: it's the very inexactness and dynamism of ecology that makes it so fascinating.

George Rushby, who later became one of the founder wardens of the Serengeti, started his career in Africa as an elephant hunter. As with most people who become intimately involved with elephant, he developed a tremendous empathy and respect for their intelligence. Yet he could never understand why crop-raiding elephant on the edges of the national parks, which needed to be shot from time to time, would return night after night despite the trauma of seeing and hearing members of their herd as they fell to his rifle. Not until more than half the herd was destroyed, did they realise it was safer to stay in the park. It always puzzled George why they did not get the message sooner.

Then again, I have to wonder what George would have said if he was told at the time that a hundred years hence a beautiful young woman would make this problem go away using a tiny insect and without firing a single shot!

It is clear then that, as intelligent as elephant are, violent or tragic consequences are something they learn slowly, if at all. As the mass starvation of elephant in Tsavo has also shown, Mother Nature's harsh lessons have a timeline, as I alluded to earlier, a natural cycle, we don't yet fully understand. So how can we expect elephant to predict the future or indeed save for a rainy day?

Speaking of hunting and intelligence in the same sentence reminds me of something that happened a few years ago. It was motivated by budgetary acumen, which is the basis of all well-run conservation bodies and justified by science ... but science does not always have the final say.

An offer was tabled at a meeting of the Association of Private Nature Reserves in which the committee was asked to consider allowing a trophy hunt of a 'big tusker' elephant in the region. This would mean deviating from the standard hunting protocol, which stated the maximum allowable weight of tusk for trophy bulls as 50 pounds per side at the time. This request for a big tusker was further qualified, stipulating that this elephant needed to have tusks weighing a minimum of a hundred pounds per side! For this concession the association would receive $500 000! Given the annual costs of combating rhino poaching alone, this was a tempting sum of money indeed.

However, members of Balule Nature Reserve, who are also members of the APNR, turned this offer down flat; in fact, a certain influential landowner within Balule threatened to take this to Parliament if the matter was pursued any further. A few of the wardens, myself included, openly voiced our rejection of the proposal to hunt big tuskers, particularly a 100-pounder. For our outspoken opinion, all the Balule wardens, along with elephant expert Dr Michelle Henley of STE, were summoned to a meeting by the then-warden of the APNR, which was to be held at Timbavati Nature Reserve's headquarters. Here, according to the agenda, we would be enlightened on the ecology of elephant and be shown how naïve we were in our understanding of herd dynamics, big tuskers, their genetic importance and, of course, the sustainable utilisation of a natural resource. However, truth be told, I suspect we were there primarily to get rapped over the knuckles for our individual conservation viewpoints, particularly for not condoning the hunting of big tuskers, a view that had influential backing in the person of a Balule landowner who also happened to be an MP. So, how dare a Balule landowner and his warden challenge a lucrative offer purely on the basis of sentiment? It was further mooted that those wardens and landowners who were against the proposal needed to be more objective, and present a scientific argument as a basis for their objection.

The APNR warden felt the proposal was in line with the reserve's policy regarding legitimate trophy hunting, which was always done in accordance with scientifically justifiable off-takes. To support their proposal and exert authority, which until now had gone largely unchallenged, a long-winded albeit thoroughly researched explanation was presented. It included scientific models explaining population dynamics and sustainable utilisation of elephant. Interestingly, some considerable thought had also gone into outlining a protest protocol to be followed by those opposing similar proposals in the future (in other words, how wardens needed to conduct themselves in protest). To cut his long enlightenment short, essentially he was of the conviction that once a big tusker had injected his 'big tusk' genes into the population, he had effectively done his job, and therefore there'd be no negative impact on the ecology of the elephant population if he was hunted.

True! ... Strictly scientifically speaking, that is.

Despite Dr Henley's 25 years of research on elephant in the APNR, and her reference to studies done on Kenya's elephant population dynamics and related studies, the warden dismissed her findings as not representative of our situation in South Africa. He reiterated that, as an ex-Kruger Park employee, he could attest to the fact that the Kruger still boasted many big tuskers despite extensive culling in the past and that this was due to their 'sound scientific management policy on elephant' ...

What bullshit, I thought. We all knew that the Kruger's remaining big tuskers existed as a direct result of their obsolete culling programme. One of the stipulations in the old culling policy was that all the big tusker bulls were deliberately moved away from the killing ground. They were intentionally spared so that tourists could have bigger specimen elephant to view and photograph – for no other scientific reason were they allowed to live! And some of those huge bulls, so spared, still grace the Kruger National Park with their magnificence to this day.

From a purely pragmatic viewpoint, I argued that a 100-pounder is a revered elephant trophy. In elite hunting circles, for this to qualify, its tusks would have to weigh at least a hundred pounds per side – so if either of the tusks weighed an ounce less than a hundred pounds, they might just as well weigh two pounds! Less than a hundred pounds would be worthless to any trophy hunter fixated on this class of elephant. The subsequent pressure on the reserve and the outfitter would inevitably compel them to err on the high side. We all know elephant tusk weights are extremely difficult to judge on the living animal. The estimates of the most experienced professional hunters can go 15 per cent either way. So the elephant being targeted, if approved, would need to carry at least 115 pounds of ivory per side. This was unacceptable to those of us objecting, and we stood firm.

My argument had no scientific support, but it didn't need any. Like many others, I simply love to see big elephant, whether they are still sexually active or not is immaterial. They are icons of the African wilderness, and like those leafless, ancient leadwood trees that characterise many of our open plains, we want to see them. I want my children to see the leadwoods, no matter that they're sterile relics, practically useless for anything but leafless bird perches or firewood, and no matter that they stand gnarled and grotesque; their unique beauty adds wildness to the panorama of the African bushveld. It's the same with old elephant. I believe they are an inseparable part of the community and should be left in peace, to be admired and respected.

KILLER ELEPHANT

Any rookie weatherman would get 100 per cent for an examination based on their prognostic accuracy for this region's weather. Unlike the Outer Hebrides, or indeed our own Drakensberg, where one can experience all four seasons in a single day, summer days in our neck of the woods are monotonously hot and languid. This particular morning's weather forecast predicted a warm sunny day over the Lowveld; nothing unexpected on that score, I thought. And as early as 8 am the temperature had already begun to climb into the thirties. Keeping cool and hydrated was on everyone and everything's mind, or so it seemed.

A mains water pipeline supplying one of the larger camps in the western section of Balule had been pulled up and damaged by elephant in their search for clean, cool water. These pachyderms have an incredible sense of smell, so when they detect the slightest moisture leak resulting from a cracked pipe, or old connection clamps rusting through, they'll dig it up and rip it out in an effort to get to the source. Needless to say, every effort is made to get these essential supply lines repaired as soon as possible. And the adage that elephant don't forget is perfectly true: once they have dug up a pipeline and obtained clean water they will return to the exact spot after you have repaired it and dig it up again. To avoid this, we lay a new section of pipe in a wide half-circle detour, a few metres wide of the site of the original break, a ploy that appears to fool the wiliest of them.

Only the slightest breeze filtered through the dense thicket of acacia scrubland, but it was enough to help cool the sweat on the backs of the two men busying themselves with repairing the water line. Except for the incessant *zizz* of cicadas, pleasantly punctuated by occasional birdsong, the only other sound was the conversation between the men engrossed in the task of digging a new trench and reburying the now-repaired line. For the two men this was a routine task: they both had a thorough knowledge of the bush and its inhabitants, and were as comfortable with this task as most people would be repairing a dog-chewed garden hose at home. Apparently neither of them had the slightest inkling of what was to happen next.

I was at my workbench doing some woodwork when the call came through. It was Steve Hearne, one of the reserve's landowners, to say a worker had been killed by an elephant near his camp. My stomach did a flick-flack as I tried to take in what he'd said. Being a Sunday morning, he needlessly apologised, saying his regional warden was away and I was the only other person he could think of turning to. Reassuring him I was on duty every day, I let him continue. I knew Steve well, and for him to sound as desperate and distressed as he did meant he needed help. I also gleaned from the tone of his voice that he could use some moral support. Although experienced in the bush and familiar with rifles and dangerous game, Steve needed formal backup, someone with a rifle to stand by in order that the police and forensic examiners could work in relative safety as they tried to ascertain exactly what had happened ... I understood completely; I dropped everything and was with him in less than 30 minutes.

According to the only eyewitness, the first time the men became aware of the elephant was when two bulls came bearing down on them at full charge. It was a sudden attack, silent and without any warning. With less than 300 metres to the safety of the camp, the two men instinctively dropped their tools and ran for it. When they realised that they would never make it, they split up. For one of the men, this turned out to be the cruellest of 50–50 decisions ever made. The man who went left was killed and the man who went right lived ... and he lived to hear as the other man died.

In my 40 years in the African bush, I'd never seen a man who had been killed by an elephant, let alone touched the body of a man killed by one. I wasn't to know that in less than a week I'd bear witness to two! What I have learned in this crash course is that no two scenarios are the same. Elephant are not stereotypical killers; they are enormously powerful and even the slightest deviation from one method of brutal attack to another can yield grossly different effects on the relative frailty of the human body.

Watching as a forensic pathologist conducts an autopsy on a screen clip is grisly enough, but for obvious reasons it is nowhere near as gruesome as reality. Nothing compares to having all your senses being brought into play when standing next to a corpse in the stainless steel environment of a well-illuminated, cold autopsy room. I suspect that of all the senses, none is quite as complex as smell. Even in our poorly endowed human olfactory receptors, the most subtle nuance of a particular scent can take you back to a place of your childhood in an instant. And the poignant memories associated with it can never be deleted from your brain's memory bank. It's the same when you stand over what was once a man, who only hours ago was looking forward to some breakfast, and now lay dead in the grass, killed by an elephant. Despite the immediate environment being scented by the crushed turpentine grass and wild lavender that lingers on the periphery, there is an overwhelming smell of the elephant's musth gland secretions and its pungent urine. Unmistakable and unique, I know these smells will cling to my memory, forever blended and associated with the odour of death.

Discernibly there wasn't much to hear, except for some unidentifiable, beautiful birdsong, possibly that of a white-browed scrub robin, and the ever-persistent cicadas, and the drone of flies that now seemed to be everywhere though they had flown in from nowhere. Then there was the sound of people talking softly, talking little. Everyone was clearly horrified as we pieced together the sequence of this tragic event as it had happened.

The soil was soft, able to hide nothing; it revealed the man's last moments of terror, of horror and death.

In my unprofessional opinion, it was apparent that the man had died a mercifully quick death when the elephant initially crushed his torso. The lack of blood from the victim's leg wounds indicated his heart had already stopped by the time he was tusked. With unimaginable power, the man's dead body had then been tossed into the air to land some 25 metres away from where he'd initially been killed; it was here that we'd come upon him. It also revealed that the victim had initially landed face down. But the elephant was clearly not finished: in a chilling final act of brutality, it knelt down behind the now-dead man once more, turned him over onto his back and then crushed him once again to make sure he was dead. This was gleaned from analysing the scratch marks on the victim's skin made by the elephant's forehead. As if coarse sandpaper, its rough hide had left marks like a giant dirty fingerprint spread across the man's chest.

Two huge holes in the soil on either side of the victim's body, made by the elephant's tusks, were indicative of the amount of force used. I measured the distance between the tusk imprints, as well as their diameter, and the depth of penetration into the soft soil. This gave us a rough idea of the length of each tusk. These measurements were used to determine the approximate size of the tusks and width of the head, in order for us to try and identify the elephant responsible. Photographs of the elephant's footprints were taken, and distributed. Like fingerprints on a human being, no two elephant have the same footprint patterns, and if the soil conditions allowed, this would be the most positive means of identifying the culprit.

Once all of these details were out of the way, the mortuary van was brought closer. As we attempted to lift the victim's body to load him onto the body stretcher, a small leopard tortoise, not much bigger than a tennis ball, crawled out from under him. I remember thinking it must have gone there and snuggled in under the poor man's body once the elephant had left the scene, otherwise it too would have been crushed like a grape.

Understandably, when confronted with such violent brutality, most people's knee-jerk reaction is to destroy the animal responsible as soon as possible. I remembered a similar incident in the Timbavati when an elephant that had attacked a worker was summarily tracked down and destroyed. As I recall, the subsequent autopsy on that Timbavati bull revealed a huge abscess at the base of his tusk, the result of an altercation with another elephant. A chip of the other elephant's tusk had broken off and got embedded there, causing a massive infection – in hindsight, a treatable condition, which long-acting antibiotics would have cured.

Bearing this in mind, I suggested to Balule's head warden at the time that we try to identify and immobilise this elephant as soon as possible, in order to ascertain the cause of its behaviour. I surmised that perhaps the bull in our situation had been wounded by an irate landowner, or indeed that there may be some other innocuous motive for its behaviour, something that could be remedied. Most importantly, I reasoned that, should it be the wrong elephant, it was much easier to reverse M99 than to undo a bullet to the brain. Instead, in consultation with the committee chairman of the reserve, it was decided rather to keep tabs on the elephant and monitor its behaviour closely, and then call in a hunter to shoot it. And although no one could possibly have foreseen the consequences of this decision, it was to prove a bad one.

The hunt for the 'killer elephant' was on. Sporadic sightings filtered through for the first few days after the incident. Reports came in from game rangers and wardens who spoke of an aggressive bull in musth charging vehicles for no apparent reason. In one instance the elephant completely wrecked a Toyota Land Cruiser. Then all went quiet – that was, until on the seventh day after the first incident, when the report we were all dreading came through: another man had been killed by an elephant. This time it was one of the field rangers in the west of Balule who had been on the spoor of the 'killer elephant', keeping tabs on him, as it were, until the hunter arrived. The incident happened less than five kilometres away from where the first man was killed.

Evidently the field ranger had been following the tracks of the suspect bull on his scrambler when he turned a corner and came upon the elephant in the road. The bull turned and charged him. Realising what was happening, the man tried to turn sharply in the soft sand and in so doing stalled the engine. There was nothing he could do to kick-start it again, his fate had been sealed when the motorbike had stalled. The elephant was on him in seconds. If I was not sure this hapless man had been killed by the same elephant, I would never have believed it. In this instance, almost every bone in the victim's body had been smashed, and the man had been repeatedly tusked to the point where he was almost unrecognisable as a human being.

Although it did cross our minds fleetingly, the thought was quickly dispelled given the viciousness of this attack; it was highly unlikely that we had two 'killer elephant' in the same area. Rather we suspected that the same bull had simply doubled back to the scene of the 'crime'. Expert trackers were later able to confirm from the elephant's spoor that it was indeed the same bull. Now there was no question: this elephant had to be stopped as quickly as possible before it killed again. We were sure that if it saw another human being it would kill again. But why, we wondered, was this elephant doing this? What had caused this highly intelligent creature to snap?

Ironically, the two victims were first cousins, who had married two sisters and who had both lived in the Lowveld among elephant all their lives.

Understandably, after the first incident there was some reluctance to react impulsively. After all, Balule is primarily a Big Five game reserve with wild and dangerous animals living in it; we all live and work here cognisant of the risks. However, it had become quite clear these incidents were not the result of chance encounters with a bad-tempered elephant in musth. This bull displayed an unusually high degree of aggression. Open displays of impatience and aggression during testosterone-fuelled cycles are well recorded, but for an elephant to purposely single out and kill people was uncharacteristic behaviour. Therefore, we had a fiduciary responsibility for the safety of the other people working on the reserve. Needless to say, the families of the two men were subsequently provided with comfort and support. They were also assured that swift action against this particular elephant would be taken.

Evidence of the elephant's erratic movement pattern suggests he may have instinctively known there was more than just interest in keeping up with him to monitor his behaviour; he must have had a feeling he was being hunted. Particularly so when having left the second victim, as the spoor evidence indicated he had not stopped to feed or drink and was moving alone, striding purposefully, like a fugitive on the run. Could this elephant have realised he'd done something out of sync with normal elephant behaviour but didn't know why?

Bennie went up in his helicopter the following morning at first light. Within an hour the suspect elephant had been located – nearly 30 kilometres from the scene of the crime and heading steadily north. I believe the elephant knew he had done something wrong and was being hunted, and I suspect he was on the run. However, I also suspect that this animal, like all except humankind, had no cognitive control over his actions. Elephant don't plan murders.

Expertly, Bennie manoeuvred the bull across some open ground where clear prints were left. It didn't take the ground team long to positively identify the individual. There was no question or doubt: this was the killer bull.

With the relevant authorities present, we could now decide what action to take. But the decision needed to be made quickly. At the pace and direction he was moving in, the elephant would have made it to the Grietjie Game Reserve within an hour. This was a concern for us as this region happens to have the highest density of people in the Balule Reserve. We could not take the risk and subsequently took the decision to put the elephant down. With the head warden and provincial authorities on board to legitimise the action, the elephant was slowly moved to an area close to a road, where he was then shot and killed from the helicopter.

A rudimentary autopsy carried out on the carcass in the field revealed that although the animal was in a heavy musth cycle, everything else appeared to be normal. He had been feeding well until the last incident, and was otherwise in excellent physical condition. However, reports from regular sightings of this bull going back at least six months indicated he had been in a state of musth for much longer than normal. My hypothesis was that this individual could not cope with the relentless testosterone levels his body was being subjected to, and the sheer frustration of no release could have driven him over the edge.

Although this story made headline news, provoking much debate among conservationists on both sides of the spectrum, there can never be a definitive ruling as to what action to take, when and where. Each situation has to be judged according to its own merits. However, what I can say is that when human lives are lost so violently and without provocation, within the area of your responsibility, it is prudent to intervene. Nothing gets one's mind quite as focused as seeing a human being torn apart and brutally killed by a wild animal.

Although wild animals do have limited reasoning power, they have no conscience and no understanding of consequences; they react on instinct. So, understanding this aspect of wild animal behaviour, the question remains, what do you do, as a conservationist, knowing that preventing another tragedy from happening is your own judgement call? The jury is still out on this one, but what I also know is that the fatherless families of these two men would have it no other way. There was no concession expected, nor was this the time or circumstance to explain to them about musth and testosterone, nor the increasing conflict between man and elephant competing for dwindling habitat.

Although elephant numbers are relatively low in the summer months, reports of belligerent behaviour by some individuals are still received. One in particular comes to mind, which also happened to be a bull in musth. In an unprovoked attack, this elephant drove its tusks through the radiator and into engine compartment of a 4x4, lifting the front of the two-ton vehicle off the ground and bending the chassis, effectively destroying the vehicle. All six occupants were badly shaken but unharmed.

Though testosterone levels are at their highest during these sexual peaks, not all musth bulls demonstrate this degree of aggression. Nevertheless, they are powerful animals, and in close proximity to humans even mild expressions of frustration can lead to devastating consequences. In Asia, mahouts are known to chain up certain working elephant during these cycles, despite it being well known that Asian elephant are relatively mild tempered.

Not all belligerent elephant are killers, and not all elephant are belligerent. One interesting example occurred at a time when wildly uneven rainfall plagued the Lowveld. Some areas would receive heavy rain, while literally across a road farmers would watch helplessly with tears in their eyes as dust devils swirled against the distant backdrop of rainbow-filled skies. Close to 120 millimetres had fallen on Olifants while, only 25 kilometres away, Hoedspruit had received a mere four millimetres!

In response, as if fast forwarded in a time-lapse sequence, the vegetation erupted into leaf, and the plains were covered in flowers. Migratory birds moved in overnight, and their familiar songs filled the humid air. Within a week we were green with new leaf and our neighbours were still grey and gloomy. However, this green would twist our feelings around, to where the grey was envied and the green became a liability. As the weeks passed, the ramifications of having better grazing became increasingly evident. Being part of a huge open system meant the game were free to migrate to wherever they pleased. And, needless to say, they were very pleased to head our way.

Naturally, large numbers of plains game, as well as buffalo and elephant, began moving into our reserve from neighbouring regions, placing a huge strain on the available resources. Of major concern from a security point of view, however, was the increased number of white rhino moving into the area. If the rhino were here in numbers, the poachers would follow. This was inevitable, and we reacted accordingly. Extra outsourced field rangers were deployed to patrol and monitor the newly established rhino middens and frequently used mud wallows. But these mud wallows were also a firm favourite with elephant and, given that we had approximately 700 on the reserve, wallowing space was at a premium. In fact, you couldn't go anywhere on the reserve without coming across elephant. To limit confrontation, I issued a caution to the Protrack anti-poaching operatives to avoid water holes and wallows during the heat of the day and late afternoon, as these were the times when elephant would most likely frequent these points.

My gut feel turned into reality one morning, a few days after issuing the directive. I answered a call from the field rangers' team leader, asking if I had a medic on the reserve. Apparently one of their rangers on patrol had been attacked by an elephant and had been injured. The extent of his injuries was not clear at that stage. My mind immediately flashed back a couple of days to an incident involving one of our shareholders, Dr Aron Frankenthal, who is not only a retired medical doctor but, as it happens, had recently had a serious run-in with an elephant himself. Although he and his guests had escaped injury, his vehicle had not been quite as lucky.

'Stand by, I'll come back to you in a minute,' I said.

I grabbed the radio and called Aron. To my relief he was still on the reserve and only too happy to assist. Calling the clearly worried operative back, I reassured him with the news that although we had no medic on the reserve, we would go one better and have a medical doctor on the scene within 30 minutes! I immediately sensed his relief from the change of tone in his voice.

While I loaded the stretcher and medical equipment from our office, which Meagan had already collected and placed for me in the car park, I arranged that Aron go directly to the base at the old rhino pens, where he could meet up with the head field ranger and get the run down. He and I then followed the rangers to the injured man.

We headed due south for two kilometres until we reached a point where we needed to leave the road and head into the bush. It was clear that only a 4x4 could negotiate the tangled zebrawood thickets and broken terrain to get to where the injured man lay. Thicker, more inhospitable vegetation you would be hard pressed to find – and as a fodder tree, it also happened to be a firm favourite with elephant. Nevertheless, using low-range gears, I negotiated the vehicle through the dense bush, until we located the injured field ranger and his companion.

Aron was already out of the vehicle, crawling into the thicket on his knees, and was at the man's side before I could reverse the vehicle into position. Despite his injuries, having been tossed into the air by the elephant, which then ran in the opposite direction, the hapless man had used these crucial seconds to drag himself into the thicket. So dense was the thicket that there was only just enough room to allow Aron to crawl in to assist the patient, assess the extent of his injuries and stabilise him for evacuation.

Engrossed in assisting the doctor by passing him the necessary equipment and preparing the stretcher, we were totally unaware of a breeding herd of elephant that had moved into the vicinity. With hardly a sound, more than 30 elephant had completely surrounded our position. It was only when those downwind from us picked up our scent and trumpeted that we realised the predicament we were possibly in. Now stabilised, but unable to move unaided, the patient needed to be stretchered onto my vehicle, which would require the assistance of all of us there. Evacuating him by helicopter from the site was precluded due to the lack of a suitable landing area in the vicinity.

The priority was to load the injured man as soon as possible, which meant we couldn't spare anyone to go out and discourage the elephant from getting any closer. For a few minutes there appeared to be a standoff as the elephant seemed to rally behind the leading cow, who I suspected was the matriarch. So in full view of her, and those immediately behind her, we took the opportunity to hurriedly load the injured man. The patient moaned in pain as we manhandled him onto the back of the vehicle with a sense of urgency and trepidation. At the sound of his cry, the matriarch moved even closer to us, stopping less than 20 metres away. With her head held high, she looked over the bushes at us, the whites of her eyes clearly visible. Then, thrusting her trunk out, she began probing the air like a mamba looking for the entrance hole to a nest full of sociable weaver fledglings. After sucking in a trunkful of air, she appeared to analyse it for a moment, and then in a sweeping snort she blew the air out. This was the first and last sound I heard her make, as she turned on her heels, collected her herd, then deliberately and quietly walked away.

Returning to the scene with a master tracker some time later, we were able to determine from the spoor that the elephant responsible for the attack was one of five young bulls, also known as pilot bulls, and not members of the matriarch's herd. The attack appeared to have been unprovoked and spontaneous. We conjectured that the elephant had been startled by the field rangers, who had come upon them while they were feeding in the thick bush, and that the bull's natural response, given his inexperience, was more defensive than aggressive.

Feedback from Phalaborwa Hospital on the extent of the man's injuries revealed that he had suffered a broken leg, bruised ribs, and some minor cuts and bruises. In my mind, this was a clear indication that there was no intention by this elephant to kill this man, even if inadvertently this could so easily have been the scenario we were greeted with. Given that I'd witnessed what an elephant hellbent on killing someone is capable of, this field ranger's injuries could be placed in the same relative category as a schoolboy having grazed his knee ...

INTRODUCTIONS AND ALIENS

As game rangers I believe we need to approach our calling with more than a protective eye; we also need pre-emptive vision, lateral thinking and, dare I say it, creative conservation methodology. There are times and circumstances which dictate when we need to relax our stance on 'immigration', when some new blood needs to be brought in to augment dwindling numbers or, indeed, to add some spice to the mix and judiciously introduce a new species into a system. In my opinion, the genome argument, so often used by sanctimonious preservationists to hide behind, is at times inappropriately short-sighted and tantamount to conservation sabotage.

To illustrate my point: award-winning vulture conservationist Kerri Wolter, of Vulpro, was asked to re-home an African fish eagle from the Thabazimbi area, as the dams there were drying up and the fish that these birds depended on were dying. As the resources rapidly dwindled, fierce competition for territory and food between the resident birds resulted in one of the eagles being injured. Since its full recovery, however, it was thought best to try and relocate it where it would not be forced into conflict again, where there were ample resources and opportunities to establish a territory, so a new release site was sought. Naturally, having spent a lot of time doing extensive research work on hooded vultures in our reserve, Kerri's first thoughts were the Olifants River, which is a well-known, prime fish eagle habitat. Needless to say, I was enthused when Kerri approached me as I knew this bird could simply be 'wild released' into the system without fanfare and would be happy here.

However, as we are part of the APNR open system, protocol requires that we run things past SANParks for approval. This we did, and the reply from senior scientists in the Kruger National Park was prompt and to the point. They refused the application based on the conjecture that the bird's genome may differ from that of the existing population of fish eagles on the Olifants River!

I may be missing something here, but having wiped the tears of laughter from my cheeks, I had a rhetorical question in response: Before man established water in the form of dams in the dry iron ore mining area of Thabazimbi and stocked the water with recreational fish, what strain of fish eagles occurred there? The answer: there *were* no fish eagles in the Thabazimbi area before the discovery of iron ore. Those eagles that found their way to those water reservoirs, where they then became established, had made their way up the smaller tributaries from larger systems such as the Limpopo and Olifants Rivers, carrying in their blood the same DNA as those found in Botswana or the Kruger ... Or perhaps this fish eagle can be re-classified a new sub-species: *thabazimbiensis* has a good ring to it. Another example of such a natural migration encouraged by man is that of the white-breasted cormorant. Originally a coastal bird, now tens of thousands populate all of our country's interior man-made water impoundments and fisheries. What about the seagulls on the rubbish dumps of cities thousands of kilometres from the sea?... Naah, life's too short. But this much I will say: if these genome criteria were as strictly applied to the many other introduced species, Balule Nature Reserve would have no black rhino, white rhino, nyala or sable antelope.

While I fully understand the threat an aggressive alien species, plant or animal, can pose to an ecosystem, and support the judicious vetting of exotic introductions, I am equally of the opinion that the perceived threat levels should be weighed against the intrinsic benefits. Each alien species needs to be categorised; they should be judged on their merits and labelled accordingly, for example, invasive (as in wattle trees) or non-invasive (as in oak trees), aggressive (as in Indian mynahs) or benign (as in European house sparrows).

As the largest region in Balule Nature Reserve, Olifants River Game Reserve has taken the lead in a number of conservation initiatives, not least the successful introduction of black and white rhino into the larger Balule Nature Reserve. Our rapidly dwindling blue wildebeest numbers were given a helping hand recently, as were the resident nyala antelope, whose low numbers have been significantly boosted. It also needs to be said that, contrary to popular conjecture, not all attempts at introducing additional species have been successful. The common reedbuck, introduced in the early 1990s, never established themselves. These otherwise hardy animals fared badly, and the last one was seen on the reserve in 2008. The introduction of 15 ostriches a few years ago was also a failure ... but some people just don't have the 'give up' gene in their DNA. This was shown in a bold and very costly project embarked on recently to bring back the iconic sable antelope to their former rangeland in Balule.

Soon after sending an update to my shareholders pertaining to the last known population of 12 sable that used to occur on our reserve in the 1960s, I was corrected on the numbers by an old-timer from this area. Founder-shareholder Graham Vickers, whose in-laws used to own the property comprising what is now known as Olifants River Game Reserve, told me there were not 12 sable in the area in 1992, as I'd reported, but in fact well over 30! Anecdotal as these recollections are, these numbers, locations and photos have since been confirmed by older landowners on the farm Seekoeigat, as well as the Weilbach family, who have been in the area for more than 60 years.

Apparently those 12 sable to which I'd referred comprised a particularly well-known herd from which 11 individuals were captured and clandestinely removed by a neighbouring landowner to our south. Environmental conditions could not have been more conducive to the task. It was at the end of the dry season; in fact, it was the tail end of the 1991/2 drought. Taking full advantage, the unscrupulous man dropped fresh lucerne bales in a crude 'crumb trail', which the hungry sable followed and were thereby lured across the boundary to their capture. From there they were loaded into trucks and driven away to be released on his other game farm in Groblersdal, which left behind incalculable destruction to the integrity of the area's population of native sable. The ramifications and ecological damage resulting from this individual's act of ignorance can never be repaired, and the costs are only now able to be calculated.

The water hole from which the unfortunate antelope were lured and captured is now located well inside Olifants River Game Reserve. Ironically, no sable antelope have visited this water hole since the lone sable cow left over from that 'capture' was last seen there 25 years ago, searching in vain for the rest of her herd. Sable are gregarious animals: they need to be part of a herd to stand any chance of survival and ward off predators. Alone and defenceless, she made for easy prey; lions were quick to detect vulnerability and killed her a few days later. However, in a testament to her legacy, this popular water hole is now known as Sable Dam.

In 2014, a small herd of sable antelope was added to the impressive list of mammals found on the reserve. From the outset it was emphasised that this project was an experimental endeavour. It was unique in that it would be motivated by enthusiasm and entirely funded by a neighbouring landowner and Olifants shareholder, Ian Black. There are no wild, predator-wary sable antelope populations in South Africa from which to source a viable herd. And as the only antelope commercially available were born and bred in sheltered environments, it was inevitable that the most naïve of them would be taken by predators. The future of these antelope as free-ranging animals would be entirely dependent on their instinctive will to survive. We were banking on the awakening of a dormant inherent fear that would cause some of them to become wary of predators – but the risks were high.

Having seen the devastating effect predation has on wild-born prey populations, such as wildebeest, we all (Ian included) anticipated and accepted that there would be losses in the learning process. From the get-go we always knew predation would be the major limiting factor to these rare antelope making it in the wild. In fact, shortly after being released, two were killed by the same pride of lions within a week of each other. A month later, a huge male leopard took one of the sub-adults. Since then, the incidents have tapered off gradually until, at the time of writing, nearly 30 months into the project. Now there are reports of sable that have learned to avoid predators; indeed, they have survived and are living in a wilderness area where there are high numbers of predators. In one instance, eyewitnesses reported they'd seen sable using their scimitar-like horns to defend themselves effectively against a pack of hyenas.

Initially, radio collars (both GPS and telemetric) were fitted to the adult sable. This allowed them to be monitored by conservationist Catherine Shutte on a daily basis during the early critical familiarisation period. Catherine plotted their movements and collected data on their progress, habitat preference and social behaviour – and, of course, information on predation. This was done for approximately three months until it became apparent the sable had settled in. So, while the cynics sneered and mumbled to themselves as the next sable fell prey to lions, all the while data was being collated and analysed. Importantly, whether negative or positive, it was nonetheless ground-breaking data, data from which we would all learn something regarding this species' introduction into the wild. No one but Ian was prepared to make the financial outlay, to risk what was needed, in order to compile this data.

Ian bought the sable in two phases. The first comprised males only, for two reasons: they were a quarter of the price, and they were bigger and stronger, all the better to ward off predators. When we thought that some of the wild-released bulls had become predator-savvy, the second batch, comprising a herd of females and a couple of males, was brought in. A total of 36 sable were finally released into Balule, after having been kept for a short while in a boma on Dinidza. To the best of our knowledge, after nearly two and a half years since the start of the programme, 19 of these precious animals are still alive and well. Two calves were born in the wild and all eyes are on them and how they will cope. The total cost borne by Ian to date is around R5 million! And his expected return? Only that a nucleus herd starts again and becomes established in the greater APNR system. Failing that, simply to know that he tried to re-establish wild sable in Balule ... where, were it not for interference, they'd in all probability still occur.

Besides the huge monetary outlay by Ian, no effort was spared by the team on Olifants to help manage this ground-breaking introduction. We assisted wherever possible in order to give it every possible chance at succeeding. The following is but one example of the lengths we went to.

A little over 22 months into the project I received a call from Ian to say one of the first batch of sable bulls released on Dinidza had been sighted in the Umbabat Nature Reserve. Apparently this magnificent animal was already causing quite a stir and stimulating huge interest wherever it was sighted. From the many photos taken of the sable and sent on to us, we could identify this individual by the frequency that had been boldly written on his transmitter collar. It was indeed one of Ian's and it was calculated to have moved nearly 40 kilometres away from the original release site, as 'the helicopter flies'.

Ian was in Scotland at the time and wouldn't be back until the following week. I rather dreaded what he was going to ask but can't say I was surprised.

'Er, Mario, could you try to capture the bull and bring him back to Dinidza?'

I mulled this over in silence as Ian continued: 'I reckon having spent nearly two years in the lion's den, so to speak, he can educate my new batch of sable with his acquired predator wariness. Then, when they are released together, the cows and calves will have a better chance of survival.'

I couldn't fault Ian's logical reasoning for wanting to bring this sable back. Predation remained the sable's main threat and anything that helped reduce this risk would help the project succeed.

It was going to be a daunting task to try and find a lone sable in more than 80 000 hectares ... and that was the relatively easy part! The procedural protocol required to traverse private land, capture, then transport an animal through two provincial jurisdictions would need official permits. Then I'd need to traverse the unfamiliar territory of three private nature reserves, and being an open system this would mean all the landowners and wardens affected needed to put petty politics aside and agree. However, contrary to my predictions and to my pleasant surprise, I was met with nothing but enthusiasm and support at every turn. Telephonically, I was able to collate all the necessary permission officially and privately: it took less than two days from the first phone call to the last.

Things needed to happen quickly, as the sable could move beyond our permitted perimeter of operation. So naturally I recruited the best man I knew in the business of aerial reconnaissance, Bennie Osmers. Bennie was also a sable antelope breeder and had a wealth of experience regarding this species. The plan was that he and I would fly to Klaserie and collect Colin Rowles, who had confirmation of the last known location of the sable. Although this was already a three-day-old sighting, we would fly a recce over the general area, and if the sable hadn't moved too far away, we surmised we'd stand a reasonable chance of locating him.

Enthusiasm helped by a tail wind got the better of us, and we touched down a little earlier than expected at Klaserie's headquarters. This meant that Colin needed to cut his lunch short; so, wasting no time, still munching a mouthful of pilchards on toast, he climbed in the little helicopter with us. Fortunately the doors had been removed to afford better visibility and, more importantly now, better airflow. Fishy breath and the usual banter over the microphone faded quickly as we began to scan the bush below us for the sable. Carefully flying GPS grids to do a thorough search soon paid off. Approximately 30 minutes into the flight Bennie located the unmistakable shape and coal-black coat of the sable deep in the mopane woodland. It was less than five kilometres from where it was last seen by Colin and right in the area of the reserve where, 50-odd years previously, viable herds of sable antelope had roamed.

Autumn colours of the unique butterfly-shaped leaves made for a spectacular contrast to the black and white magnificence of this iconic antelope. Like a monarch of the mopane, the lone sable created a poignant image I'll never forget. He stood there proudly, as if he belonged there, inseparably part of these surroundings, so clearly at home. I was overwhelmed with a sense of guilt, uncomfortable that we were about to wrench this beautiful animal out of paradise ... I couldn't help feeling we were about to disrupt an experiment on the brink of success.

There were no other sable in the region, and a lone sable's vulnerability to predation would be accentuated without the combined advantage of herd's extra senses for protection, but this was little consolation. All things being equal, I would rather have moved the other sable to his position, but I was in no position to make this call at the time.

We moved quickly. Once the sable had been located and his position punched in, we returned to Olifants, where I was dropped off to collect my Land Cruiser. Bennie flew on to refuel. I then drove through to Mica, collected a transport crate, and continued through to Klaserie. We planned that Bennie would give me a head start then fly on to Hoedspruit and collect veterinarian Pete Rogers and his assistant, Janelle Goodrich, from where they would rendezvous with me close to the sable's location. I would be driving through unfamiliar country, so co-ordination and communication were crucial.

Despite the rather vague road directions given to me, I made good time. Like a choreographed event, I pulled up at a prominent junction in the road to see the helicopter approaching. Janelle climbed out and unloaded much of the medical equipment we'd need. Once all the gear was loaded we climbed into my vehicle and followed in the direction the helicopter flew as it went in search of the sable. Approximately 10 minutes later, in virtually the same spot we'd initially found him, the sable was located and darted. Unfamiliarity with the roads in Klaserie was of minor concern to me, particularly as Bennie had a bird's-eye view, and we had ground-to-air communication. Skilfully he guided us in closer while moving the staggering sable to where it finally went down, literally a couple of metres from the roadside, where we were then easily able to treat and load it.

Fortunately all had gone smoothly: if we'd needed any more time than was spent, due to any unforeseen glitches, we would have had to call off the entire operation for another day. We had timed it to the wire. The sun had already slipped out of sight and the yellow helicopter's black silhouette diminished to a speck, its throbbing rotor now silent as it was absorbed into the fading light of sunset's red afterglow. I drained the last of my tepid Valpré before starting the vehicle, briefly pondering if they would spare me a thought when they were back home in less than 30 minutes and cracking open ice cold beers.

In case you were wondering why in my book it happens that whenever leaving us after a long day's work the intrepid helicopter pilots always seem to fly into the sunset, like a Texas Ranger in a Zane Grey novel – well, it's simply that Big Game Heli's headquarters are due west of Balule. So, romantic images aside, it was back to reality as I turned my headlights on and slowly began the long haul back to the sable camp on Dinidza. I was alone in my Land Cruiser with a lonely, somewhat bewildered sable bull in the trailer behind ... my thoughts now focused on him and getting him back safely.

Shortly after being released with the group of sable on Dinidza, the 'wild' bull was challenged and beaten by one of the bulls that had been brought in with the harem of cows. Having been fed on a diet of lucerne and scientifically formulated pellets known as 'Boskos', this bull was heavier and stronger than the relatively lean 'wild' bull. Having spent nearly two years adapting to the semi-arid conditions of Balule and, latterly, the poor winter veld of Klaserie, he was not able to compete. So once again our hardy, bush-wise sable found himself on his own.

As I write this, nearly a year has passed since bringing that sable back from Klaserie. As it happens, I have just received an email along with photographs of our wayward bull from Colin. His conversation was disparagingly short and to the point, stating that the same bull was back again and that, as the sable was of no conservation value to him, we were welcome to take it back again. However, I had come to know better; I had learned an important lesson in innovative conservation. To my mind this brave animal had returned to a particular region in Klaserie, back to where wild sable used to occur, back to where he belonged, to where something primal had instinctively drawn him. And, like a salmon that leaves the vast ocean and swims back upriver to find the same tiny pebble-strewn stream of its birth, this antelope instinctively knew where his destiny lay. This time I decided not to interfere ... *Que sera, sera!*

In terms of the project's aim, as envisaged from the outset, this sable's introduction into the 'wild' has been a remarkable success. Particularly when we consider that he and his parents were bred in the protected husbandry environs of a sable breeding ranch, and up until his release he had never known what it was to be a wild sable, to defend himself against predators or to go hungry. Nevertheless, despite the plethora of cynical scepticism that dogged this project at every turn, this survivor has proved the exception to the rule; he adapted and has ever since been trying to teach us something. Why the hell there are still those that won't take heed now beats me. But more than that, I could kick myself for not listening to my intuitive gut feel on the previous occasion. Every thought since seeing him screamed to me of this animal's contentment, and to leave him well alone. This time, however, I know better ... I am listening.

Any 'tame' or gregarious antelope that has endured more than 1 000 predator-filled nights in an area with some of the highest lion and leopard densities in the Lowveld can indeed be considered 'predator wary' and integral to the system. More importantly, this animal has given this particular introduction experiment the recognition it deserves. Irrespective of financial outlay, it has proved that it is possible for naïve prey animals to learn fear, to know what to fear and to avoid becoming an easy meal. Besides the predation hurdle, this remarkable animal took the worst drought in living memory in its stride. Therefore, if for no other reason than that, it deserves our utmost respect.

In my view, this sable has demonstrated more than its conservation value and that the sceptics were at least partially wrong; it has demonstrated that the question of their survival in the wild may not be as bleak a picture as is painted by the pundits who have all but given up on the rapidly dwindling wild populations of sable and roan antelope in the Kruger National Park. Hopefully future decisions regarding experimental introductions will lie with those without blinkered viewpoints and who are intelligent enough to realise the potential of nature's powerful dictates if given half a chance.

In 1993 there were over 800 wildebeest in Balule Nature Reserve. Then, in 2003, 85 wildebeest were captured and sold. This was an ill-considered decision from which the reserve's wildebeest populations have never recovered. By 2012 all the internal fences had been removed within Balule. Larger predators could now access previously closed areas, where they actively targeted wildebeest and giraffe, particularly the former. It wasn't long before there were fewer than 150 wildebeest left. Clearly the capture and removal of those 85 at the time tipped the population off the knife's edge, and from there it was down the slippery slope into a predator sink.

But it appears all is not lost. Again it was Ian Black who, of his own volition and at his own cost, reintroduced over 200 wildebeest back into Balule in a phased release programme stretching over three years. Although blue wildebeest are relatively easy to source and cheap to purchase, as facilitator of this project I made a point of obtaining them from an area where the population is predator wary, as they were all to be 'wild released' into an area with a healthy number of lions. Fortunately the wildebeest sourced were from the southern portion of the Timbavati Game Reserve where, needless to say, all the major predators abound.

All indications are that, despite some predation, particularly on the calves, their numbers appear to be stable. Interestingly, the wildebeest have moved far and wide within the open system, as is to be expected of an intrinsically migratory species.

Since my earliest days on Olifants, it has been home to a small population of approximately 20 nyala. These strikingly beautiful and exotic-looking antelope are relatively common in the Pafuri region of the Kruger, northern KwaZulu-Natal and north-western Mozambique. I have no records of any introduction of these antelope in terms of numbers or point of release on Olifants, so I must assume that this small population moved in from the neighbouring Kruger National Park. I suspect they may have followed the Olifants River system many years ago, probably migrating in search of food during a severe drought.

The nyala on our reserve appear to be habitat specific. Preferring the broken hill country and riparian habitat along the Olifants River, nyala are seldom found inland in the relatively flat open country. Originally they could be found in small groups numbering two to four individuals and were only seen on rare occasions either on their own or in the company of impala. Not surprisingly, the shareholders wanted to see more of them and suggested we bring others in.

When formal proposals were made to bring nyala onto the reserve, initial fears from the sceptics and naysayers was that they would compete with their smaller cousins, the resident bushbuck, but it appears this was unfounded. Since the introduction of another 35 nyala six years ago, their numbers have almost doubled, and they have spread far and wide into Balule with minimal impact on other species. Census figures year on year indicate there has been no apparent effect on bushbuck numbers, which are still seen in good condition and living cheek by jowl alongside nyala. Predominantly browsers, nyala have adapted and done extremely well, particularly in the thick bush environment along the Olifants River. It has to be said these beautiful antelope add a rich diversity to the mosaic of this beautiful slice of Africa.

To conclude the topic of aliens (and some interfering conservation authorities), a subject close to my heart is trout. If asked what I prefer doing when taking some time out from the bush, the short answer is that I invariably head to 'alien country' with my fly rod. Locally I will make a relatively short journey to the highlands of Dullstroom, the Drakensberg or, less often, the Eastern Cape in search of trout. And on very rare occasions, when the budget can stand it, I go to the other side of the world in search of the same aliens.

Sad to say, though native to the Atlas Mountains of North Africa, trout, introduced to South Africa over 120 years ago, have now been declared an alien species to be eradicated. More importantly, while our ill-advised conservation authorities are busy waging a sanctimonious war against these innocuous little fish in our country, they remain comparatively paralysed as precious indigenous icons weighing more than two tons are being poached to extinction at a rate of nearly four animals per day. And, more recently, elephant and lions are becoming the new targets. Other lesser-known but unique animals such as pangolins, vultures, and species of reptile too numerous to mention here, are being threatened with extinction, plundered for the illegal muti and pet trades. The environment is mined to irreparable destruction and 'fracking' looms on the horizon. This while our increasingly scarce rivers, now devoid of 'terrible trout', have become nothing more than conduits for home-grown raw sewage!

Yes, I'm a closet 'alien' trout fisherman ... Scourge, deride me, I care not! As conservationists in South Africa, we need to get our priorities right, as the coming chapters will reveal.

AN OLD WARRIOR MOVES ON

Back in 1988 there were no rhino on Olifants River Game
Reserve. At the time, fences still existed between us and our
neighbouring reserves. Klaserie already boasted a good number of white rhino, some of which had been introduced years before
and were now being augmented with others that had moved in from
the Kruger and Timbavati. In short, their white rhino population was
already well established.

Balule Nature Reserve had yet to develop, remove the boundary fence with Klaserie and thereby become a member of the APNR.
Furthermore, within the embryonic Balule, a myriad of fences between
the various regions still remained. Essentially then, never mind the
eco-political hurdles still to overcome, it was primarily the physical
barriers like the fences that prohibited natural recruitment of rhino.
At Olifants we couldn't wait for the fences to come down, though the
timing was very unclear. If rhino were to be established on our reserve,
we'd have to source suitable breeding animals and stock it ourselves.

Preparations began immediately to procure a viable group of white
rhino. A huge holding pen comprising four compartments was duly
financed and erected to house the newcomers. These bomas had to be
well constructed, robust and comfortable, as the rhino would need to
spend a few weeks in confinement while settling down and getting accli-
matised. In fact they were so well built at the time that these same pens
are still standing to this day, not only as a monument to this extremely
successful project, but ironically now serving as an operational base

and headquarters for Protrack's field rangers, who are our outsourced anti-poaching team.

The first rhino purchased by Olifants River Game Reserve was an adult bull named Boy Boy. It was apparent he'd been hand-reared, as he had absolutely no fear of people or vehicles. A few Land Rovers still proudly bear the affectionate rubbing scars from his horn, which left deep gouges in the fairly soft aluminium bodywork of these vehicles. Soon afterwards, an adult cow we named Mary was purchased and brought onto Olifants. We suspected she was pregnant, so we released her into the open reserve after a relatively short while in the pens. The third white rhino to make his home on our reserve was also purchased as an adult, a particularly large and powerful rhino bull. Having noticed considerable interest in this rhino by a hunting outfitter at the Natal Parks Board auction, Olifants simply had to have him. And as is true at most auctions, when you really want something, passion rules the head: although pushed to a premium, we still managed to outbid the hunter. So, in all likelihood, this rhino would otherwise have ended up on some foreign trophy hunter's wall.

Unfortunately for Boy Boy, once all the rhino had been released from the bomas, this new bull proved too much for him. The resulting conflict was completely one-sided, so much so that if we had not moved Boy Boy out of harm's way, the new bull would eventually have killed him. Our field rangers named this dominant bull Msimbi, from the Zulu word for iron. Boy Boy was moved back into the pens for a few weeks until he recovered, and a new home was then found for him on a game farm near Gravelotte.

Nearly 20 years later, having ruled unchallenged for all this time, we thought Msimbi's day had finally come. It happened to coincide with an influx of virile young bulls from Klaserie. Discreetly the old bull withdrew, simply shifting from his prime territory and into the marginal areas that comprised the shallower, less fertile soils adjacent to the railway-line road. He knew his limitations, it seemed.

It may very well have been Murphy's Law, call it what you will, but the fact is that even though it had taken over 20 years to happen this was the day one of my biggest fears would be realised, the day I received a call from Kaapmuiden's train traffic control centre to say that a train had collided with one of our rhino.

The shock of the news was numbing: it felt like someone had suddenly injected novocaine into both my knees. Nevertheless, I managed to jump into my truck and floor the accelerator. It was the end of July, the middle of our dry season, and the Land Cruiser's back wheels spun on the loose gravel, taking enough rubber off to bring my replacement tyres in a month earlier than budgeted for, the least of my worries at that stage.

The infamous bend along the Palm Loop has been responsible for some truly sad moments for me. However, nothing I'd experienced to date was to be quite on the same scale as what I anticipated finding. Pictures of horror in my mind, extrapolated from experiences of other large animal versus train collisions I'd witnessed during my years on Olifants, jostled against memories of a time when I worked for an eternal optimist who, removing the ever-present toothpick from between his teeth, would smile and say: 'The picture is never as black as it's painted, pal.'

If only I'd taken this old cliché to heart, I thought to myself as the vehicle ground to a halt, I would have saved myself a considerable amount of unnecessary anguish. No horror scene greeted me, no broken, mangled animal, only the heat rising off the blue-grey crushed granite supporting the lines and the smell of old grease used to lubricate a junction in the line.

Although there was no sign of the rhino, I could clearly see where the incident had occurred, where the rhino had tumbled down the embankment, falling head over heels after being hit. On its way down it had dislodged two discarded concrete sleepers before ending up on the road. Here I noticed a small pool of blood in the soft sand, clearly indicating where the rhino had lain, obviously in a state of shock, until it managed to gather itself and walk away. The spoor also indicated the rhino was favouring its right front leg. Judging from the direction it took and the size of its tracks, our trackers and field rangers were sure this was Msimbi.

Nothing escapes unscathed from a collision with a train, even one travelling at a relatively slow speed: these 'iron horses' are simply too heavy and too hard. But this time it was apparent the exception had proved the rule; this train had collided with another form of iron. Msimbi had made it clear he was dominant on the day he arrived, and he had remained the dominant bull all these years. Contrary to everything I'd researched regarding what is considered the average period of tenure in this role, Msimbi was clearly in a league of his own. I estimated he was about 12 years old when he was bought, so calculated that he was at least 32 years old now. This extended period of supremacy may have had something to do with the fact that the reserve was fenced off until 2005, but then again maybe not, as he did smash through in the late 1990s and kill one of Klaserie Nature Reserve's rhino bulls in horn-to-horn combat.

With Msimbi having had no successful contender in all those years, I guess it would be safe to say the majority of the younger rhino we see on our reserve today are his progeny. However, the helicopter game census at the time indicated an unnatural leap in numbers, 41 to 52 from year to year, a clear indication of recruitment from Klaserie. What we also noticed was that the majority of the newcomers were young adult bulls, and despite one of these bulls being captured and removed, its territory was filled in less than a week! This suggested that available prime habitat, for white rhino in particular, was becoming scarcer as their numbers grew, which in turn would lead to territorial competition and conflict, as suspected.

My field rangers, among whom was master tracker January Mahlaule, began to track the wounded rhino, and it wasn't long before he was located approximately a kilometre away from the railroad, lying down in some really thick raisin bush. Through my binoculars I could clearly see the notch in his left ear, the notch Gerrit Scheepers had cut when the rhino was microchipped nearly 12 years previously. It was, as I'd feared, our old stalwart, Msimbi. I then did what I didn't want to do, but knew I had to, in order to ascertain what the extent of his injuries were. I clapped my hands and got him to stand; this he did with relative ease, but as he moved off I could see he was limping on his right front leg. The next thing I remember doing was calling Gerrit, who again dropped everything to come and assist, particularly when he heard who the patient was. Unfortunately Gerrit's little plane was in for a service, so he had to drive through to the reserve. Nevertheless, he was on the scene in less than two hours.

As always, it was a great relief to have Gerrit in on a crisis like this. While he prepared the dart, we did the mundane stuff, like carrying the medicine box, water and ropes, and getting the blindfold ready. Quietly, we stalked into position; Gerrit crept forward on his own, to minimise noise. A short while later I saw him lift the dart gun to his shoulder. *Phhhitt!* The dart landed perfectly on target. Within a few minutes, the usual short high-stepping gait indicated Msimbi would be down shortly. He hadn't moved more than a few metres from where he was darted. Moving in quickly we covered his eyes, which has an immediate calming effect. Then, as a precautionary measure, we secured one of his back legs to a stout tree using the rope.

Gerrit wasted no time in attending to the immobilised rhino. Despite the dire nature of what we were dealing with, I couldn't help thinking how amazing it was that this huge, magnificent animal, which a 1 000-ton train could not lay low, had collapsed in minutes to three milligrams of M99. Moving around to his right side, we could clearly see the blue and yellow paint from the locomotive smeared across his flank; it told a vivid story. It also told us that he'd taken a raking blow; he was not hit square-on as we'd suspected. By manipulating the rhino's huge leg, Gerrit confirmed that, although nothing was broken, there was damage to the shoulder muscles and tendons, something only time and whatever medication we could administer there and then would help to heal.

In the weeks that followed, daily monitoring of his movements by our field rangers revealed that Msimbi was covering up to five kilometres in a night. Within two weeks he was walking without any outward signs of injury, the limp all but gone. Old 'Iron' was back on the beat, we all thought, and I guess so did he. But as a prize fighter circles his opponent, looking for the slightest sign of weakness or vulnerability before throwing a punch, so did one of the younger bulls that had moved into the area notice what our human senses could not pick up on. There was a chink in the old warrior's armour, and although 99 per cent healed from his clash with the train, the one per cent shortfall was probably all the younger bull needed to gain the confidence to challenge Msimbi. And as is true of most situations involving physical competition and stamina ... 'Youth is King'.

Two months after the train incident I received a report of a rhino that was limping badly. I assumed it was Msimbi, and that he'd stumbled and torn the newly healed muscle, which although having been on the mend for eight weeks already was probably still a little brittle. Nevertheless, Meagan and I took a drive out to see for ourselves. We arrived to find the old bull grazing peacefully on the extreme limit of his territory, and although he appeared to have a slight limp, he was able to move with relative ease. We stayed with him for nearly half an hour, until it began getting too dark to see without the aid of a spotlight, and at that point we decided to drive home.

I didn't sleep well that night.

Less than 18 hours later, another call came in, this time not from a concerned shareholder but from our tractor driver. Using his cell phone, he called to say he had a visual on a 'sick' rhino in virtually the same area Meagan and I had left Msimbi the previous evening. From his description and tone of voice I could tell this was serious.

Gerrit, and every other vet I knew, was down in Cape Town on a veterinary conference at the time. However, resident Hoedspruit vet, Dr Hein Müller, although extremely busy, could tell from my tone that I needed him urgently, so he agreed to come out immediately.

Msimbi was in such a bad way that he could not lift his forequarters off the ground. In fact, he was lying flat on his side when we first approached him. Hein then simply walked up to within a few metres of the stricken animal and immobilised him for closer examination.

It appeared from the gaping wounds on his left shoulder that he may have been shot and wounded, but this was quickly disproved when Hein, who has hands the size of a bunch of bananas, was able to insert his fingers deep into two of the gaping wounds. Judging from the other relatively superficial scratches and injuries, it was clear that another rhino was responsible. Msimbi's shoulder was broken, and most of the connecting tendons and muscle tissue had been torn in the conflict.

It was clear that the old bull was done; Msimbi's reign had come to an end ... and I didn't need a vet to tell me. But he did anyway.

Hein's prognosis was as I expected. He told me the rhino's injuries were such that he would be unable to stand on his own; as a result, he would not be able to eat or drink. In this state the rhino would die in less than a week, he said. The thought of this rhino I had known for nearly 20 years being left to die as nature decrees – slowly, through lack of nourishment, and in agony – was unacceptable to me. To hell with the pragmatism of natural science this time, I thought. Wasn't the train catalytic in this? Hein suggested that the most humane option was to put the old boy to sleep, a gentle and painless option; I gave the nod without hesitation, my throat too swollen to speak ...

It was the only rhino I'd ever had to kill.

I recalled the wise old adage once more. The picture was not as black or bleak as it could have been, and I took solace from the following. Rhino live on average 35 to 40 years. Msimbi had lived happily and largely unchallenged for well over 30 years, 20 of which were in our reserve, where he was loved, admired, cared for and protected. Altogether, it has to be said, this is an unusually good innings for a wild rhino bull. During his reign he not only gave us lasting memories of what he was, but in his progeny the genes and irrefutable legacy of his iron bloodline will continue through the generations.

In light of the threat to this species, due to unscrupulous poaching for their horns, I leave you with this modicum of comfort: like the gladiator Msimbi was, he left the arena with honour and dignity. He'd lived by the horn, and died by the horn ... not *for* his horn.

OPERATION BLACK RHINO

The introduction of white rhino into Olifants River Game Reserve back in the late 1980s has been recognised as a huge success. Both in terms of establishing a healthy population of these iconic creatures on the reserve, as well as for white rhino conservation in the broader context, it is an accomplishment we are all extremely proud of. Encouraged and motivated, after about 10 years we proposed that the shareholders investigate the possibility of introducing the endangered black rhino into the reserve as well. However, it transpired that a minimum of five black rhino would be required as a viable group. Unfortunately, finding compatible individuals, and the cost involved in having to purchase this number, put a serious dampener on the project.

It took an innovative scheme known as the Black Rhino Range Expansion Project to pave the way to making this dream a reality. At the helm was Dr Jacques Flamand of the World Wildlife Fund (WWF). What an opportunity! Basically, the expansion project, sponsored by the WWF, needed suitable areas to establish viable populations of black rhino (and still does).

On 6 March 2009, I wrote to Dr Flamand indicating our sincere interest and commitment to bringing black rhino onto Olifants Game Reserve, which together with Olifants North Game Reserve formed the biggest of eight regions making up the 44 000-hectare Balule Nature Reserve. I also mentioned that Olifants North had just completed Parks Board specification holding pens. More importantly, I described the habitat to Dr Flamand, saying that the broken hill country and corkwood woodland through which the perennial Olifants River flowed comprised a wide variety of browse, which I believed would be ideally suited to black rhino. Though I waxed lyrical with enthusiasm, I fell short of mentioning how little I understood of their ecology and that I had no practical experience to base my assumptions on. To take a little credit, though, I'd done some research on black rhino habitat preferences, particularly with regard to their dietary requirements, which revealed that they are known to utilise over 200 species of plant, many of which are toxic to other animals. Deep down there was never a question in my mind, I knew that Balule would provide an ideal habitat for black rhino.

Two years later the first of a number of high-level scoping visits to Balule was undertaken by Dr Flamand and his team of experts. This led to Balule being shortlisted, and eventually our reserve was selected from many other hopefuls, even managing to pip the prestigious Sabi Sands Game Reserve to the post. Moreover, we'd been given an opportunity to really shine as a relatively new member of the Association of Private Nature Reserves, comprising the well-established Timbavati, Klaserie and Umbabat nature reserves.

Although we'd qualified with room to spare, we were acutely mindful of the huge responsibility being undertaken. What would it be like when the honeymoon was over and we were left babysitting 19 black rhino that belonged to someone else? I began to envisage the practicality of what this actually entailed. Dr Flamand reassured us that if he or his colleagues had had any doubts whatsoever at the outset, he would have moved on in search of other suitable areas and project minders. I took solace from that. After all, the buck stopped with him: his reputation and the continued success of this project depended on his judgement and gut feel.

The recently developed Olifants North Game Reserve was desperate to establish white rhino in its region, so this project could not have come at a better time. The region featured predominantly rugged, hilly bushveld with a wide variety of browse and minimal grass plains, which is at best marginal habitat for white rhino, but ideally suited to black rhino. Olifants North was encouraged to seize this opportunity offered by WWF and look at the black rhino programme. Chairman Jurgen Elbertse wasted no time in taking the initiative and burst out of the starting blocks to run with it.

Through commitment to the broader conservation significance of such a project, the directors of both Olifants North and Olifants Game Reserve managed to formulate an agreement with the rest of Balule Nature Reserve. A total buy-in was a prerequisite to effect and co-ordinate the introduction, which proved a daunting task. Getting the other six regions to come to the party was no mean feat, and little did we know at the time but this was only the precursor to what was going to be required to make the project a success. To begin with there were huge financial implications, not the least being the daily moni-toring and the welfare of these precious animals. We were taking on responsibility for well over R15 million worth of endangered animals, animals that faced an added threat from ruthless poachers after their horns. Without the enthusiastic support of the rest of Balule and the commitment of the regional wardens it simply would not have been possible. Being part of the greater open system, neighbouring Klaserie, Timbavati and Umbabat private nature reserves were also brought in, albeit as passive, non-contributing participants.

After months of preparation, November 2011 saw 19 black rhino (11 cows and 8 bulls) successfully translocated from the Eastern Cape and introduced into Balule Nature Reserve. Footage was posted on YouTube of rhino in harnesses dangling below helicopters, which proved to be one of the most innovative and least stressful methods used to capture them and transport them in and out of inaccessible mountainous ter-rain. They were then flown to a receiving area where they were loaded onto trucks and prepared for the 30-hour road journey to Balule.

Upon arrival, they were released at carefully chosen sites, each of which was strategically located within a three-strand section of temporary electrified fence, an area that covered approximately half of the reserve. Although this fence was primarily erected to keep the rhino away from the railway line, and to prevent them explosively moving out of the area upon their release, it also contained the habitat type most suited to black rhino, and where it was hoped they would establish middens and settle in ... The long and the short of these experimental precautions is that they worked!

Basically, the pioneer group of black rhino we received is on loan and will remain the property of the Eastern Cape's Great Fish River Nature Reserve. However, as they establish themselves, settle down and breed, 50 per cent of their progeny then belongs to Balule, unless losses of the initial stock occur, in which case they are replaced with progeny. Ideally then, if all goes as expected, black rhino populations will grow to the point where this and other projects are able to provide animals to other recipient areas that fit the criteria and qualify for an expansion population in the future, and so on.

Administrative preparation began, which included compiling a comprehensive black rhino management plan and the employment of a full-time monitor. Credit for the latter must go to Meagan, who as far back as 2008 recognised the talent of a certain Sinhle Mathebula, particularly for his interest in the ecological facets of nature conservation. As a young student, of his own volition, Sinhle studied the plight of red-billed oxpeckers outside protected areas, the results of which improved awareness of this bird's importance to local communities' domestic stock. No longer are these precious birds merely targets for herd boys' catapults. This soon led him on to bigger things when he was employed by Dr Michelle Henley of Save the Elephants to help monitor the movement of collared elephant in the Timbavati, Umbabat and Klaserie nature reserves. It goes without saying that under Michelle's mentorship and experience he grew in confidence; it was now time for him to seek bigger opportunities.

Sinhle was approached to monitor Balule's black rhino and took on the challenge with enthusiasm. The measured success of the introduction would hinge on effective daily monitoring, and he was up for the task. Black rhino are thick bush specialists, not the easiest animals to keep tabs on. To this end, each rhino was fitted with two transmitters. It being impractical to fit a collar on a rhino's neck, it was decided to fit an experimental foot collar on either of the hindlegs, with a second transmitter implanted in the anterior horn. Nothing was left to chance regarding keeping up with their movements, the idea being that if one transmitter failed we'd have a backup. It was essential that, for the first three months at least, we knew exactly where each rhino was every day.

Having Sinhle focus on the black rhino took a lot of pressure off the regional wardens, who would otherwise have needed to spend hours every day checking up on the rhino in their various regions. Sinhle would relay his daily monitoring stats to project co-ordinator Melodie Ahlers, who would collate the data and compile detailed monthly progress reports, which were then submitted to the WWF.

A few rhino tested the temporary three-strand fence once or twice during the first week, but the attempts were half-hearted and of short duration; after this they quickly settled in and made themselves at home. Interestingly, although only two rhino were released on Olifants River Game Reserve, a third rhino joined them from across the river in the first week and has never returned. Besides the three we now see regularly in the broken hilly country between Olifants River and the railway line, there are two 'wild' black rhino bulls that are seen occasionally east of our reserve's biggest water hole. We suspect they may very well be two bulls obtained from Swaziland and released in Klaserie over eight years ago.

Watching a black rhino feeding in really thick bush is a rare privilege. Often they will munch so intently on the plethora of browse that you are able to creep up quite close to them, and their noisy chewing is sometimes the only giveaway to their exact location. Further proof that this is prime habitat for black rhino is apparent from their condition factors, which are high; their general demeanour and apparently peaceful goodwill also speak volumes. I know this is not exactly a scientific deduction, but there it is. Since removing the fence, only one rhino has moved beyond this line and then only for a few hundred metres to a water hole close by where it drinks and then returns. Prior to the introduction of black rhino, there appeared to be a definitive line, which I referred to in my first book as the 'Commiphora curtain'. It is an imaginary line roughly demarcating two broad vegetation types, which I have always perceived as the point where white and black rhino habitats merge. It was along this line that the habituating ring fence was erected. I suspected, however, that as winter progressed, the rhino would widen their range slightly in order to access more browse, and inevitably some overlapping between the two species would occur.

It wasn't all a happily-ever-after story, and even from the outset there were accidental losses and injuries. A black rhino bull died in transit before reaching Balule when its head got stuck in a crate meant for transporting much larger white rhino. But the next incident can only be described as one of the worst cases of mistaken identity in the bush.

One of the landowners in the west of the reserve was out one day, hunting meat rations for his staff. At 82 years old, his failing eyesight would give him just enough of a visual to make out some form of shape and colour to shoot at, and he was relying almost entirely on the staff he'd taken along with him. So when the meat-hungry staff urgently hissed the word 'warthog' through clenched teeth, and pointed in the direction of some thick bush, the doctor lifted his rifle, and as the cross-hairs of the telescopic sight steadied, he pulled the trigger. At a range of about 25 paces it seemed easy enough, but when he went up to look at the pig he'd bagged, he saw that in fact he'd shot a young black rhino cow between the eyes. The rhino didn't feel a thing when the bullet ended her life as she lay sleeping under a guarrie bush.

This was a conservation disaster, a 'blue on blue' of incomprehensible proportions, one that no excuse could condone, and for which none was proffered. Essentially a culmination of circumstances beyond our control. Looking back now, that temporary shift of focus allowed me to get over the shock. It allowed the blood to cool a little, preventing me from saying something I may have regretted or had to answer for later. Not that it had cooled down by much. But mistakes can happen to anyone, and this was indeed a genuine error, one for which full compensation was paid by the landowner, without hesitation or excuse. And as devastating as it was, we couldn't allow this incident to negate the hard work that continues to go into making the important black rhino expansion project the huge success it otherwise is.

A couple of months after the release, the first black rhino calf was born on Olifants North, and less than a month after that, another was born on Olifants. However, not all had gone as smoothly as we would have expected. Sinhle reported that he had observed a black rhino cow defending her newborn calf from being harassed by a couple of hyenas at one of the water holes. A few days later he found the same mother on her own: there was no sign of the calf. Thinking she may have hidden the baby rhino, we monitored her closely for the next few days. Nothing. We checked for tracks of the calf in the rocky terrain where it was last seen ... still nothing. A couple of weeks later, without a shred of evidence and with heavy hearts, we finally had to accept that the second calf born to the project had been lost. Given the earlier observation made by Sinhle of members of the local hyena clan's attempts to take the calf at the outset, we suspected that in all likelihood it was lost to predation.

In a freak accident, during a re-collaring operation on Olifants North, a rhino in a semi-tranquillised state fell awkwardly down a steep slope. In the tumble, her horn hooked under a horizontal tree trunk, snapping her neck. In another instance we had the unexplained death of a cow, thought to be of natural causes related to her digestive tract. Tragically, her orphaned calf, which was too young to fend for itself, had to be sent to a rehabilitation centre, where it remains to this day.

In order to get a physical condition assessment, we needed to get a visual on each rhino at least once a week. As these animals are notoriously quick to charge, this can be a dangerous business, and there were some close shaves, times when it was only thanks to Sinhle's tree-climbing ability that he would be able to monitor another day. For moral support on these days he took January Mahlaule along with him.

One day, from spoor alone, January was able to ascertain that one of the rhino was dragging what he suspected was a wire snare ... And horror of horrors, despite intensive monitoring, it had happened right under our noses!

We reacted immediately, and with the aid of telemetry were soon able to locate the rhino. I picked up my binoculars, focusing on the back leg, and there it was, just above its foot collar, a thick wire snare tight around its leg, trailing a piece two metres in length. However, closer inspection revealed it was not as severe as it could have been; fortunately the wire did not appear to have cut into the leg. Nevertheless, it had to be removed as soon as possible in case it tightened and cut off the blood supply to the rhino's foot.

For some reason or other, every helicopter in the area that I would normally be able to call on was unavailable: they were all out doing something else, being serviced or in another country. Local vet Dr Pete Rogers was on holiday in the Kruger Park at the time but did say that if we could pick him up with a helicopter he'd come in a flash. Verbal authority to dart the rhino was obtained from the authorities, so it was all systems go ... if we could find a helicopter, that was. Hours later we managed to locate a Bell LongRanger which had been chartered by an Arab racehorse breeder for their managers to visit a game lodge in Sabi Sands. Through the pilot, we approached the clients with a proposition. They would be allowed to observe the darting process, if we could use their helicopter for a couple of hours or so. Knowing the whole round trip would be about three hours, this would be a huge cost saving – it was a no-brainer. So when they agreed, I was elated.

A Bell LongRanger is not the ideal machine for this kind of work, but it had to do, and *do* it did. As it turned out, however, flying into the Kruger to pick up Pete was not as simple as you would imagine. It looked as though we were going to need a chainsaw to cut through the reams of red tape. The conservation community in the Lowveld is a small one, so thanks to some level-headedness, and through personal contacts in the Kruger Park, the chopper was able to fly in and pick Pete up. Half an hour later they landed on our airstrip and preparations were made to immobilise the rhino. All the while, Sinhle, clad in his day-glo orange vest for easy spotting from the air, was keeping track of its position. Not long after that, in typically rough terrain, the rhino cow was darted and the snare removed. Although the whole operation had taken more than six hours to organise, the snare removal procedure took less than 15 minutes. Pete then administered the antidote, and within a minute the rhino was up and away, probably wondering what all the fuss was about.

The importance of daily telemetric monitoring and the weekly visual assessments was once again demonstrated when, only a few weeks after the snare incident, another one of our rhino, this time a bull, was noticed with a swollen back leg. Closer examination revealed there was likely to be a problem with the foot collar – or, indeed, that another snare could be the cause. By now Sinhle, tasked with focusing on this rhino, had noticed that it had an almost imperceptible limp. Yet again there was no question: we were required to act immediately, immobilise the rhino and determine the cause and extent of the swelling. As it turned out, we weren't a moment too soon: apparently the foot collar had packed with mud, which had then dried, causing some constriction, this in turn caused swelling, and so the collar began to cut into the flesh with each step. Ugly though the wound was, it was fortunate that the tendons at the back of the foot had not been severed. According to Dr Rogers there was still a chance that the wound would granulate and heal ... we had got to this rhino just in time!

Motion-detecting cameras were set up at a water hole that this bull was known to frequent, in order to monitor its progress. We set the cameras so that we'd get some close-ups of his foot as the healing progressed. I'm pleased to report that, as we'd all hoped, the wound granulated well and within two months the rhino had recovered completely.

In light of this incident, some important lessons were learned. The effectiveness of the foot collars versus the risks involved will be discussed, and a decision will be made regarding their continued use. In the meantime, I devised a concept foot collar that would overcome the problem and presented it to the Balule Committee in July 2012. The design was innovative, yet simplistically robust and practical. Most importantly, it was animal friendly, something the present foot collars are not.

Possibly owing to the fact that it would need to be engineered from scratch, I didn't hear back from anyone regarding my proposed design. In fact, much to my annoyance, replacement collars arrived a few months later. Though we'd hoped the use of this type of foot collar would be abandoned, it was not. But having no say in the matter, we were contractually bound to carry out the refitting of those collars either lost or damaged. To add to my stress, the collars that arrived were hopelessly too small! Worst of all, they were constructed of the same stiff belting that had caused the horrific wound on the bull rhino's leg in the first place. However, as the cow we were working on was already immobilised, and lying in an awkward position in really rough terrain, I was anxious to get the job done so that we didn't have to dart her again the next day, seeing as darting black rhino is an extremely risky business and to put her through more unnecessary trauma was just not worth it. Necessity is the mother of all invention, so in my desperation to make the collar fit, I was able to remedy the situation by sacrificing one of the four collars. Cutting the strap of one I was able to use sections of it to lengthen the remaining three. In fact this 'bridge' actually made the belt fit without a 'step': a smoother design and an improvement on the original.

Despite the setbacks and challenges we faced at every turn, our commitment to establishing black rhino in Balule has been nothing short of resolute, and needless to say, we have grown in confidence with the project. The rhino love their new home and have produced a total of nine calves. Our pride in what has been achieved has been kept moderately understated, though we all feel this is another conservation success story that needs to be shouted from every rooftop at every opportunity and not whispered about in hushed tones, behind masks in dark corners, to only those we trust ... But we dare not. In the interest of heightened security measures, we need to remain circumspect with details pertaining to the numbers and specific locations of these precious animals.

To this end, no expense was spared to bring one of our bulls back from the state-owned land across the river. Here he was in danger of falling foul to meat poachers; not only would he be opportunistically killed if stumbled upon, but the area was infested with hundreds of cable and steel wire snares set for buffalo, hippo and giraffe, snares with a breaking strength that could easily hold a black rhino. Essentially, once this rhino broke out of Balule Nature Reserve's protection he was a 'dead rhino walking', doomed without our intervention.

Time was of the essence – and just to add to the pressure, the rugged terrain and lack of road network in the area compelled us to use a helicopter to airlift this rhino back to Balule. This would be the first time in the private sector of conservation that airlifting a rhino would be attempted ... Daunting? You betcha!

Expensive and risky as it was going to be, the head warden of Balule, Craig Spencer, was up for it, and we all supported him. Olifants donated money from its rhino fund for some helicopter hours and fuel. Johan Grobbelaar, who is in charge of anti-poaching and security on Grietjie, and a small team of rangers helped by keeping track of the rhino on the ground. Regional warden Rian Ahlers, whose contacts in the helicopter world are well known, jumped at the opportunity to help. And finally, to everyone's relief, Pete Rogers would be doing all the veterinary work. It was all systems go.

For two days the team at Hoedspruit Air Force Base was on standby to help with their Oryx helicopter, but on the day allocated the rhino could not be located before nightfall. All the while he was moving further and further north, away from the reserve and into hostile territory. On the morning of the third day, he was located using Big Game Heli's little Robinson R44. Once tranquillised, the rhino was trussed up and harnessed for the lift. However, the local military machines were otherwise deployed at this stage, so an ex-US Air Force Huey, primarily used to fight forest fires, was organised and brought in to do the lifting.

Adrenaline flowed as everyone there stood open-mouthed in awe, all holding thumbs, as the unique sound of those twin helicopter blades took up the strain and the rhino was lifted into the air. When mouths closed and the saliva flowed again, the dust made a gritty paste ... but no one cared. Elated, they watched as the helicopter lifted the rhino high into the air before moving off slowly in order to avoid swinging the precious cargo around. The powerful helicopter flew westwards along the Olifants River, back into the heart of Balule. Fortunately for a few awestruck Olifants shareholders, this route took the dangling rhino right over their chalets.

The culmination of a few milligrams of M99, passionate conservationists, and expert pilots flying the most useful transportation machine ever invented had made this dramatic rescue possible. Fully tranquillised and hanging upside-down, the rhino had no idea of what was happening until 30 minutes later when, having been lowered to the ground at the drop-off point, he was unharnessed and given the antidote. Seconds later he stood up, looked around somewhat bemused, then, without the slightest stagger, took off as if he knew exactly where he was going, completely oblivious of the previous three days of anguish his walkabout had caused us all.

In an incredible demonstration of the power of social media, a video clip taken of the rhino suspended beneath the helicopter as they flew over one of the chalets was posted on Facebook before the rhino had reached its destination!

Melodie Ahlers compiled her monthly report and submitted it as usual to Dr Flamand, who had nothing but praise for the commitment of the team involved in the rescue operation. I'm sure he also felt a sense of pride that his project was in good hands, that his gut feel about Balule being a suitable recipient for the WWF's black rhino expansion project had been the right decision.

When all is said and done, the black rhino introduction into Balule has to be labelled a success. It also needs to be said that despite the relatively heavy viewing pressure, the black rhino on Olifants in particular are seen regularly by visitors and shareholders. And despite Dr Flamand's initial trepidation regarding their sensitivity to unnatural activity, such as vehicles and trains, they appear to be unaffected by either. In fact, one of the most popular venues for three of our black rhino happens to be within 50 metres of the railway line! One black rhino cow in particular, named Buza, can only be described as an absolute honey and provides hours of viewing pleasure to hundreds of people. Though not a term generally used to illustrate the temperament of this species, she is the sweetest-natured individual imaginable. However, we are aware that Buza is rather unique and that her docile and tolerant demeanour is not characteristic of these notoriously short-tempered animals.

Some months later, on the way down to visit our son Dino at Rhodes University, Meagan and I planned the trip to take us on the longer scenic route via the Great Fish River Nature Reserve area in the Eastern Cape. I was intrigued and wanted to see what the area looked like, as this was where our black rhino originated. Besides being astonished at the distance the rhino had travelled to get to us, it was most interesting for me to see the relatively lush vegetation and rolling terrain making up the habitat type that used to be their home. But I also realised that any animal that can utilise well over 200 species of plant has to have survival tattooed on its genes; it's no wonder they are thriving in the relatively harsh, dry conditions found in Balule.

Interestingly, black rhino feature in almost every account and diary of early explorers and hunters, all the way from the Cape to the Sudanese desert; they are indeed a supreme example of adaptability and survival. So how can we allow man to destroy this magnificent example of evolution in the ecological blink of an eye?

VULTURES ARE A
DEAD GIVEAWAY

It's often the most innocuous clues left by careless criminals that eventually lead investigators to their doors. The mind of a trained detective plays a key role in these instances. Moving down another dark alley, but still in the same neighbourhood, we find ourselves embroiled in a league of criminal activity that ranks with the worst horror crimes imaginable. It is becoming increasingly apparent that there are striking similarities between the profiles of rhino poachers and those of serial killers and assassins. Pre-eminent among these shared characteristics is that both are dispassionately ruthless killers and target-specific. Adding to our nightmare and frustration, they are super fit, disciplined to a fault, cunningly elusive, and night-time is their habitat of choice ... However, we cling to the fact that they are also human beings and, as such, will make mistakes. Add greed to the mix and you have the ingredients for a fallible stew.

The realisation that our reserve is not immune from the rising scourge of rhino poaching hit home on a crisp May afternoon back in 2011. One of the reserve's shareholders out on a game drive reported a dead white-backed vulture hanging in a tree. I'd received word, only a week before, that these birds were being poisoned in the Hoedspruit area and mutilated for certain body parts, which were then sold on and used in the traditional medicine (muti) trade, so I responded immediately and went out to investigate.

Not known as one of nature's prettier people at the best of times, the huge bird made a macabre spectacle as it lay tangled in the branches of a small knobthorn tree. Its two-metre wings were spread awkwardly, festooned in the grotesque contortion usually seen in animals that have not died peacefully. Now, hanging only three metres off the ground, it belied the graceful image these birds usually exhibit as they soar effortlessly on superbly designed wings at altitudes more commonly associated with jet aircraft and cumulus clouds. I believe it must have tried to land in the topmost branches, as they usually do. Thrashing in its death throes, it may have fallen and tangled itself in the lower branches of the tree, which enabled me to reach the unfortunate bird and remove it quite easily. At this point I still had no reason to suspect anything untoward. Huge electric pylons close by had accounted for a number of vulture casualties over the years, and naturally this was my first thought.

More often than not we are drawn to death on the veld not by one or two individuals but by hundreds of vultures, either as they circle over in a silent, feathered vortex or as they wait patiently perched on leafless trees for miles around, where from a distance the twisted branches seem to bulge with these huge birds like giant dried fruit in a long-dead orchard. Little did we know that this single dead vulture would reveal what a hundred living birds might not have been able to in this particular scenario.

I carefully placed the dead bird in a bin-liner bag as it needed to be taken in for a routine autopsy at the local vet as soon as possible. Taking the shortest route back to camp, I made my way along a faint track that went through a shallow depression cutting along the edge of a huge muddy pan. It was there that I saw another sick-looking vulture at the water's edge. Hobbling around and tripping occasionally, the poor bird was clearly in serious trouble. Froth oozed from its beak and nostrils, bubbling with each laboured breath. I'd seen this before in domestic geese that had eaten lawn treated with ant poison, and my stomach turned at the realisation that these vultures were showing the classic symptoms of some kind of agro-chemical poisoning.

Holding the bird against my chest, I looked down at its black eyes which were blinking up at me in confusion and pain, its sharp, curved beak agape as if in a silent scream. It offered neither resistance nor defence. Here was a bird that regularly undertook marathon flights of hundreds of kilometres each day of its life to search for food, a bird now crippled, unable to cover a couple of metres properly, let alone fly.

Subsequent investigation led us to another three dead vultures in the vicinity of the dam. However, these birds also happened to be in close proximity to the carcass of a lioness which had been killed by three new male lions that had taken over our resident pride's territory approximately a week earlier.

Of course suspicion and conjecture as to the possible reason for the vulture deaths immediately focused our interest on the closest source of carrion, which was obviously the carcass of the lioness. Having been decomposing for over a week, it was literally under our noses, so to speak. All eyes and thoughts were focused on the fact that there may possibly be something amiss with it. Having seen the carcass a day or so after she had died, and seeing the terrible wounds inflicted by other lions, it was clear to me what had killed her. This conclusion was backed up by the fact that another lion carcass, a younger male, was found the same day. He had been killed in the same manner and was lying less than two kilometres away from the lioness. (Incidentally, using whisker patterns and ear nicks, this particular lion was later identified as the same male lion suspected of being the cub killer.)

Initially there was some concern that muti poachers had opportunistically laced the lioness carcass with poison in an effort to kill vultures. Thousands of vultures and hundreds of short-tailed eagles are killed every year in Africa in this way. The latter species, which are close to endangered status, are simply left to rot, as it is primarily the vultures these murderers want. Everything else that dies is of no interest or concern to them.

Confusing the issue were the spoor and feeding patterns noted of smaller mammals in the vicinity. Black-backed jackals, civets and mongooses had also fed on the lioness, so I was also looking for these other, less conspicuous scavengers lying dead or dying close by, but a thorough search revealed nothing. Two things bothered me. First, there weren't more vulture carcasses in close proximity, and second, there was no sign of any other dead or dying creatures. I remained convinced that those vultures we'd found were poisoned elsewhere and had come down to the water hole for water and died there.

Our trusted and highly experienced field rangers were also not convinced that the problem lay with the lion carcass and supported my suspicion that the source of the poison was further away and less obvious. But my immediate concern was to try and find any more dead or dying vultures: if found early enough, the sick birds could be saved with treatment. So I left finding the source of the poison up to my competent rangers. It wasn't long before they called me in on the two-way radio.

Getting onto some high ground, we noticed about 30 vultures sitting in the prominent trees way off in the bush, not too far from the pan where I'd rescued the poisoned vulture, and approximately 400 metres from the lion carcass. I sent my field rangers in to investigate around the bases of those trees in order to try and locate any more unfortunate vultures that may have succumbed. In the meantime I rushed the one surviving vulture to Hoedspruit, where Dr Pete Rogers managed to pull the bird through with the miracle of early detection, experience and Atropine. The other carcasses, which had been kept cool but not frozen, were stored in Meagan's air-conditioned office overnight. Needless to say, it took a couple of weeks before the smell dissipated completely, as vultures are naturally quite smelly birds – and understandably so, as most of their feeding activity is spent with their neck and head deep inside rotting carcasses.

The dead birds were sent to Dr Gerrit Scheepers, who did a preliminary examination upon their arrival. Based on his experience, the initial diagnosis was that the deadly agro-pesticide Aldicarb (Temik) could be the possible culprit. Gerrit then sent tissue samples off to the pathologists for a detailed analysis and confirmation.

Later that morning an investigating patrol was sent in search of more vultures, but none were found. Instead they uncovered other shocking evidence that confirmed one of our greatest fears: our defences had been breached and our reserve violated by rhino poachers. Cable snares plaited together to form a steel rope as thick as a man's thumb were set within earshot of the same water hole where the vultures had been found. Poachers were targeting our rhino, and the bastards were right in our midst plying their treacherous, deadly trade. No rifles, no helicopters, no chainsaws, only simple, silent and equally deadly strangulating cable snares, cable so strong it was capable of restraining an animal many times the size of a white rhino!

I made a phone call to Big Game Heli, and a helicopter was scrambled; Meagan made another call, and yet another heli was put on standby. Within 25 minutes the helicopter was on the scene. Half an hour later, regional warden Rian Ahlers and his newly acquired German shepherd tracker dogs were brought in. A number of Balule's regional wardens were on the scene, as was Klaserie's Colin Rowles, who was on standby with his team of well-trained anti-poaching rangers. Everyone around realised the seriousness of what was happening and that their area could be targeted next. The support was incredible!

Unfortunately, having recently come up from Pretoria, Rian's tracker dogs were new to their handlers, also working in the heat of the day, in unfamiliar terrain and without a scent article, was not a good start. However, the female did manage to locate snares that had been set for smaller game in the vicinity. All indications were that the poachers were long gone. From their fresh boot prints our trackers were able to interpret that they had lain low when they'd heard the chopper searching the area.

That night was full moon, which the poachers used to their advantage to cross the Olifants River. Then they moved along the myriad game paths through the dense mopane woodland of state-owned land, from where it's a hop and a skip onto the R40 main road and the nearby community of Mashishimale. Alternatively, they could choose Phalaborwa's urban surrounds, where they would simply have been able to melt in, absorbed among the masses. Either way they would be lost to us.

Fortunately, we were able to react quickly and thwart what could have been a far greater tragedy. Another 12 hours and the scene may have resembled that on Selati Game Reserve a couple of weeks earlier, when a black rhino was caught in a cable snare and killed. Knowing what these careless killers leave behind, a thorough sweep of the area over the next two days enabled us to remove well over 50 snares in two 'mopping up' patrols. Only two impala had been caught and strangled in the snares; fortunately, a third was found alive and rescued – though a small victory in the scheme of things, we felt elated to have been able to save its life. Two grapefruits, suspected (and later confirmed) to have been laced with poison, were found near the bigger snares targeting rhino.

I believe an attempt was made by the poachers to poison the vultures by lacing the two snared impala remains with poison. Conjecture has it that this may have been done in an attempt to get rid of these early warning sentinels, so that they could target the rhino undetected by the eyes in the sky and, as a bonus, get a few bits and bobs for the local witchdoctor. Fortunately, they did not leave much for the vultures and only a few birds got enough poison ingested. This time their greed had backfired, but we were painfully aware that next time they may not be so sloppy!

This was not the end of it. We had discovered the tip of the proverbial iceberg, one that was going to be floating in our sea for the foreseeable future as an ever-present danger and threat. It had been a wake-up call for all of us; it tested our resolve and above all showed us not to be dismissive of small clues, no matter how subtle or innocuous. And that we needed to lift our heads occasionally. To this end, every ranger now carries a pair of binoculars and checks the skies every morning for vulture activity.

Evidence of a hurried retreat by the next gang of poachers a couple of weeks later showed that the helicopter search that we had instituted was extremely effective in terminating their activities. Perhaps not in the sense that the poachers were caught fleeing the scene and subsequently apprehended, as we so desperately would have liked, but at least it demonstrated to those bastards cowering in the bush like rats in a hollow log that this honey badger would claw through and eventually get them. We wanted them to see the helicopter and the manpower we'd deployed; they needed to know we meant to protect our wildlife at any cost.

In the meantime the rest of the ground crew were sweeping for the snares set by the poachers before they ran. From the air the helicopter located their camp not too far from our boundary with Klaserie. Our anti-poaching unit's search around the periphery of the camp revealed heaps of incriminating evidence: more snares, a bottle of poison, salt, sugar, maize meal, clothing and other human detritus, all hidden in rock crevices or stuffed down disused aardvark burrows. Not far away from the campsite, we found the skinned remnants of a zebra carcass, which had been completely encircled with snares specifically targeting lions, leopards and hyenas. Obviously these killers had diversified their target market and extended beyond rhino horn: their ill-gotten gains would now include lion and leopard bones for the Asian market, as well as hyena body parts and lion fat, which are in huge demand by local witchdoctors or sangomas.

Thankfully we were able to avert any predator casualties at this trap. Another 50-odd snares were found, among them four thick cable snares targeting rhino, which had been set around a rain-filled wallow; however, again we were able to remove them timeously.

The next day we found an old day-pack that poachers had hidden while making their escape. It contained interesting paraphernalia, including some de-worming tablets, painkillers, a military water bottle, women's clothing, marijuana and a hat. Most interesting, however, was a small stash of witchdoctor's muti which I was told by our anti-poaching rangers is ingested to make one invisible! It looked a little like dried faeces and in all probability was just that. Needless to say, no field tests were conducted to determine the authenticity of this observation. Also found, which proved to be the biggest game changer, were five live nine-millimetre pistol rounds. At least one of the poachers was probably carrying a firearm!

Mopping up operations revealed that, all in all, the poachers may have spent two weeks in the bush and had set well over 150 snares. However, from the evidence found, it was apparent that they'd managed to get away with relatively little. The known tally included five vultures, seven impala, two warthogs, a zebra and two hyenas.

For a couple of weeks everything went quietly back to normal. Feedback from professional anti-poaching intelligence on the 'outside' indicated that Selati Game Reserve and surrounding farms near Gravelotte were being revisited by those poachers suspected to have been pushed out of our area. Unfortunately, this was the same reserve where in all likelihood it had been these same poachers who had successfully poached a rhino with cable snares before. However, we began to believe that our anti-poaching strategy was having a stifling effect on their forays into our reserve and that they would leave us alone ... Oh, how wrong we were.

THOSE WHO WILL NOT LISTEN ...

We had begun to believe that the message of our field rangers' resilience had trickled through the bush telegraph and been received by those planning to target our reserve's rhino. It was little more than three weeks since the first poisoned vulture was discovered on our reserve, exposing an undercurrent of treachery in our midst, heralding the trauma of the future.

Under our noses, this gang of poachers had gone about their ghastly business with impunity. The scale of it shocked even the most hardcore men in the team; we tortured ourselves asking how this could have slipped in under the radar for so long. There was no one but ourselves to blame: had we possibly been guilty of the 'it can never happen to us' syndrome, allowed complacency to creep in? Nevertheless, a valuable lesson was learned: we resolved never again to allow our vigilance to wane ... And it hasn't.

Despite being put to flight, and their camp, equipment and snares destroyed, the poachers had seen too much. The damage was done; they'd had a taste of the easy pickings, and the possibility of greater things was just too tempting for them to ignore. Our warning had fallen on deaf ears. So it wasn't long before what we suspected was the same gang entered our reserve. However, this time we were better equipped: not only had we employed technology able to help us detect their incursion in time, but most importantly, our field rangers were mentally prepared and determined to arrest these men before any rhino could be killed or a single snare set. It was a challenge and our guys were up for it.

Early on Wednesday morning, 29 June 2011, field rangers on a routine patrol drew my attention to suspicious spoor that had been observed close to the Olifants railway bridge. As this point of entry formed a convenient bottleneck, we had recently installed a Bushnell Trophy Cam motion-detection camera to cover it. To the best of my knowledge this was the first time an American hunting camera had been used specifically for rhino anti-poaching work in South Africa. At the time, this was all the camera trap technology available. Today dozens of relatively sophisticated camera traps, sending real-time MMS images to our cell phones, are strategically deployed throughout Balule. I'm pleased to say that most of the other reserves have done the same, with excellent results.

With bated breath, we huddled around Meagan's computer as she downloaded the camera footage. Dozens of train images, a few images of our field rangers on patrol, and a lone lioness ... Meagan stopped scrolling on three grey, grainy images that sent shivers down our spines. We stared disbelievingly as she enlarged the frame and zoomed in, revealing the ghostlike figures of three balaclava-clad men carrying what appeared to be thick cable and backpacks. According to the camera's timer they'd triggered the motion detector as they entered the reserve at 6.20 the previous morning. These images spoke volumes. The wavy twist of the cable snares draped over the shoulder of one of the suspects was the same as that of those we'd recovered on previous snare sweeps and which had killed two rhino on Selati Game Reserve. These were most likely the same poachers returning intent on setting these snares; this time they would be coming to specifically target and kill rhino. These poachers knew where they were going, what they wanted and where to set the cable – but now so did we!

Confirmation was made when our trackers identified their shoe prints as the same as those from three weeks previously. There was no question: despite our show of force and determination to keep them out of the reserve, the same arrogant bastards were back for more. As they knew the lay of the land, they would lose no time setting those cables. We needed to apprehend them as soon as possible, in order to minimise the potential danger to our rhino and, of course, other game. Although we knew this gang was targeting rhino, they were also using Aldicarb poison indiscriminately.

Clearly we needed to be more decisive: the message this time needed to be clearer than the last. My field rangers, good as they are, also know their limitations. Realising this was a task too big for us to handle alone, I called for help from local wardens and the South African Police Service (SAPS). A Squirrel helicopter loaded a ground force, comprising the Special Operations Unit dealing specifically with rhino poaching in the Kruger Park, and was on the reserve within a couple of hours. Colin from next-door Klaserie dispatched his team of field rangers to help and was hovering on the cutline, on constant standby for us if needed. The noose was beginning to tighten.

We had been on the poachers' spoor all day, but despite deploying two helicopters and a Foxbat fixed-wing aircraft, we were unable to locate them. In the meantime the team on the ground was painstakingly tracking their every devious move. This was before the days of canine assistance, so deciphering the subtle signs of their anti-tracking technique took heaps of valuable time, which gave the poachers the advantage and enabled them to keep ahead of our team. (Of the variety of tricks used by them, we have found that the most common is to wrap socks over their running shoes on sandy sections. Then, walking on the balls of their feet, they leave indistinct scuffs that blend in easily with old elephant, rhino and hippo tracks. Hopping from rock to rock and using the roughest stony substrate are others.) With daylight fading fast and the men depleted, the decision was taken to set up an observation post and play the waiting game. Despite a determined effort by all, it was apparent that the rhino poachers had gone to ground. They had not crossed the river as all the known exits were covered and the floodplain was clear of any spoor exiting the reserve.

While the exhausted Special Operations members were taken back to Olifants to be fed and housed overnight, Jabulaan Makhubedu, head of our own anti-poaching team, pulled me aside. He said the team had decided to position themselves at the bridge as they anticipated the poachers would try and escape across the river that night. So their plan was to arrest the poachers when they tried to cross the bridge at the bottleneck. Knowing how exhausted I felt, I admired their strategy and determination, so without hesitation I agreed.

An hour after sunset, I sent my driver with supper, coffee, chocolate bars and warm overcoats to the bridge where my field rangers had settled in to wait for the poachers. I instructed him to make a show of the vehicle arriving and leaving. The ruse was to fool the poachers, who we suspected were watching the bridge from the surrounding high ground. We needed them to believe we'd come to collect our tired, hungry field rangers and take them back to base, allowing them to think their usual escape route was left unguarded.

These killers were no amateurs; they had been hunted before; they too had made a study of our tactics. Cautious as ever, they waited another three hours before making their move. But our field rangers' discipline held; they gave nothing of their presence away. When the poachers were satisfied it was all clear, they stealthily crept out of their hillside positions and made their way down to the bridge without a sound. Leading the trio with handgun in hand, the front man carried little else. Behind him, armed with an axe, the second man was clearly also prepared for confrontation. The last man carried a backpack with their essential equipment and in his right hand he carried a blood-stained machete.

Their soft-soled running shoes made no sound, but they knew there was no way they could remain silent walking on the gravel, which they needed to do in order to access the narrow entrance to the bridge itself. Walking on the lines or sleepers would have been deathly quiet, but in the prevailing darkness, this tactic would mean having to drop their eyes and concentrate on each footfall, something they couldn't afford to do. Instead, they must have lost their nerve, deciding to rush the bridge so that if there were men there, they would catch them off-guard – and once past that point and on the bridge, they must have gambled that we would not shoot them in the back. It was also chillingly clear by their weaponry that the poachers were not entirely convinced that the field rangers had all left, and that they were prepared to shoot or hack their way through to the bridge to escape.

I tried to picture the scene in my mind's eye. Three men running towards you on loose gravel, in pitch darkness, can sound like a stampede. It must have been terrifying for our field rangers. An old .303 Lee-Enfield rifle was all that stood between them and certain death as three armed poachers ran towards their position. High on marijuana, the poachers completely ignored the call from our field rangers to stop, instead they answered by firing blindly in the direction of the challenge. The ranger in front had no option but to shoot at where the muzzle flash emanated from, hitting the man closest to him, virtually at point-blank range.

The copper-jacketed 175 grain bullet ripped clean through the man's heart, killing him almost instantly, breaking his spine as it exited. The pointed projectile now angled off its path of destruction and turned broadside on, smashing through the second poacher's hand. It was a paralysing blow; the axe he was wielding simply fell from his now useless hand and clattered harmlessly onto the mound of coarse gravel that made up the foundation supporting the train lines. The third man had already dropped everything he was carrying and run, and was now followed closely by the wounded man. A cocktail of adrenaline, endorphins and marijuana gave them legs our tired field rangers simply could not match. In a few seconds the inky-black night and thick riverine bush closed in behind the fleeing men and swallowed them whole.

At 10.54 pm, Meagan and I were woken by a call from one of our field rangers. It was Joachim Timani. Almost inaudibly, he uttered five words.

'The poacher. He is dead!' Timani always spoke softly.

Meagan and I got dressed and drove down to the cottage where we roused three senior SAPS officers of the Special Operations Unit and drove them to the scene with us. This was the time when we needed experienced people to assist, and although I was reluctant to involve Meagan, truth be told it was comforting, because when confronted with a situation like this you need all the loyal support you can muster. We arrived on the scene not knowing what to expect, or how we'd react to the sight of a dead human being. My mind was racing with questions. I'd seen men killed by elephant, lions and hippo, and others fatally stabbed in drunken brawls, but this was to be the first fatal incident involving a rhino poacher.

We now had to deal with the situation and find out what protocol to follow. Also, Meagan and I quickly found out that everyone is gung-ho and full of bravado when it comes to how to tackle rhino poachers. 'Shoot the bastards' is the lament often heard, but when the shit actually hits the fan, and you look around for support, you find yourself surrounded by a sudden emptiness, as we did that icy cold morning. Nearly everyone, it seemed, had somewhere else they needed to be or something they had to do.

We arrived to find the victim lying close to the bridge; he lay on his back as if asleep. One of the SAPS officers collected the weapon, then checked for signs of life and found none. The dead man's balaclava hid his eyes, and although tempted, I just couldn't bring myself to lift it up and look at his face. Sparse beard stubble dotted his chin and surrounded his lips, which were slightly parted as if he was still breathing. I expected to find a lot of blood but saw none except for a little around the entrance wound on his chest.

There was little else for us to do while we waited for the local police and the mortuary van to arrive. So I lit a small fire, knowing we had at least three hours to stand there in the bitter cold contemplating the situation. I was shocked at how little emotion Meagan and I felt at the time. Perhaps our response would be delayed, I thought. Knowing that we had thwarted the killing of our rhino, an undeniable feeling of relief prevailed. Nevertheless, I couldn't help thinking how unnecessary this man's death was ... If only he had listened.

As can be expected with any unnatural loss of human life, the resulting investigation proved time-consuming, difficult and expensive. We
needed the best legal representation. Needless to say, Olifants' board
gave the 'no expense spared' go-ahead. Coert Jordaan, an attorney
who specialised in anti-poaching shooting incidents in the Kruger
National Park, was contacted. At first we were told he couldn't take
the case, as he had a number of scheduled court appearances the next
day. However, after much pleading and persuasion from Meagan, who
had also promised to fly Coert to and from the scene, he relented and
rearranged his entire schedule to help us.

The next call we made was to Mike Pingo of Sunrise Aviation, our
intrepid game census pilot. Without a moment's hesitation or grumble,
he refuelled his JetRanger that night in preparation. Then, scrambling
the helicopter in the pre-dawn light, he flew Coert from Nelspruit that
same morning. This mode of transport wasn't a question of dramatics
but was necessitated by the pressure being brought to bear by local
police detectives, who were demanding a statement from Timani. At
that point in time, it would have been inadvisable for him to have made
a statement without the best legal representation we could muster. We
owed our brave field ranger that much.

Having left Nelspruit at first light, Mike and Coert arrived in
Hoedspruit as police were trying to take Timani in for a statement.
Meagan and I sat there chewing our fingernails until we heard the helicopter approach and fly overhead. What a beautiful noise! We then
whispered to Timani, 'Go to the toilet – and take your time.' This
bought just enough time for Meagan to drive out and collect Coert on
the nearby airfield.

Though the police appeared slightly taken aback by our efficiency
and professionalism, as a matter of procedure a murder docket was
opened. This required Timani to be taken to Phalaborwa Magistrates'
Court in order to apply for bail. So, while Meagan drove through to
Phalaborwa following the police van carrying Timani, I got to go with
Coert and Mike in the helicopter. On the way we took a quick detour
along the Olifants River and spent a couple of minutes hovering over

A black-backed jackal sizes up an abandoned buffalo calf. PHOTO: L CLEARY

The author and veterinarian Dr Pete Rogers (*right*) with an injured lion. PHOTO: G DU TOIT

A hippo cow and calf, two of the many victims of train collisions on this railway line's infamous 'death bend'. PHOTO: M CESARE

Treating an injured giraffe on Olifants River Game Reserve; *(left to right)* Jabulaan Makhubedu, Dr Gerrit Scheepers, the author and Neil Hulett. PHOTO: M HULETT

One of the 'big tuskers' that trophy hunters are prepared to pay huge sums of money to kill.
PHOTO: C COCKING

One of the reserve's black rhino is airlifted to safety after having wandered into hostile territory.
PHOTO: J GROBLER

An average-sized breeding herd of elephant on Olifants River Game Reserve. Note the healthy number of calves. PHOTO: M CESARE

After an absence of 24 years, sable antelope were reintroduced into Balule. PHOTO: D JOCELYN

Invasive but necessary, a radio telemetric transmitter is implanted in the horn of a white rhino. PHOTO: M CESARE

A well-placed camera trap reveals the ghostly figures of three rhino poachers moving into the reserve.

A white rhino, tranquilised with M99, is steadied before going down to have a microchip implanted and a DNA sample taken. PHOTO: C CAMPBELL

Helicopter pilot Benjamin Osmers (Bennie) skilfully manoeuvres a darted rhino towards the loading area.
PHOTO: F FISHER

The late Benjamin Osmers, helicopter pilot extraordinaire, conservationist and friend.
PHOTO: M CESARE

Author and Leonie Hofstra (*right*) with a rescued rhino calf the day after its mother was brutally killed by poachers.
PHOTO: Z HAJDINJAK

Mary and her calf. Mary was one of the first rhino introduced into Olifants. PHOTO: N HULETT

Sinhle Mathebula, Balule's black rhino monitor, takes time out to educate schoolchildren about nature conservation. PHOTO: M CESARE

Pictured here with cable snares set to target rhino are *(left to right)* the author, Jabulaan Makhubedu, January Mahlaule and Glenn du Toit.

The author and Saba on the bank of the Olifants River. PHOTO: M COX

At 17 months old, Saba successfully tracked down this rhino poacher. The poacher was arrested before he was able to kill any rhino. PHOTO: PROTRACK

Janelle Goodrich of Provet prepares to administer the tranquiliser antidote after treating this rhino for a poacher's bullet wound. Saba looks on in bemusement; this was her first live rhino. PHOTO: D CESARE

Some of the Black Mambas, an all-women team of anti-poaching rangers who have achieved world renown. Seated with his muzzled Belgian Malinois is Mambas founder and Balule head warden Craig Spencer.
PHOTO: PROTRACK

Olifants field rangers undergo regular musketry training. PHOTO: M CESARE

While the Olifants River creates a pretty picture as it flows through the reserve, low water levels make it relatively easy for rhino poachers to wade across. PHOTO: M CESARE

the scene of the shooting incident. It was an excellent opportunity to give Coert a crucial bird's-eye view of the scene in order to explain what happened, how and where.

We waited in the passageway of the magistrates' court with Timani while a rather corpulent magistrate and Coert went head to head in her chambers. The solidly built double brick building did little to muffle the ranting; all I can remember her screaming hysterically was, 'This is a planned murder!' followed by a moment's relative quiet. Then, again: 'No, this is a planned murder!'

Our hearts dropped, but Coert had been there, done that and got a box of these T-shirts before. He remained composed and persisted with his awesome knowledge of criminal law and the legal system's nuances until Timani was granted R1 500 bail and released. The court date for the hearing was set for the following week in Phalaborwa, from where the hearings were shifted to Hoedspruit Magistrates' Court, much to Coert's relief. He was confident that at least Timani would get a fair trial in Hoedspruit.

The prosecution team was hellbent on convicting Timani of murder. It was a traumatic time for all of us, particularly Timani. However, I was with him at every hearing, assuring him of our reserve's support at every opportunity. Having spent a total of 21 hours in court, I am pleased to report that Coert got Timani acquitted after four months and five court appearances.

Rhino anti-poaching: 1 ... Rhino poachers: 0!

Glib as this may sound, the outcome of Timani's case would be setting a landmark legal precedent. All eyes were on this case: I suspected that the rhino poaching syndicates in the area as well as the anti-poaching world were waiting for the outcome. Had it gone against Timani, the result would have reverberated negatively for those fighting the good fight, demoralising hundreds of dedicated field rangers and placing thousands of rhino at higher risk.

We were lucky enough to gather a good deal of detail about the other two poachers' ordeal. According to reports from the anti-poaching units, the day after their accomplice was shot the two men were still at large and on the run. Our field rangers had followed their blood trail and tracks through Balule, along the Olifants River, all the way to the R40 road, a distance of approximately 35 kilometres! There it was evident that they'd managed to climb aboard a taxi. However, the wounded man was in such agony that he admitted himself to hospital in Tzaneen where he was promptly treated, arrested and cuffed to his bed. All gunshot patients are reported to authorities by hospitals as a matter of course. The second man was arrested at his house shortly afterwards.

Although we could not positively identify the two men when they appeared in court, we knew it was them ... And, most importantly, they knew we knew.

Despite not being charged with any crime, they'd both been pursued by a crack team of trackers and field rangers. Although the man with the hole in his hand could not give a plausible explanation for the wound, he denied being at the scene of the shooting. Focused primarily on Timani's acquittal, we declined to pursue the lesser issue and prove otherwise. Nevertheless, the poacher and his accomplice had spent the best part of four months in jail, and one of them will never be able to use his right hand to help him kill a rhino or set a snare again.

Timani had managed to stop two rhino murderers with a single bullet! A cartridge that was designed over 120 years ago, fired from a rifle that had already seen service in a world war and was older than he was. He still undergoes regular trauma counselling. Killing a fellow human being, even in self-defence, plays on one's conscience, never mind how tough you may think you are or how just the cause.

FIRST RHINO POACHED ON OLIFANTS

It was a pivotal moment when we realised that the meat and muti poachers, who invariably used steel wire or cable snares, were no longer our reserve's greatest poaching threat. Snare poachers were unselective, and in that random approach lay their predictability and weakness. But the world was changing; the stakes were now much higher, and the demand for rhino horn in particular had become insatiable. We were now up against the big guns – literally and figuratively.

What we were facing now was a completely different animal: a breed of killers focused on a specific target, like a pack of dogs following a bitch on heat; little seemed to deter them. Even the death of a comrade at the hand of our field rangers did not send a clear enough message. All they did was learn from their rival gang's mistakes, up the ante and change tactics. Up to that point we'd been hoping the message to avoid our area was clear, but the latest incursion took most of that wind out of our sails. They were entering our reserve with the sole intention of killing rhino for their horns, and nothing would make them deviate from their intended targets. These poachers were clearly in a league of their own; their organised, Spartan efficiency made us realise the rules of this despicable game had drastically changed. We were up against experienced, organised criminals, assassins and hitmen from a seemingly endless source.

Ruthlessly intent and totally focused on the task, they never made a fire, established a campsite or left a trace of litter. Besides simple day-packs, they travelled light. Most of them wore old running shoes, which left only subtle imprints as clues to their movements and were also quick and easy to remove when crossing the river. For some unfathomable reason, All Star seemed to be the brand of choice.

It is the same when you need to study a legal document or agreement, which until the moment it actually affects your life lies glossed over in a file at the bottom of a drawer. Now pertinent, you study each word in context; you find the content understandable and even absorb the legalese like a sponge. When we studied the blurry photos that our hidden cameras sent through we had to read the images, understand and interpret them quickly, so every nuance was analysed and the unconfirmed detail was at least speculated on. Lives could depend on this.

Analysing the latest grainy, ghostlike camera-trap images of three poachers entering the reserve revealed their body language in detail. The message was clear: we would have a fight on our hands to keep rhino from getting slaughtered. In that message was not an iota of ambiguity. Other subtle clues allowed us to make more assumptions. For example, we noticed their wide, determined stride, the spacing between them as they walked, and the way they carried the rifle. No stooping, no sideways glancing; their straight-backed posture as if marching on parade suggested an arrogant confidence, which sent an involuntary chill down my spine. It was apparent from this that these men were ex-militia: either that, or they had done this before.

Thanks to a perfectly positioned camera trap set by Pieter Pretorius, Grietjie's regional warden at the time, the earliest images of these men revealed their first incursion was around midnight on 15 September 2011. It also showed they'd left a few days later empty handed. At this point, the standard camera trap was upgraded to include one that sent MMS images to a cell phone. One of our shareholders knew someone who knew someone else at MTN who, once given the GPS co-ordinates of the cameras, helped our cause by prioritising the images sent to our phones. Effectively this meant there was absolutely no delay. And although these cameras' positions were changed regularly, the general area was priority ring-fenced so that it did not affect this vital capability.

Upgrading to more sophisticated cameras that incorporated this feature was the best decision we made. When the same men entered and triggered the camera a week later, we weren't a week or days behind the foray. We were now in real time: in fact, often we were so close behind them there were times I could swear I smelled their smoky, sweat-soaked clothing. Realistically, though, we knew they were already in the killing zone ... of the rhino, that is. Catching a poacher who has not killed a rhino you can tie him to is as good as taking someone to court for trespassing. The best we could do in these situations was to thwart their forays, chase them back, and prevent our rhino from getting killed.

At this point we usually called in a helicopter. These incredibly versatile machines are arguably the best way to respond in these situations. The poachers, who at that stage had no idea they were triggering cameras each time they entered, must have wondered how the hell we were onto them so quickly. Invariably, with a helicopter in the air the poachers would go to ground, which allowed us time to tighten the net and deploy a tactical reaction force if needed. These were known as disruptive tactics and essentially placed the poachers on the back foot, effectively changing their mind-set from killing mode to survival mode. Their priority was now to escape the pursuit; killing a rhino became the last thing on their minds.

While the helicopter flew grids across the river, our field rangers went into the area on a clandestine, hot-pursuit foot patrol. However, it took an inordinate amount of time to track in the rocky terrain, and we only had a couple of hours of chopper time left. As expected, the poachers made for the boulder-strewn hills that characterise much of state-owned Doreen, where they hid themselves like rock rabbits until nightfall.

Instead of running for the R40 main road, as we half expected them to, the wily bastards crossed the river onto the southern side (our side) and sat it out until around midnight. In a demonstration of their calculating discipline, they didn't expect us to consider this brazen tactic ... And they were right! Later, when we had left the area, they felt safe enough to cross back through the river, exiting the reserve the same way they had entered. As if in defiant mockery of our efforts, the images of them leaving were triggered around 1 am.

For the next couple of weeks all went quiet, and we resumed routine patrols, albeit with heightened awareness. Besides the few camera traps on the boundary, it remained extremely frustrating that we could not keep tabs on incoming movement through Doreen. Though we sneaked in anyway, they were stolen hours, we needed more time to do a thorough combing each day. Inevitably, it wasn't long before Carel Jailbird of Doreen bumped into our field rangers on one of these attempted sneaks; they were investigating vulture activity on the property, and he threatened to charge them with trespassing if he found them there again.

This man had hated our field rangers ever since they'd arrested him for illegally hunting a leopard on state land, a charge for which he was convicted and his weapons confiscated. Needless to say, having a criminal record has been a bitter pill for him to swallow. In this particular instance our field rangers were actually on the railway servitude road where they are allowed to patrol. So, confidently, but with the cordiality undeserved by such a scoundrel, they responded by telling him that they were in fact on Transnet's property and had full authority to be on that section and could proceed all the way through to Phalaborwa if deemed to be necessary. As it turned out, when the man had left, they took a sneak look anyway and found the fresh remains of an elephant that had been professionally hunted the previous day. We checked with the authorities, such as they are, and were informed that a permit had indeed been issued. His paperwork was all in order … Surprise, surprise.

Relentlessly driven by greed and amassing fortunes in cash, the poachers were unable to resist the temptation to try again. Close to midnight on 7 October 2011, three men, armed with a rifle and an axe, triggered the cameras as they came back into Doreen. Once again, they sat patiently and waited for us to reveal ourselves. Satisfied that things had quietened down sufficiently, and knowing our focus would be to check along the 'front line' for strange movement, they made good their incursion. Under the cover of darkness, the poachers sneaked across the Olifants River into our reserve. Having waded through the river, they walked barefoot through a landowner's bush camp while the occupants slept. Possibly this was an unconscious display of confidence, or an attempt to avoid the surveillance cameras that they somehow now suspected were at the bridge.

Once their feet were dry, they slipped on their running shoes. From there they followed well-worn game paths into the hilly terrain, habitat that was more suited to black rhino than white. Fortunately, at that time there were no black rhino in the area. The poachers continued eastwards, heading towards the Klaserie/Balule boundary. At that time of year, this area is relatively well watered and, as a result, is known to support one of the densest populations of white rhino in the reserve. These bastards knew exactly where they were going! Once in the area they would simply wait until daylight, then track down and kill rhino … Simple.

Despite their concerted attempts at anti-tracking, when walking in the dark even the most experienced poachers are unable to conceal all their tracks, some of which were observed by our tracking team the following morning. Ironically, at this point in time I was on my way to a meeting in Hoedspruit to discuss the formation of a co-coordinated anti-poaching response team – with the provisional name Game Reserves United (GRU) – which was to be set up in all the private reserves to help combat this scourge.

Included on the agenda was a presentation by Lorinda Hern about Rhino Rescue Project's innovative horn treatment, which renders the horn toxic to human consumption but is harmless to the rhino and lasts for up to four years. As fascinating as this concept was, I found my mind wandering back to those poacher's tracks; I could not concentrate so, against protocol, left my phone on.

Later, during the meeting, I took a call from one of my field rangers

stationed inland. He informed me of suspicious spoor, tracks and movement consistent with poachers. I could tell this wasn't a matter-of-fact,
heads-up call; in fact, it was the urgency in his voice that concerned
me, and then when he phoned me for the second time, saying he was
sure the poachers would be going back across the river that evening,
I knew we needed to act quickly. Embarrassed at the interruption, I
actually leaned across and showed Andrew Parker, who was chairing
the meeting, what it was about. Even though the image of the poachers
on my cell phone was grainy and indistinct, he understood completely:
Sabi Sands Game Reserve, where he was CEO, had recently lost eight
rhino to poachers.

Earlier on in the meeting, ex-Special Forces officer Dap Maritz
emphasised the need for getting the GRU task team operational as
soon as possible. Using our situation as an example, he pointed to me
and said, 'As Mario sits here, he knows there are poachers using an
area he cannot access with his team. The poachers know this and use
the hilly terrain that characterises much of the state-owned land to
their advantage. From there they observe our field rangers' movements
using binoculars and then launch well-planned poaching raids into
Balule Nature Reserve.'

I broke in, explaining my frustration that the lessee of this land, who
had himself been convicted of illegally trying to hunt leopards there, now
bore a huge grudge against our field rangers and, as a result, would not
allow them to patrol the area. Strictly speaking, this was tantamount to
aiding and abetting; nevertheless, I would welcome a less confrontational
arrangement, and some possible mediation from GRU to assist Balule in
this area, in the interest of combating rhino poaching.

Straight after the meeting, I informed Grietjie's regional warden that
the poachers were still in the area, and that they would almost certainly
go out past his cameras that night; if so, we needed to move quickly
and lay an ambush. I also told him that, as we spoke, my anti-poaching
team were deploying themselves to set up an observation post downstream of the bridge where the suspicious tracks were seen crossing
that morning.

Concealed in an observation post on the southern bank of the Olifants River, the field rangers knew that given the time and light available there would have been little point in trying to track the poachers over rocky terrain. Instead, they decided it would probably be better to sit tight and intercept them when they returned to the relative safety north of the river on Doreen, where once through the river they might drop their guard.

The poachers, still unaware of the camera, had now triggered the infra-red motion detector, sending more images straight through to our cell phones. It was now just after 8 pm. The SAPS and special crimes unit were immediately alerted by SAPS reservist Eugene Engelbrecht, who then scrambled a task team from Phalaborwa to help us set up an ambush on the R40.

At approximately 10.30 pm, the special task force of the SAPS arrested the poachers on the R40 as they exited the area at a known rendezvous point. A .375 Magnum rifle, a bloody rhino horn, and an axe were seized, as well as other incriminating evidence. Two of the suspects fled with the smaller horn but little else. Although there were now two rhino poachers in custody, and a pick-up truck, a fresh rhino horn and the 'smoking' rifle seized, there was still no carcass. Usually in rhino poaching incidents it is the other way around. Sadly, though, we knew that whichever way things were going down, and as euphoric as it was to make a bust of this magnitude and rarity, out there, somewhere on our reserve or in Klaserie, lay a faceless, dead rhino.

Finding the carcass was top priority: it held the vital clues and forensic evidence that would link the suspect to the crime; nothing else was as important at this stage. The next morning we had a helicopter up to try and locate the carcass. Colin came in from Klaserie and anxiously joined the search while I directed him and Bennie over the most likely hot spots in our region. Despite three hours of flying, and a ground sweep by field rangers of the area where we presumed they would most likely have targeted the rhino, no carcass was located. Despondently, we went home to strategise, deciding to move the search area further south the following day.

That evening, at around 10, I received a call from Eugene to say that the interrogation of the suspects resulted in them deciding to co-operate and reveal the whereabouts of the dead rhino. One of them said the rhino lay about five kilometres south-east of the river from where they had crossed. With this information, our field rangers went in on foot early the next morning and were able to locate the carcass of a white rhino bull. It lay where the first flight line with the helicopter would have started that morning, approximately 200 metres away from where we'd stopped flying the previous day!

I approached the scene with trepidation. It was my first poached rhino, a tragic sight, more grotesque and pitiful than pictures do justice to and one I won't go into detail describing. We have all seen enough. Colin and Bennie hovered overhead to get the GPS co-ordinates. Even back then, in my heart I hoped it would not be one of 'ours'. But the reality is that a rhino bull can cover more than 100 square kilometres just marking his territory, a territory that usually covers numerous man-made cutlines and reserve boundaries. So one day he may be ours, and tomorrow someone else's. But to an opportunistic poacher he is simply a lucrative target, wherever he happens to be.

The ground-to-air radio crackled, the lilt in Colin's voice was evidence of his lifted mood and relief. Later his body language showed a more relaxed man, this was not a Klaserie statistic to report on, and the realisation brought him a palpable sense of relief. At the time I wanted to cry, but in hindsight I can't say I blame him. No warden wants this statistic on his report card. Little did I know it at the time, but this was my first experience of the emotional strain being brought to bear on those wardens whose areas are hard hit by poaching. Sabi Sands' Andrew Parker, who happens to be one of the finest conservationists I know, was one of the hardest hit – and for no reason other than the rhino numbers being relatively high in his areas of responsibility. The poachers knew this and targeted these high-density zones specifically.

While we waited for the forensics team to examine the carcass in more detail, our field rangers secured the crime scene and immediate surrounds as they had recently been trained to do. This was to prevent any corruption of evidence and DNA. Once the scene was secure, I left one of my field rangers there while the rest of us backtracked the rhino's last movements to try and locate shell casings or some other clue that might help us narrow the event down to where, when and how. While on the spoor, we looked up to see dozens of vultures dropping out of the sky onto something about a kilometre away ... My legs went lame and the saliva in my mouth dried up as I realised there could be another rhino down that we had missed! As we hurriedly closed in on the scene, vultures took off in every direction, abandoning what they had dropped out of the sky for. In a trampled clearing lay the scant remains of what was yesterday a cheetah kill. I never thought I'd be so happy to see a pile of cleanly picked impala bones in my life.

A gentle drizzle the night before blurred the edges of what little clues we could find. Despite this, we were able to determine where the rhino had initially been observed and from where the first shot had been taken, then a little further on we located where the second and fatal shot had been fired. It was this second bullet, located using a metal detector, that had sealed the poacher's fate. Now marked as exhibit four, it would link the rifle to the crime and, we hoped, enable a conviction that would send the poacher and his accomplices away for many years.

Inexplicably, possibly due to the terrain and wind direction, no one had heard the poachers shoot the rhino. To add insult to injury, a light aircraft leaving the reserve that day had flown right over the poachers and the fallen rhino, its occupants blissfully unaware of the brutal slaughter happening a few hundred feet below their aircraft. These chilling facts were later gleaned from the suspect in custody, who revealed that they thought the aircraft was sent to look for them. It was also at that point, he told the interrogators, that the smaller of the two horns had been left behind in their haste to get away from being spotted from the air. However, we found this was not the case: when we located the carcass, both horns had been removed. I suspect that as the aircraft continued, getting further away, the brazen bastards continued to hack off the horn that they had only temporarily stopped removing.

Carrying both horns in backpacks, they then made their way back to the broken hilly terrain where they holed up about 500 metres downstream of the bridge. Evidence suggests they waited there until nightfall before crossing, and may also have taken the opportunity to move out of the reserve when they heard our team heading home, knowing that even if we'd left a couple of men behind it was dark enough for them to wade quietly across the river undetected.

Purely for interest's sake, the helicopter pilot, Bennie, measured the distance from the rhino carcass to the river, using the train bridge as a reference point: the GPS reading was 5.1 kilometres, and the poacher had told us it was five kilometres! This kind of accuracy is scary, and if not coincidence then it certainly raises the question of whether the poachers are using GPS to locate middens and popular wallows. And, if so, who is supplying them with the co-ordinates?

Five months later, almost to the day, I received a call from the investigating officer at the SAPS to inform me that the DNA sample collected from the carcass matched that of the horn found in the suspect's possession. Also, ballistic tests of the poacher's rifle proved that the bullet recovered from the slain rhino's shoulder was fired from their weapon. So, not even the likes of OJ Simpson's lawyer would've stood a hope in hell of getting these poachers off a 15-year sentence behind bars.

A couple of weeks later, we attended the sentencing hearing in Phalaborwa. And as hard as I tried to make eye contact with the poachers, they would not look at me or my field rangers when their sentence was handed down. Their heads remained bowed and their eyes fixed on their shoes even as they were led from the docks.

The investigating team are confident they will round up the whole gang, including the buyer/exporter. It appears that all involved are Mozambican nationals. However, extradition and cross-border negotiations will take time.

It is clear, and has been for the last 20 years, that the lack of management on state-owned land across the Olifants River from Balule Nature Reserve, particularly the farms Doreen and Rhoda, continues to pose the biggest poaching threat to our area by continuing to provide a safe haven and convenient access for poachers to launch their attacks from. Everyone knows this. It's all a question of 'small steps', so among the myriad of other approaches to consider, I believe the Associated Private Nature Reserves, in conjunction with SANParks, need to use their credible reputation to help control activities on this area north of Balule, as they do elsewhere. After all, the same big game that move in and out of the APNR and the Kruger National Park also wander over to Doreen and Rhoda. We are collectively vulnerable ... and responsible. A note of caution was sent to our neighbouring regions, as a warning to those who allow the 'Sandton Security Syndrome' to lull them into thinking that as long as your neighbour is less prepared, or is more vulnerable, he is more likely to be robbed than you are. As this recent incident has shown, nothing could be further from the truth. Determined rhino poachers have shown that if they want to get there, nowhere is too far for them to go, and they will negotiate seemingly difficult obstacles to get what they want. They will walk right over you, and crawl in right under your nose – or worse – to get to their quarry.

Tragic as it is, we try to take some comfort from the small victories; we console each other by saying that with the present rate of birth versus mortality, and if we could bust one poaching gang for each rhino killed, we could win the war. However, if we pushed this to two, the rhino population would be unsustainable; anything beyond that and the extinction of wild free-roaming rhino would be simply a question of time.

RHINO CONSERVATION AWARDS

Johannesburg was calling once again. This time it was not to attend a board meeting or visit family. Rather it was to attend a special function I'd been invited to at rather short notice and totally unexpectedly. Although the 'City of Gold' is where I was born and grew up, I return to its environs reluctantly and only when I absolutely have to. However, this auspicious occasion was an absolute 'have to'!

Meagan had flown down to Grahamstown for a few days to visit Dino. And as much as I would have loved her along with me to hold my hand, her basic instinct as a mother held sway; this time the pull of the herd was not as strong as the instinct to protect her young.

The horizon glowed pink as I climbed into the Land Cruiser and began the six-hour road trip to Johannesburg. Destination: Emperors Palace, of all places. No, not to gamble or watch a show, but to attend the Rhino Conservationist of the Year awards ceremony, hosted by the Game Rangers Association of Africa (GRAA), of which I am a professional member. As it happened, I was a nominee in one of the categories.

The submission for an award had been initiated by shareholders Neil and Morag Hulett and supported by the directors of Olifants River Game Reserve as well as the GRAA, and I had been nominated along with some of the continent's top wildlife conservationists in the category 'Best Awareness and Education'. I had no idea what to expect, or quite how extensive and prestigious this event would be, until I arrived and joined the other nominees, their relatives, friends and the guest speakers. Daunting as the occasion was, I have to admit the surrounding support and optimism left me with butterflies in my stomach while the names were read out in the various categories, especially during the announcement of the category in which I was nominated. And although I did not walk away with an award on the night, just having my name on that list and being included among the deserving nominees was indeed an honour in itself.

Needless to say, I was humbled by the occasion and will remain grateful for the acknowledgement by my peers, the association, and particularly the people of Olifants River Game Reserve, who continue to entrust me with what I consider to be no more than my duty in the struggle to conserve these magnificent animals.

It turned out to be a superbly organised awards ceremony. High-profile dignitaries, among the many attending, gave speeches that were passionate and heartfelt; in particular the ever-pragmatic General Jooste of SANParks, who spoke most eloquently, with hardly an 'er', and seemingly off the cuff. Deserved winners were applauded for their efforts in the various categories, followed by speeches made by influential, committed conservationists on the latest statistics of rhino poaching and what we can do to stem the tide. Also encouraging were the promises made by the relevant government representatives who spoke with due concern on the crisis. They appeared to have a grasp of the urgency and realised the need to expedite criminal proceedings against poachers and syndicates. It was clear they knew, as did those of us on the ground, how important the timeline was. There clearly was no time for diplomatic protocol to take precedence over this crisis, particularly between Mozambique and South Africa. Cross-border procedure needed to be expedited. It was also becoming a humanitarian issue for families of poachers; people, as well as rhino, were needlessly dying as we waited for the next course and as we sipped our wine. And all of us there knew that the time for talking was over: time was running out.

In the meantime, a world away, reality prevails. Fighting the good fight, field rangers are getting their boots on the ground, weapons in hands – and sweating, there's always lots of sweating – often for little or no reward. Then, for some, there's the aftermath and inevitable reality that awaits them after an incident. The stench of rotting flesh that fills their nostrils during the all-too-crucial autopsies carried out on poached rhino carcasses, a crucial prerequisite for successful convictions.

If ever there were two worlds in one country, ours has to be the epitome of that cliché. While a mood of constructive optimism prevailed among those present at the banquet, and as we sat listening, in a plush hall, on comfortable chairs, at tables decked in crisp white linen and silverware, the barbaric antithesis of this scenario was unfolding less than 500 kilometres away. Killers, gathered in a seedy tavern, were planning their next incursion to kill more rhino. Driven by greed and huge financial reward, a gang of men, among many others in the Lowveld, under the same moon, were focused on the brutal destruction of our rhino. These rhino poachers were planning to worm their way deep into the heart of our reserves. Having just done their technical preparation, they would swing past the sangoma for some added spiritual protection. With the drop-off and pick-up points arranged, they would move towards Olifants.

With their running shoes tucked away in backpacks, the three barefoot poachers waded through the murky Olifants River and across the muddy floodplain, into our region. While this was happening, more than 20 other groups moved into the Kruger National Park, many of them from Massingir in Mozambique, some crossing paths with others on their way out, their backpacks stiff with bloody horns. Closer to home, other gangs made use of the convenience of well-built roads and were driven by Audi, BMW and Volvo to drop-off points close to Sabi Sands, Manyeleti and Klaserie, to mention but a few remaining bastions of these precious animals, all targeted almost simultaneously.

The next day, I awoke in a strange bed to a birdsong-less quiet … reality prevailed. I didn't stay for breakfast; instead, I focused on leaving before the traffic built up, hoping to make the Alzu One Stop in time for a double espresso with hot milk as the sun came up. I drove past the depressing coal mine dumps and belching power stations with more than an inflection of optimism this time. I couldn't help but feel encouraged by all the goodwill and passion that had rubbed off from the previous evening; it was a refreshing change from the sea of cloudy pessimism my boat sails in most of the time of late. As usual I was keen to get back to the bush, though these days I realise it's not for the same reasons I used to want to get back home.

At 12.07 pm I received a call from Protrack's field rangers, who camp out permanently at strategic pickets in the bush, reporting that they'd heard a gunshot west of one of our water holes. I'd been home a couple of hours and, having just changed into my khakis, was settling down to enjoy a cold beer that never happened. Having quickly confirmed that nobody was hunting or shooting for rations in the area, I knew there could only be one explanation.

Protrack's tracking unit and field rangers immediately began making their way to where the shot was heard. Within 10 minutes the team was on the scene of the shooting, which happened to be a popular rhino midden, located near a natural mud wallow. From the spoor they were able to ascertain that there were two poachers involved and both were now following the blood-spattered spoor of a rhino bull. Although the rhino had been wounded, it was moving quickly, so fast that the poachers were actually jogging in its tracks. Once I was given the direction the rhino was running, heading for the four power lines, I drove up to the area as fast as possible to try and intercept the poachers. At this point, they were so intent on following their quarry they were unaware that they, in turn, were being followed by our field rangers. In the meantime I'd called in for helicopter support, and while I positioned myself covering the high ground with good visibility for a kilometre in either direction, our field rangers covered the section over the next rise. If the poachers broke cover, one of us would see them.

However, given the unavoidable time lapse, minimal though it was, spoor indicated that the rhino had already crossed under the power lines, heading south-west, minutes before we were able to get there – and fortunately way ahead of the poachers, as it turned out. Despite being chased at a run, the bull had managed to put some distance between himself and his pursuers. The poachers must have heard my vehicle approaching, at which point they abandoned the hunt and began heading north, back to the Olifants River. We were only able to determine this fact later when we backtracked their spoor. In the meantime, unknowingly, we assumed that if we backtracked the rhino's tracks, which were easier to follow at speed, we would possibly make contact with the poachers as they tried to finish it off.

We split into two groups: one would pursue the poachers, while the rest of us would focus on finding the rhino, but not until we'd had a quick look-see with the helicopter. Bennie did what only this master pilot could have done in an effort to flush the poachers – but to no avail. He turned the little Robinson and headed south to look for the wounded rhino. Ten minutes later the ground-to-air radio crackled with Bennie's voice.

'Mario, we have located the rhino.'

My heart sank into my knees. But before I could envision another carcass, Bennie qualified the statement.

'He is near the old rhino pens and, although still moving quickly, he appears to be limping badly.'

My focus shifted instantly. Although I had no idea how badly the rhino had been wounded, I guessed that if it had made so much ground, and at such pace, there could be some hope. I was now intent on saving the animal, if possible. So, while our field rangers and the Protrack team carried on tracking the poachers, my next call was to Dr Peter Rogers, who immediately put down his knife and fork, swallowed his last mouthful of Sunday lunch and came to our assistance. Half an hour later Bennie picked Pete up at the Hoedspruit airstrip and flew him back to us. In the meantime we had obtained one of the GPS radio tracking collars originally destined to be fitted to one of our black rhino. This was an emergency; the details could be sorted later ... we'd simply order another collar. Thinking ahead, I surmised that if by some miracle we were able to treat this rhino, and possibly save his life, he would need to be monitored closely for movement data, signs of improvement and possible follow-up treatments.

The white rhino bull was located within minutes, darted, and identified from his ear notch. He had run nearly five kilometres with a poacher's bullet through his leg ... incredible! Although the bullet had passed clean through the upper part of the front leg, missing the bone, it was a large calibre, possibly a .458 Magnum, the velocity of which caused extensive swelling of the wound channel. Pete did the best he could to sterilise the wound and prepare the animal for the lengthy healing process that would hopefully follow and culminate in recovery. Long-acting painkillers, antibiotics and anti-inflammatories were administered, which had obviously kicked in by the time the rhino stood up, effectively masking the extent of the injury and allowing him to walk away with only a slight limp.

In the meantime, as the sun began to sink low on the horizon, we knew the poachers were getting ready to try and escape under the cover of darkness. Stopper groups, co-ordinated and set up by Protrack's reaction unit and Balule wardens, did their best to anticipate their exit point – not an easy task with approximately 10 kilometres of roadside bush to cover – at best a calculated gamble. Soon all units were in position in the north, covering their chosen exit points on the R40. Here they would lie in ambush all night. Other field ranger units, including our own team, covered key points on the southern bank of the Olifants River and the bridge.

The poachers, now on the run, must have anticipated we would be waiting for them on the most likely entry/exit routes. No doubt they also knew it would be an almost impossible task to cover a 10-kilometre river front at night, so they simply crossed well upstream from their usual crossing point for the first time, knowing it was a relatively quiet section of the reserve. At first light the following morning, our trackers found where the poachers had waded through the waist-high murky river, regardless of the hippo and huge crocodiles in that section, again a clear indication of the level of their desperation to evade us. The site they chose to cross was also known as the 'Picnic Site' on Grietjie. It was where a schoolboy, celebrating passing his matric exams, had been taken by a crocodile in front of his classmates and never seen again … However, we can be absolutely certain that if these poachers don't suffer some similar misfortune, natural or otherwise, they will be back!

We made every effort to keep a close eye on the injured rhino for the next few days, but despite rhino monitor Sinhle's best efforts, the telemetry let them down; so it was back to basics. Our field rangers would have to do without expert tracker January that morning, as he was called in to track down the rhino. Although the spoor indicated that he had moved a lot, it was apparent the medication had worn off. January was able to interpret from the spoor that the rhino was favouring his injured leg. But miracles aside, we had expected this prognosis. So, without pushing him, we were able to confirm that he was eating and drinking well, evident by his healthy dung piles. I made contact with Pete and scheduled a follow-up treatment in a week or so.

Two years later, having made a full recovery, Sable Bull, as he is now known, was repeatedly attacked by a dominant bull coming into the area. The wounds inflicted were severe, and had we not intervened Sable Bull would have been killed. A natural progression, one may argue, but strictly speaking a poacher's bullet had given him the slight, almost imperceptible limp that was enough to warrant him being challenged and subsequently beaten. However, before the inevitable could happen, he was recaptured in August 2015 and translocated across the river to the Olifants North region. Two days later, the rhino crossed back onto the south side, where he chose to stay in an area not normally frequented by white rhino but which afforded him the respite he needed to recuperate and gain his strength. As I write, he is on the south bank of the river near my house and has apparently recovered completely.

We hope that Sable Bull will stay where he is for now. Though not in ideal white rhino habitat, at least he is relatively safe and not completely alone. He has been photographed in the company of black rhino at one of the well-used watering points. One of these rather rare photos shows a seemingly affectionate Ebony and Ivory nose-to-nose 'greeting' between the two species. With luck, he will heal to the point where he is once again in 'competition condition' and able at least to hold his own against other white rhino bulls. Only time will tell.

THE 'KERATIN KLONDIKE'

It had been well over a year since the poacher was killed and his two allies had spent their months in prison. During the time that followed we assumed that word of their ordeal at the hands of our field rangers was being spread far and wide. We all lived in the hope that such a drastic and decisive response would have sent a clear message to even the most determined poachers. Unfortunately, however, even if it had reached those planning the destruction of our rhino, the spiralling demand and huge rewards obtained for their horns still makes some think the associated risks are worthwhile.

We couldn't say we'd not had an inkling of what was in store for us. The latest spate of incursions by rhino poachers into the reserve demonstrated a level of determination and persistence the likes of which we'd not experienced before. However, this did not demoralise our anti-poaching rangers; if anything, they began to treat each invasion with progressively more contempt and resolve than the one before. More importantly, with each incident they learned that little bit more about the 'enemy' and their tactics.

Initially it seemed that incursions peaked during the full-moon phase. As is true of most guerrilla tactics, rhino poachers have responded by exhibiting increasingly erratic patterns and becoming less predictable. Needless to say, our security is placed on full alert in times of high incursion probability or when acting on information and intelligence gathered. For the duration of these anticipated forays, we sleep fully clothed, removing only our boots, ready to respond with a minimum of delay.

The summons to duty is a fairly muted call, nothing dramatic or repugnantly appropriate. Yet the response is the same as if a bomb has gone off. On my phone it's an innocuous tweet that announces the grainy images of poachers, caught on hidden cameras at some ungodly hour, as they move into the killing zone. I haven't asked my colleague what his is; there hasn't been much time for small talk ... Except of course when Valentino Rossi won the Dutch MotoGP at Aspen.

Driving to the staff village, we then mobilise our field rangers. Once awake, the men quietly and quickly get their things together. No urging is necessary; what follows is a methodical, practised routine, an organised rush. Some of these men have been with me for over 23 years. They know from experience that these operations can last anything from six to twelve hours, sometimes longer, and there's no coming back for anything left behind.

To a man they approach each mission as though they have a huge axe to grind. Although accustomed to the fact that death is a part of life in the bush, they are angered by the brutality of rhino poachers. Finding the hornless, bloated carcasses of three rhino in March 2012 visibly upset them; it also hurt their pride. These men feel, albeit needlessly, that they were made to look like failures at their job, and they are desperate for the slightest opportunity to set the record straight. After a quick discussion on strategy and deployment tactics, we drive out together, later splitting into two or three mobile groups. Once deployed, communication between us becomes everything.

After losing those three rhino, we upped the ante. Routine perimeter patrols now focus on likely target areas, and strategic observation and listening posts are manned 24 hours a day. To this end, we have two rangers camping in the bush in thorn shelters at random locations, from where they radiate, conducting wagon-wheel-like daily foot patrols. At first light each day, units from the posts based on the boundary comb the most vulnerable known entry points, checking for any signs of incursion. Although we have a good idea of *where* they will hit again, it's the *when* that remains the challenge.

Technology is playing a huge role in providing us with vital early warnings of incursions, particularly camera traps, which despite their limitations have proved to be invaluable tools. More expensive, but equally important, is the monitoring of the rhino themselves. Besides proactive measures taken in the form of the controversial horn 'poisoning' and dye treatments of many rhino in our region, five adult white rhino were also fitted with GPS satellite foot collars, which have allowed us to monitor their movements on a daily basis. In addition to this, the system is also equipped with a 'geo-fencing' alert programme, which sends an MMS to our cell phones immediately when a rhino strays into a 'hot' area. This is another tool in our box, and although not quite the silver bullet yet, these strategies make a quicker reactive response possible.

Imagination, battery life and cost are the only limitations in electronics. However, even with the most innovative technology available, there comes a point when some devices can become too technical and cumbersome to be practically applied in the bush. Or, indeed, fitted to the rhino themselves. I'm not advocating that we simply fight fire with fire, rather that we employ appropriate technology that is effective. Simplicity and reliability are key, particularly expert trackers and sure communications. Having said this, however, it was the monitoring of the satellite-collared rhino that alerted us to the presence of poachers when data downloaded from one of the collared rhino indicated there'd been no movement for nearly 12 hours. I was able to use Google Maps to calculate the rough location of the static signal. As it was a clear, warm morning and there were no vultures or other signs to make me think the worst, I was beginning to hope that this would turn out to be a technical problem. So we systematically checked every rhino midden and mud wallow in the area, in case the rhino had thrown its collar. When no collar could be located, we decided to follow any large rhino tracks found in the vicinity, hoping to make visual contact. Careful tracking revealed the fresh tracks of a rhino bull, indicating it had moved in the last few hours. Later, much to everyone's relief, it began registering 'normal' movement beamed down via satellite. But we did not call off the team yet, as the tracking effort by our rangers to locate the rhino had provided us with other crucial information we would otherwise have missed.

During the intense search for the rhino, we found other fresh tracks: the unmistakable anti-tracking spoor of poachers! Somehow they'd managed to sneak across the river without triggering a camera, and their entry went undetected by our patrols as they'd used rocky terrain to access the area. But now having to move through the relatively sandy terrain favoured by white rhino, their spoor was more difficult to conceal. Nevertheless, it was disconcerting to realise that we probably would never have found the footprints in the middle of the bush had we not also been searching for that particular rhino.

In the war against poachers it has become clear that nothing works effectively if used in isolation. It usually starts with early detection and fresh information. Then, from the moment a camera trap captures an image and communicates it to our cell phones, to calling in the anti-poaching rangers so that an appropriate response can be planned and executed, the digital radios become indispensable. Ground-to-air radios are also used to good effect when disruptive operations are underway, using a helicopter in conjunction with ground teams and trackers. Cell phones are an excellent backup as a silent tool. Radios are noisy and not for clandestine use. Many a time a poacher has been put to flight by untimely chit chat on the radio. Incidentally, we have found that poachers do not operate where they have no cell phone signal.

The following is an example of the judicious employment of a combination of surveillance technology, expert tracking and reliable communications, which was used to good effect one morning. Knowing the poachers had triggered a particular camera, our focus was immediately sharpened on the location. The intense tracking that ensued revealed the faint scuff marks of an All Star running shoe. Although merely a scuff or two among thousands of other natural marks made by the myriad of creatures in the bush, these were in the wrong place, and the attempt to conceal them was evident. Only one animal on earth does that.

No technical instrument known to man can emulate the analytical mind of a master tracker, just as there is still nothing to beat a dog's nose in scent trailing a rhino poacher. Communicating the information about the tracks, specifically direction and age of spoor, via cell phone to the rangers deep in the bush enabled them to use the timeline to calculate where the poachers were likely to be. In so doing, they were able to head them off and actually make visual contact. A minute later and the poachers would have passed by unnoticed. Unfortunately, in attempting to circle them and confront them head on, they were lost to the thick bush. (If this was a conventional war, the enemy would have been shot and killed at that point ... game over. But if you shoot a poacher in the back, you will be charged with murder.)

Bennie was called in and air support was with us in less than half an hour. A determined chase ensued, but tracking was hampered by the extremely rugged terrain. Despite Bennie's expert low flying and the experienced spotters on board, the poachers went to ground and escaped detection. However, the disruption of their poaching foray was complete; there'd be no rhino dying that day. Curling themselves up into tight balls, the poachers hid in the thickest bush. Then, as the heat died down, they moved a bit further. Later, under the cover of darkness, they waded back across the river and escaped.

Anticipating that we'd be waiting for them at the most likely spots, and not wanting to run the gauntlet through the battery of .303, .223 and 12-bore weaponry that makes up our field rangers' arsenal, they chose instead to wade through the relative safety of a chest-deep section of the Olifants River. It leaves one with a modicum of comfort to know they fear you and your field rangers more than the huge crocodiles they knew they had to wade past that night.

We'd hoped that by now they'd got the message that we were determined to go to extraordinary lengths to protect our rhino. Naturally we assumed it would be some time before they targeted our area again. Nonetheless, we diligently continued our routine daily patrols along the river and target zone, effectively narrowing the area of focus. As it happened, our assumption was wrong: the respite was shockingly brief.

A week later, what we assume was the same gang entered the reserve again!

Unbeknown to us, this time the poachers had spent one and a half days unsuccessfully trying to kill a rhino. I suspect that a combination of intensive patrolling in the area and a miserable cold front that blew in on that weekend (making rhino less dependent on wallows and water for cooling and therefore more unpredictable and difficult to locate), must have had a hampering effect on this incursion. Also, something we inadvertently did must have spooked them, causing them to leave in a hurry and cross the bridge in broad daylight. This was highly unusual, but in so doing they unknowingly triggered a perfectly positioned camera trap, resulting in one of the clearest images of these elusive, arrogant killers ever captured.

Intelligence gleaned from this single image proved to be invaluable. The rifle barrel sticking out of the bottom of the lead man's jacket was clearly that of a large-calibre weapon. And the steel-handled axe in the second man's hand needed no elucidation as to its intended purpose. These images provided excellent surveillance in terms of how much they were able to tell us about the suspects. However, for a change I looked beyond the images, beyond the chilling arrogance and the weaponry. What I was able to take from these images, besides the obvious, was more important to me as a manager of a team of field rangers on the front line, the custodians of our precious rhino. I discovered that a long-held suspicion of having a mole within our staff ranks was completely unfounded. It was evident from all the images I studied that the poachers had no idea there were cameras at the bridge. Had there been collusion, they most certainly would have known to avoid them.

Once again, a little before midnight on 20 June 2013, an MMS to our cell phones showed the same three poachers coming in! This time we were alerted within minutes of them triggering the cameras, and they still had no idea we had been warned, so we planned to track them and make an arrest. Unfortunately, our clandestine plan was compromised by the unauthorised movement of a vehicle in the vicinity. A classic example of 'too many chiefs' and another important lesson learned, something I promised myself wouldn't happen again … And so we continue to improve.

However, the poachers now knew we were onto them, which meant they would simply move more stealthily and employ anti-tracking tactics to evade us. The arduous task of tracking them would now be made extremely difficult. Essentially we now had to go to plan B to keep them from killing any rhino: to chase them out of the area, even if it meant they would get away once again. So, reluctantly, we had to bring the chopper in earlier than we wanted to and put the poachers to flight once more. Poachers are reluctant to shoot knowing you know they are in the area. We banked on this fact often.

Given the resistance the poachers met with each time, one might have believed they would be scared off or simply try somewhere else. Not so: less than 12 hours after being chased out, they returned! This time one of the camera traps set up near the main R40 road was spotted by them and hacked to pieces when they entered. Thinking this was the only camera, they confidently continued, unknowingly triggering another camera further down the fence line. This time we decided to track them relentlessly, to hunt them down until we confronted them, when hopefully one of the poachers would attempt to use his weapon on our rangers, at which point appropriate action could ensue. We all began to feel that nothing short of this level of response, each time they tried, would bring an end to their relentless onslaught.

Moving confidently into our area, which had previously been avoided owing to relatively high vehicle movement by our shareholders in game viewers, the poachers had now crossed the line, literally and figuratively, a clear sign they were ruthlessly more determined than usual. We knew it was only a question of an hour or so, and a rhino would be killed. At this point the only edge we had was that the poachers still had no idea we were quite so close behind them; yet despite this and some expert tracking by our rangers they remained elusive. Ever cautious, they employed anti-tracking methods at every opportunity and, in so doing, could move much quicker, too fast for even our best trackers to keep up with them. As it was, our trackers had been on their tracks for nearly eight hours; they were thirsty and exhausted, and concentration was beginning to wane. I couldn't risk it any longer ... I called for Bennie and his little yellow helicopter once again.

Soon the throb of its rotors could be heard approaching in the distance. I couldn't help thinking what a comforting sound this machine made in a crisis. Landing with just enough time for us to scramble aboard and connect our headsets, ace pilot Bennie flew like a man possessed. Not surprisingly, he seemed to be taking this incident personally ... and besides having lost rhino on his own game farm to poachers, this would be the third time he'd be hunting these same poachers on our area in the last two weeks!

My son, Dino, had brought some sandwiches and coffee for us. Colin Rowles and I hadn't eaten for hours. There being a spare seat in the helicopter, and us needing every pair of eyes we could muster, I asked Dino to join us. He was 19 years of age at the time, and this would be his first time in a helicopter ... Talk about a baptism of fire!

We soon spotted three white rhino, which were likely being targeted by the poachers, lying in a sandy drainage line about 300 metres ahead of the trackers and ground crew, totally unaware of the danger only minutes away. The poachers had to be between the two, we thought. As the helicopter came in closer, the three white rhino stood up, and Bennie used the rotor wash to gently move them out of harm's way. Apparently not a moment too soon as we were later told by the tracking team that tracks indicated the poachers had been sitting upwind of the unsuspecting rhino, waiting for the right time to shoot.

Leaving the rhino running safely out of harm's way, Bennie climbed away, turning tightly, and headed back to the spot where the poachers were now likely to be hiding. In gravity-defying curves and dives, that tested every pop rivet's integrity in that R44's frame, the little machine became a hunting tool in his hands. Like an African hawk-eagle trying to flush a covey of spurfowl, throwing all caution to the wind and literally swooping in on the most likely thickets trying to flush them, Bennie dropped the helicopter down to the treetops; he rotor-washed every tangle of brush that could possibly conceal a poacher ... nothing.

We blew out everything from scrub hares to warthogs; everything, it seemed, broke cover, except for the men we were after. There was no time to take in the exhilarating flying; my focus was under each bush and inside each aardvark burrow. My index finger never moved from the microphone button; I was desperate to be the first to shout, 'Got the fuckers!' We tried for nearly two hours without success. When low fuel and fading light compelled us to land, my finger, although numb from the cold, was still poised over the microphone button. Dino hadn't had any time to get sick; in fact, he loved every second of Bennie's exhilarating flying skill.

Without shutting off, Bennie said farewell as we climbed out of the helicopter. Standing there in the dust we watched him lift up, then nose his machine down and head for home. Fading quickly, they became a speck against the orange backdrop of the western skyline, and though I could no longer hear the throb of the helicopter, Bennie's parting words still rang loudly in my ears …

'Mario, if we'd had a good dog working with the ground tracking team today, we would have had those bastards today!'

In contrast to the ugliness of what could have described that day, a beautiful winter sun began to edge behind the mountains, taking with it what precious tracking light remained, and as dusk abruptly enveloped the mid-June bushveld, a chilly darkness set in. Reluctantly, the ground team were compelled to call it a day, and although disappointed it hadn't ended as we so dearly would have liked, at least we were comforted by the fact that no rhino had died on the day. We also knew the poachers were cowering in some thorn thicket with their noses in the dirt, wondering how we always knew where they entered and how quickly we were onto them.

Knowing we would be after them again at first light, if they persisted, the poachers decided to get out of the area shortly after dark. Our rangers were expecting them to do this and set up an all-night ambush, covering both sides of the bridge using night-vision equipment. Nobody would be able to cross undetected. Another ambush awaited them further inland and yet another on the main road. Frustratingly, the poachers out-manoeuvred us: they took a route never used by them before and escaped once again!

Our camera traps often reveal three men entering north of the river, but usually only two sets of tracks are found hunting rhino in the reserve. On a couple of occasions, when the camera trap has captured the images of the poachers leaving our area, the images have shown only two men, but images taken by cameras set up closer to the main road have revealed three men. So where does the third man go? I suspect he sits on one of the many hills across the river/bridge area, watching us when we deploy, and keeps his cohorts informed of ambush points to avoid. This is much like baboons do with a *brandwag*, or lookout, posted while the troop forages or raids crops. Typically, one of the troop will sit in a vantage position – usually at the top of a tall tree or outcrop, commanding a 360-degree view of the foraging troop below – and will bark when warning of danger, a primitive but effective early warning system. Unfortunately, evolution has bequeathed the poacher's lookout a cell phone ... It's simply too much of a coincidence that they know when to use the bridge and when not to, and where we plan to deploy ambush teams.

Unfortunately, we're in a war: clearly a one-sided war where the enemy enjoys the protection of the law and exploits it to full advantage. Until this changes, the odds are stacked in the poacher's favour. Despite this and six separate incursions, our counter-determination to protect the rhino has been more resolute, and so far our disruptive tactics have prevented them from killing our rhino with impunity. However, it seems that with each incursion that we thwart they appear to get more desperate, and desperate, greedy people make mistakes. Although our rangers will be waiting for that, it's only a question of time before poachers change tactics again. If the preceding accounts have left you feeling a sense of frustration and helplessness, then you are welcome to join the club!

As it was in Alaska's Klondike, when the hunt for gold brought out the worst in men ... now that keratin is more valuable than gold, how far will we allow this hunt to go?

BENNIE IN THE MIST

I pulled the ringing cell phone from my shirt pocket, scowling at the words 'Private number' glaring arrogantly back at me and reflexively scrolling for the 'reject call' option. In my experience, 'blocked' or 'private' numbers invariably belong to insurance sales people, or loan sharks looking for defaulters. But this time something made me tap the screen and answer the call. 'Hello?'

'Good morning, is this Mr Mario Cesare?'

'Yes it is,' I replied.

'Sir, you are speaking to Captain Maseki of SAPS Polokwane.'

'Good morning Captain, how can I help you?' I enquired, somewhat curious, as we'd had no direct dealings with Polokwane SAPS so far – none that I was aware of anyway.

'Those two poachers apprehended in October 2012, the same day they killed a rhino on your reserve, have been sentenced to 15 years' imprisonment respectively. So, as the case is now closed, the confiscated rhino horn belongs to you; it is awaiting your collection at our office,' came the reply.

I vividly recalled the moment when the sentence was handed down and the accused had refused to make eye contact with me. This call from Captain Maseki was finality, a job well done. Case closed. My faith in the authorities had been restored.

'Thank you, Captain, I was actually at the sentencing hearing in Phalaborwa,' I said. 'I will make the necessary arrangements for collection of the horn and contact you as soon as possible. Please give me a cell number where I can reach you, not an office number, please,' I added.

Practically, it all sounded simple enough: I would just drive through to Polokwane, pick up the horn and drive home. I'd done the trip a couple of times before, and it was always a rather pleasant drive, enduring a few hours at most. I loved the changing landscape of the drive.

Initially the road takes you through some ruggedly beautiful bushveld, studded with awe-inspiring granite outcrops which rise like mini volcanoes out of a sea of mopane woodland. It is here, in these hills, that some of the biggest leopards in South Africa are to be found. No doubt the multitudes of cattle farmed in the area prior to the rare game species breeding ranches that have since taken over contributed in no small measure to this phenomenon. Then quite abruptly, as if crossing an invisible border, the landscape changes and the scenery is dominated by huge citrus farms and opulent tropical fruit orchards, which stay with you all the way to the subtropical town of Tzaneen. Leaving the warmer Lowveld behind, the scenic route gradually wends its way up through the mist belt to Magoebaskloof, where its twists and turns compel you to slow down – a good thing if you want to enjoy the montane forest and not miss the tiny, mystical hamlet of Haenertsburg.

Only an hour away from big game country, you will find yourself cruising through rolling hillsides with hedge-like tea plantations; essentially this is the start of the Drakensberg range, which from there traverses the entire eastern half of our country. Once through and over its peaks, having crossed a few icy-cold, gin-clear streams, which still hold rainbow trout, you carefully wind your way down to the contrasting flatlands, where warmer country greets you once again. Here, overgrazed thorn scrub and scrawny cattle will accompany you to the outskirts of the sprawling city of Polokwane.

But I knew this trip was not going to be a sightseeing tour. We'd stop only when absolutely necessary, only when hunger threatened our concentration, and this would then be remedied with a quick lunch at the Coach House, near Tzaneen … Maybe. But the nagging security threat that transporting such a dangerous cargo posed kept hammering away at my thoughts. Whichever way we looked at it, the risks were high; there was simply too much at stake to be complacent about the detail. So, somewhat reluctantly, the scenic road trip, with its prospect of lunch at a nice restaurant, was abandoned and replaced instead with what proved to be an experience unlikely ever to be repeated … not by me anyway.

I'd allowed for a couple of weeks to apply for the necessary permits to possess and convey the horn from the Department of Environmental Affairs and Tourism (DEAT) in Polokwane, before making firm collection arrangements. A month went slowly by and no permits materialised, so I reapplied. When three months had elapsed and still nothing had happened, I informed our committee of the situation. We were afraid that the longer the horn was in the custody of SAPS, the greater the chance it had of getting 'lost'. Thanks to legal eagle Louise Cleary, a letter demanding 'permits or else' was hand-delivered to our local branch of the Limpopo Department of Economic Development Environment and Tourism (LEDET) in Klaserie. Needless to say, all the necessary documentation was in my hand in less than three days! Apparently the official drove to Polokwane himself, collected the permits and microchipped the horn at the same time.

The moment the permits were in my possession, I contacted Bennie to arrange a date and time to fly us to Polokwane and collect the horn. Being the height of game capture season, helicopters were scarce and Bennie was fully committed. However, he understood the urgency and managed to squeeze us in for the following Monday morning, the 28th.

Two days and six phone calls later, I finally managed to make contact with Captain Maseki to confirm the venue and collection date. After listening patiently, he told me that a certain Captain Pitjeng was the person I now needed to contact for the horn, which I duly did. Getting down to the detail, Captain Pitjeng then informed me that the horn was not lodged with the SAPS but at some nondescript office building on Thabo Mbeki Street, opposite McDonald's. He also wanted to know what time I'd be arriving and how I was going to convey the horn. Not wanting to be too specific, I told him sometime between 8.30

and 10.30 am but managed to avoid disclosing how we were planning to get there, transport the horn and the route we'd be taking to and from the pick-up point.

Besides chartering the flight, support and backup plans on the ground needed to be put in place. Two well-armed and trusted security officials from Phalaborwa, who will be known only as Eugene and Nella, were contracted to drive ahead of us very early on that Monday morning. Once there, they'd scope the offices out before we arrived; if all legit and cleared, they would then pick us up at the airport and escort us through to collect the horn. Although this may sound like cloak-and-dagger stuff, planning on this level called for belts and braces, so I had yet another contingency plan in place. We'd also reserved a hire car from the airport, so that if for some reason our security detail was held up, or couldn't make it on time, we'd at least have transport. What could possibly go wrong?

Sunday night found me glued to The Weather Channel. The forecast predicted heavy mist and light rain for the route through the mountains and on to Polokwane. It wasn't looking good for the following day's flight. However, when I spoke to Bennie he said not to worry, he knew the route through the mountains and these conditions often cleared quite quickly; nevertheless, he'd assess the situation again in the morning. So, for all intents and purposes, the flight was still on.

Monday morning dawned grey and ominous. My assistant, Glenn du Toit, and I were already waiting on the cement slab-cum-helipad behind our offices. And although Glenn's usual banter helped make light of the situation, it was somewhat veiled, as he too had watched the weather forecast. Bennie was someone who was never late and, sure enough, at 6.45 am, as arranged, his yellow R44 swooped in, and without much ado the three of us were in the air. Destination: Polokwane.

Conditions appeared promising as we flew north-west over some familiar bushveld. However, approaching the high country around Magoebaskloof we could see that the mountain plantations ahead were shrouded in thick mist. Here and there, the valley bottoms were only just visible, and I was thankful we were in a helicopter, but more than that I was confident we were being piloted by one of the best in the business. However, sensing a smidgen of trepidation, Bennie said he knew of a valley or two that were sometimes negotiable even in these conditions, but that if the mist closed in on us we'd simply land and have a cup of coffee with a local forester until it lifted. Apparently he'd done this before when flying the CEO of Lego through to Tzaneen one day. Although this revelation provided some measure of comfort, we took more from Bennie's ability and attitude, at the time.

As predicted, the valleys he negotiated the helicopter through were clear enough, and soon we'd wound our way through the forest-covered mountains and were descending into the low country. But as we did so it was apparent that we were not out of the woods yet, so to speak: the flat lands were covered in a cotton-wool blanket of mist, which spread in front of us all the way to Polokwane. Then, to add a squirt of adrenaline to that which was already coursing through our veins, we had no radio communications. Despite trying every frequency Bennie knew, there was no response from the air traffic control, neither civil nor private. (It was probably a self-declared day off for ATC due to fog.) We were completely on our own: a little yellow helicopter in a sea of grey.

Undeterred, Bennie continued flying. He was obviously familiar with the area around the Polokwane airstrip and confidently brought the chopper down lower. We came in slowly, cautiously flying only a couple of metres off the ground on the one edge of the runway. The sound of the rotors, *whuppa-whuppa-whuppa*, cutting through the grey shroud that separated us from the short grass below the bubble was all I could focus on for a while. Then the rotor pitch changed as the helicopter slowed down ... We were going to land. The terminal building was only just visible through the mist as we touched down, and except for the two ghostlike figures of security officers Nella and Eugene, it was deserted. Looking back as we drove away, we could just make out the lanky figure of Bennie standing alone next to his helicopter. He was on his cell phone, probably letting his worried family know all was fine.

Driving out towards the city, I turned to Nella and asked if we should phone Captain Pitjeng to tell him we were on our way.

'No, wait until we are only five minutes away, then we will call him,' he said.

This I duly did, about 15 minutes later, on Nella's cue.

'Good morning, Captain Pitjeng. This is Mario from Olifants River Game Reserve; we will be at your office in five minutes to pick up our rhino horn.'

The response was an unexpected moment's deathly silence on the other end of the line, followed by an all too familiar utterance ... '*Eish!*'

Captain Pitjeng had decided to go to Johannesburg that weekend. Not just that, but he would only be back on Tuesday and was the only person with the key to the safe that contained the rhino horn! Fortunately, Nella knew the head honcho at the depot and we were soon in his office, where I explained that this predicament was due entirely to Captain Pitjeng's negligence. And given the effort we had made, and the costs incurred, I explained that repeating this was not an option. Against all legal protocol I demanded the horn be released to Nella and Eugene the following day, irrespective of whose name the permits were in. This was duly agreed to in writing, and the horn was unceremoniously brought home along the scenic route.

This horn, along with the eight others Meagan and I had temporarily stored in a fireproof vault on the reserve, now resides in a vault in Johannesburg, aptly named 'Fort Knox'. Formerly part of the American Embassy, this depot has probably got the highest security rating in the country. Prior to this arrangement, only Meagan, I and one of the directors of the reserve had the keys to the safe on the reserve and were privy to the location of those horns. Needless to say, this was a huge responsibility which we are all now free of.

Ahead of the 2016 Convention on the International Trade in Endangered Species of Wild Fauna and Flora (CITES), where a decision would be made on whether or not to legalise the trade in rhino horn, the South African Government realised there would be a huge source of tax revenue in this product if pro-trade was opted for. And although the decision eventually made would go against the trade, as a result Parliament issued an instruction to the DEAT that all horns in private hands, across the country, needed to be audited with immediate effect. Besides the fiscal control, the intention was to compel all owners of horn to conform to a measure of legitimate ownership and compliance. Unfortunately, this move also exposed the whereabouts and numbers of even the most judiciously concealed and vulnerable stockpiles of rhino horn.

As a result, numerous horns have been stolen from private reserves and farmers' homes since. In the single biggest heist in our country's history, close to 50 rhino horns, valued at nearly R380 million (Asian end), were stolen from the DEAT's regional offices in Nelspruit shortly after this audit. And this was accomplished without a clue being left to follow or a single shot fired! Being so close to Mozambique, I can guarantee that neither those horns nor the culprits will ever be found.

For the rest, wardens, rangers and farm managers were left vulnerable as their stockpiles were exposed for auditing. Even their staff now knew how many horns were on the premises and where they were located. A dangerous situation indeed, as it would be opportunistic thieves, the bottom feeders of the criminal world, who would pose the greatest threat. If these wanton killers were to hear a rumour bandied about the beer halls and shebeens, word would spread faster than a Nike sale, and the unfortunate caretakers of rhino horns would be in imminent danger. The anxiety we voiced at the outset may have been perceived by local authorities as the overreaction of owners and wardens, but the ramifications were manifest in the following horrific incident.

One night, about a week after this supposedly clandestine audit, the warden of Sabi Sands and his wife were attacked in their home on the reserve. The attackers were specific: they demanded only rhino horns, which many criminals assume all wardens keep in their safes along with their weapons and personal valuables. As it happened, there was not a single horn on the premises. Frustrated and angry, the murderous bastards stabbed the man's wife repeatedly and cut the warden's throat, leaving them for dead. Fortunately, their children were at boarding school at the time and were spared the ordeal. I am pleased to conclude that both the warden and his wife survived the brutal attack after lengthy hospital treatment.

Some wardens I have spoken to have considered keeping one or two horns available, just so they have something to appease any would-be criminals if challenged.

BLACK RHINO DOWN

When the last wild rhino was killed in Zambia's Luangwa valley and Zimbabwe's wild population was down to less than a handful, rhino poachers shifted their focus to the rich hunting grounds 'down south'. Incidents of rhino poaching escalated from 1993, when 14 rhino were poached in South Africa, to present levels of nearly 1 000 rhino killed each year in our country's national parks, particularly in the Kruger National Park and those of northern KwaZulu-Natal.

Although we had yet to feel the full brunt of this onslaught in our own backyard, incidents in private reserves adjacent to national parks were on the increase. With the Kruger just 29 kilometres from our boundary, I suspected it would only be a matter of time before our rhino were targeted with the same aggressive persistence. As predicted, the poachers came and began to target and kill rhino in Balule Nature Reserve, which culminated in the loss of our first rhino to poachers in 2011. The tally to date is 29 rhino, of which 28 were white rhino and one a black rhino from the newly introduced population.

One may well ask, in light of the arduous task and the resources needed to try and protect the rhino we already had, what the hell were we thinking when we brought another 20 rhino into Balule. What's more, not just any rhino but the endangered black variety and, wait for it ... not even our own! However, all logical considerations aside, as conservationists we could not allow rhino poachers to dictate the bigger conservation strategies to us. As daunting as the project was, we simply refused to dance to their tune. Instead we decided to approach the future with renewed optimism and fortitude. As a result, Balule Nature Reserve became proud contributors to one of the most meaningful conservation initiatives in the world, and as wardens we were happy to man up and accept the challenge.

While Balule had qualified as participants in the Black Rhino Range Expansion Project with room to spare, we were mindful of the pioneering nature of this endeavour. All eyes were on us, the 'new kids on the block', and how we would manage and monitor these endangered animals once they were released into our care.

Given the limited numbers to begin with, we were all too aware that losing a single black rhino, for whatever reason, would be a huge setback, so every precaution was taken to minimise the risk. However, given the complex logistics and hazards associated with capturing, transporting and accommodating animals of this size, we understood that injuries or even fatalities could be expected at the outset. Once released into the wild to fend for themselves, calves in particular would be vulnerable to predation. But when an adult bull was lost to poachers two years into the project, it laid our best monitoring plans bare; it was a devastating blow.

On 15 January 2014, shortly before 8 am, my cell phone rang. It was our rhino monitor, Sinhle Mathebula, and before I could say good morning he uttered those dreaded words, words you half expect to come in the dead of night, not on a beautiful sunny morning ...

'Black rhino down, both horns taken,' he said, his quivering voice barely comprehensible.

Shock and instant nausea prevailed as I listened to the detail. You never get used to hearing bad news; it always drains your blood and dries your mouth ... always!

In a sad twist, this was to be Sinhle's last patrol as monitor for Balule's black rhino project. He had monitored these rhino with passion and dedication for more than two years, and this morning he went out on what he thought would be another routine patrol. All the rhino were individually known to him: particularly this one, which having established a territory was usually easily found. However, this morning its telemetric transmission indicated a static signal – usually explained by a collar thrown or transmitter lost … or by the animal ceasing to move. Upon closer investigation, this time it was clear why there was a static signal. Tragically, Nkondela, as he was known, had fallen foul to a poacher's bullet only hours earlier. Under the last vestiges of darkness, possibly even as late as pre-dawn light, he'd been killed and his horns hacked off. The blood that pooled under what remained of his head had only just begun to congeal, which meant that the poachers were, at the most, three to four hours ahead of us.

A few hastily cut raisin bush branches, the leaves of which were only now beginning to wilt, had been used in an attempt to cover the carcass, no doubt to prevent detection by a helicopter patrol or vultures. It was the first time poachers had covered a carcass in our region, indicating that they knew they needed to buy time to make good their escape. In order not to contaminate the immediate area, which now comprised a crime scene, it was cordoned off. Preservation of detail was vital, and this routine protocol was strictly observed until the authorities arrived. So we could only do a cursory inspection from a discreet distance until the forensic team and police arrived, whereupon they would authorise an autopsy to be done to procure any forensic evidence and allow a select few of us in closer to positively identify the particular rhino from its distinctive ear notches or implanted microchips.

I left Sinhle at the carcass to wait for the anti-poaching task team and the police to arrive while I drove to the run-up pad at the top of the runway close by. There I parked my Land Cruiser, got out and proceeded to walk down the runway towards the windsock. The words of a master tracker I once worked closely with resounded in my head: 'If it doesn't fly or swim, it can be tracked.' So with the sun in my face I hoped there'd be angled light to cast even the lowest shadow across a print, a faint chance of picking up some indication of the poachers' exit route.

Whether it was that my old eyes were still up to the task or because I was so desperately determined to deal with more than clutched straws

I don't know, but there it was: the faintest imprint of the sole of a relatively small but much-worn running shoe, which seemed to jump out at
me. Ironically, it had cut across the spoor of a rhino, forming a straight
edge where nature would have left a round one ... It was this that drew
my attention to the spot. Checking the opposite side of the airstrip I
found another set of tracks clear incoming and outgoing prints. They
were virtually on top of each other; however, these prints were much
larger and were clearly made by a combat-type boot. There had been
at least two poachers. In the meantime, the anti-poaching reactive task
team had been mobilised and was soon on the scene. I pointed out the
tracks of the poachers, then left them to follow the spoor and try to
determine not only where the poachers had come into the reserve but,
more importantly, by what route they intended escaping.

Subsequent investigation by the forensic team revealed our rhino
had been shot with a single .375 Magnum hand-loaded bullet, which
was recovered virtually intact. This was not the same calibre used in
the previous incidents: again, chilling evidence that there could well
be more than one gang at work in the area. Later that day I heard
that another two rhino had been killed near Gravelotte: one near
Andover and two in the Southern Timbavati. Six rhino poached within
a 50-kilometre radius of Hoedspruit in less than 24 hours!

Why the poachers targeted this black rhino may well have had
something to do with our anti-poaching strategy at the time. With our
resources stretched over a wide area, we focused our anti-poaching
efforts on the relatively high number of white rhino concentrated in
the eastern section of the reserve, inadvertently leaving a window
open in the west, which was primarily black rhino habitat. We'd
assumed that maintaining telemetric contact with the black rhino
every day would keep this base covered. Needless to say, the incident
caught us off-guard: a mixture of shock and helplessness prevailed
among us all; this could have been prevented – we felt we had failed
to protect this rhino.

While we were following the tracks of these poachers, another set of fresh tracks was being followed by the Klaserie anti-poaching unit some 15 kilometres to the south-east. Comparisons made of the footwear via MMS showed this was a separate group of poachers, not the ones we were chasing. It wasn't long before that gang was caught up with and fired upon by Klaserie's well-armed rangers. Despite a number of shots having been fired, the poachers managed to escape unscathed. Given the tally of rhino killed in the Hoedspruit area the previous night, it was clearly a synchronised foray, indicating that at least three gangs were involved.

Still reeling from the shock, we desperately searched for clues. Conjecture was rife; everyone wanted answers as to why this relatively small-horned black rhino was targeted so deep inside the reserve, while many larger white rhino, closer to the poachers' entry point and escape route, were simply passed up. Backtracking revealed the poachers had moved a long way to get to this point; they'd moved swiftly through heavily populated white rhino country and targeted this animal. Why? Simply put, they knew there was an excellent chance it would be there. Over the last couple of years, hundreds of people had had regular sightings of the black rhino at Warthog Pan. It was no secret; the movement of these black rhino to and from this water point became predictable to the point of high probability. This also meant that the reserve's shareholders were most likely using this knowledge to view the rhino, which was comforting from a monitoring point of view. However, the proximity of the water hole to a road with unfettered access, and to the railway line with its myriad of maintenance crew members and train drivers, meant that hundreds of people using this route in and out of the reserve also had knowledge of these rhino and their movements.

Using radio telemetry tracking of signal transmitters located in the horn, as well as foot collars, the black rhino were located each day, as stipulated in our contractual agreement with the WWF. However, the rugged terrain favoured by the black rhino sometimes prevented our receivers from picking up a signal. It was then that our master tracker from our field ranger unit, January Mahlaule, would be called in to assist Sinhle by tracking the rhino spoor and physically locating the animal. The two men got on well as a team: Sinhle admired January's tracking skill and bush knowledge and made no secret of the fact that he wanted to be a wildlife guide one day.

In an environment typically fuelled by egos and testosterone, decorum invariably takes a backseat. Needless to say, the head warden at the time felt as we all do when confronted by the senseless death of a rhino. Up until now all the incidents had involved white rhino, but now, for the first time, he had lying at his feet the faceless carcass of one of the precious black rhino. With all his composure lost to bitter anger and frustration, he began jumping to conclusions, looking for a scapegoat, anybody to blame for this embarrassing tragedy. In his mind there was no question: it had to be an inside job – and who better to focus the blame on than those who knew these rhino intimately, the very men who were entrusted to monitor and track the black rhino every day.

His misguided and irrational finger-pointing culminated in accusations being levelled at January, one of the reserve's finest anti-poaching rangers, who he suspected was in collusion with our trusted black rhino monitor, Sinhle.

I didn't know it then, but outbursts of this type were early symptoms of the psychological effect that rhino poaching was beginning to have on those of us drawn in and exposed to this scourge every day, myself included. Although some were able to hide it better than others, I was beginning to see through the facade. No matter how much we tried to tough it out, it ate into our souls and began to suck the joy out of living and working in the bush.

Writing the necessary reports always puts me in mind of the awful task of those military men who have to tell families that their sons have been lost in action. Someone needs to step out of the trenches, maintain composure and remain emotionally detached when necessary. That someone has to open the picket-fence gate, walk up the pathway and knock on the front door. Then, with cap in hand, maintain all the composure they can muster as they inform those near and dear of their recent loss. In consolation, they provide assurance that everything possible is being done to thwart any further senseless violence and brutality. And who more conveniently placed to do this than those of us fresh from the front line, equipped with the details and first-hand information? Nobody else wants this task; nobody wants to report a failure.

However, our devastated faces are not enough for some, and despite every assurance that our anti-poaching units are doing everything possible to minimise losses, the response is usually a polite nod of cursory understanding, which lasts until the moment our backs are turned. Walking away, you feel the heat of their frustration as it burns between your shoulder blades and through into your heart. Insinuations of doubt and mistrust are bandied about in bars, at braais and around boardroom tables. And while some aspersions may be speculatively subtle and reticent, others are unashamedly blatant and outspoken.

Perhaps I should have been more intuitive and seen that what was manifest among colleagues, between employers and employees, was symptomatic of the constant pressure, of being held accountable for that which is not essentially our forte. It's a classic 'catch-22' situation: most of us know we are in over our heads and our reputations are exposed to elements of this fray on two fronts, but we cannot simply give up.

Shortly after the black rhino poaching incident, Sinhle resigned and moved to Umlani Trails in the Timbavati Private Nature Reserve, where he took up employment as a ranger. It had been a lifelong dream of his, and despite heightened suspicions from all quarters owing to this sudden move I knew differently. Subsequent polygraph tests conducted at APNR level by Timbavati's polygraphist completely ruled Sinhle out as a suspect. I received these results three months later via our head warden at the time and, as expected, without so much as an apology. Today Sinhle Mathebula is still happily working at Umlani, where he now holds a senior ranger's position.

I'd recruited January some 10 years previously for his bush savvy and tracking skill. In those days, wire and cable snare poaching was the main threat to the larger wildlife in our region; to counter this we needed men on the team who thought like poachers and knew the bush as well as they did – or better. Having previously worked for a professional hunter in the area, January was familiar with local conditions and knew his way around dangerous game. On two occasions he'd saved men's lives: once by shooting a wounded leopard and once by diverting a charging buffalo. As rhino poaching began to escalate, it became clear we needed brave, reliable men to help us combat the scourge. January not only ticked all the boxes in this regard, but his weapon-handling skills were unmatched. Needless to say, he proved to be an invaluable member of the team.

A week after the black rhino poaching incident, which resulted in unfounded aspersions cast on January's integrity, an incident occurred that would reveal suspicions of this man's collusion with poachers to be unfounded. Some sceptics have argued that what followed (to be related in the following chapter) was an elaborate, albeit risky, attempt to throw us all off his trail. However, I think not ... You be the judge.

RHINO POACHER SHOT

Since the usual full moon alert the week before, each night had been getting progressively darker. Being overcast, tonight was particularly dark, and except for the regular rumble of huge 16-wheelers transporting magnetite from the mine in Phalaborwa, the R40 was quiet. Nearing midnight there was little in the way of other traffic on the road as the seemingly innocuous Toyota Corolla tucked into the grimy slipstream of one of these trucks, like a pilot fish under a huge shark. At a given point the car would begin to drift back, then, as the truck disappeared over a rise in the distance, the small red sedan slowed down and pulled off the road, grinding to a stop at a known marker.

Three men got out and hurried to the back of the car, where they quietly opened the boot and retrieved two backpacks. The larger pack contained two loaves of sliced white bread, two litres of Coca-Cola, a well-worn pair of All Star running shoes and a brand-new hunting knife. In the other was a well-used axe, a plastic bag with six rounds of solid-point ammunition, a small torch and a screw-on silencer, which was wedged in under an old brown overall.

Wrapped in a camouflage jacket, stashed behind the back seat, was a battered Czechoslovakian-made Brno .375 Magnum rifle. The weapon was removed and placed against the fence line by the third man, who then rushed back to the two men still at the car and, mumbling a word or two to them, handed each a golf-ball-sized transparent plastic bag, the contents of which resembled marijuana. Then he got into the car, which was still running, and slowly drove away onto the road and into the night. Only once up to speed, and some distance away, did he switch the headlights on.

Climbing over the game fence, on the corner pole, was child's play. Within minutes, the two men had shouldered their respective backpacks and the rifle, which was simply pulled through between the bottom strands. Lifting his T-shirt, the man taking the lead tucked his nine-millimetre pistol back into position: it had dislodged from the comfortable recess in the small of his back when he'd jumped down from the fence pole. Both men pulled out their cell phones and turned them off to preserve battery life. Then, without a word, they set off in single file, the man behind carrying the rifle by its barrel, balancing the weapon on his shoulder in a practised, familiar manner.

They hugged the fence line, heading due south for a short distance, until the Eskom pylons loomed silver grey against the inky skyline. From there they angled sharply eastwards and simply followed the power lines, which took them almost to the bridge. Their usual route, through the Olifants River itself, had been cut off. Heavy rains upstream had resulted in the river coming down in flood, which left the poachers no alternative but to enter the reserve across the 400-metre-long train bridge spanning the river.

Their strides were purposeful, if a little careless, their minds filled with confident arrogance since the sangoma had assured them they were going to get a big rhino and, as long as they each kept that little plastic bag of muti on them, they would remain invisible to the field rangers. The two men could already feel the weight of the bloody rhino horns in their backpacks; for now, their minds were filled with excited anticipation of success and thoughts of what they were going to buy with their share of the spoils. Once they'd crossed the bridge into rhino country there'd be no time for dreaming: they would need to avoid detection while they focused on finding and killing rhino.

Rhino poachers plan their incursions well in advance. Besides procuring the usual transport arrangements, equipment and information, part of their strategy is to seek advice and protection from sangomas, who are revered and consulted extensively before such forays are embarked upon. Thankfully these bone-throwing accomplices have limited technical skills and so have little or no power over the infra-red motion-detecting sensors of our camera traps. A little after midnight, in spite of the 'invisible-making' crap in their respective pockets, one of our strategically placed cameras' infra-red beam triggered, sending an MMS – a ghostly grey image of two armed suspects heading south towards the train bridge – through to my phone. It was as though a silent bugle had sounded a signal that the battle had commenced.

We'd calculated the time it took at a fast walking pace to get from this camera to our rangers' observation post; we knew there were only minutes to spare before the poachers reached the far end of the bridge and began crossing on the narrow walkway, straight towards our men. The field rangers on duty, guarding this bridge 24/7, were notified immediately and briefed that the two suspects on their way in were armed and dangerous. To confirm this, I sent the image through to January's phone.

Moving from the relative comfort of the observation post, which is situated approximately 50 metres from the bridge itself, January and his partner, Lucky Makhubedu, walked quietly down to the bridge. January checked that the volume on his two-way radio was turned right down and did the same with their cell phones. Routinely, he slipped a shell into the breach of his Winchester pump-action shotgun and quietly pushed the slide forward, while Lucky loaded his .303 rifle and got into position to apprehend the suspects.

My instruction to both men followed accepted policy and procedure and was clear as it always is.

'Even if they shoot at you, or try to attack you, do not shoot to kill, aim only for their legs. Never shoot a man in the back, and never shoot a suspect more than once, unless your life is in imminent danger.'

Less than 15 minutes had ticked by since the camera trap had been triggered. I'd just thrown my weapon and my grab-bag of essentials into the Land Cruiser when my cell phone rang. It was January.

'Maybe I've made a mistake,' he stammered. 'I think I have killed a poacher.'

'I will be with you in 10 minutes: don't move, don't answer the phone and don't phone anyone else; wait until I get there,' I said.

I arrived to find both field rangers at the south end of the bridge. My headlights fell on January sitting on the railway line with his head down, obviously traumatised, a picture of utter dejection. Lucky stood close by, shining his torch down the maw of a seemingly empty bridge. My phone tweeted again; this time there was only one suspect in the camera trap image: it was the other poacher, carrying the rifle and running for his life ... or, as I rather suspected, to an appointment with a certain sangoma he wanted to have stern words with.

I walked up to January and sat down on the cold steel track next to him, then, scrolling down on my phone, showed him the image that had just come through.

'Tell me exactly what happened,' I said quietly.

'We got into position soon after you called, and within a few minutes we heard them. Although there was no sound of their footsteps, we knew they were getting closer to us because the metal of the old walkway creaked. It was really scary; right up until the moment, we could make them out clearly enough to challenge them. I could see the man in front was carrying something in his hand, which he lifted and aimed in our direction: it was clearly a handgun.'

'OK, so what did you do then?' I asked.

'I shot, aiming low for the legs as you said I should, and the man in front collapsed immediately, but when I looked again he was gone. The second one carrying the rifle turned and ran back the way he'd come. I thought the man I'd shot had fallen into the river. I shone my torch at the spot, and I couldn't see anybody, but I saw there was something moving between the tracks; I could not be sure it was the man I'd shot at and wasn't going to approach in case it was and he was still able to use the handgun and shoot us.'

'You acted bravely, January; you did the right thing under the circumstances, protecting your life and that of your partner is always top priority. Importantly, you have done your job as a protector of the reserve's rhino, and as a result of your actions there will be no rhino dying today.'

January appeared to be unconvinced by my overview of the situation. Perhaps I simply didn't have the skill to tell him what he needed to hear at that point, but what I did say came from the heart: it was not merely consoling; I meant every word. Nevertheless, I could see that the realisation of what he had done was beginning to sink in, and he needed to be taken away from the scene as soon as possible. Also, he was definitely in no frame of mind to make a statement to the police. So without any further ado, I instructed one of my colleagues to take him back to base.

Walking up to him once again, just before he was driven away, I assured him the whole reserve was behind him, that they'd support him as they had done in Timani's case, whatever the outcome.

As they drove away, I walked back to the bridge and shone my flashlight in the area where January indicated the poacher had been shot. However, any thought of approaching the spot was averted by a droning in the distance, which I recognised as the powerful diesel-powered locomotive of a train approaching. When nearly two kilometres of train had rumbled past us, and the world had fallen abruptly quiet again, I shone the flashlight back on the bridge. This time, something under the train lines moved in the beam; whatever it was, it was reddish-orange in colour. My heart sank; I thought the suspect may have been hit in the torso by a stray pellet and was bleeding, and as much as I hate rhino poachers and wish all of them were no longer with us, I couldn't help wanting this one to be alive, because I knew that if he died the charge against January would be murder.

When the police eventually arrived, nearly four hours later, we moved in under escort to investigate. We found the suspect huddled in a recess under the tracks between the sleepers. It was apparent that both his legs were broken. Although crippled and unable to move, he was very much alive. I breathed a sigh of relief when I saw that what I had initially thought was a blood-soaked shirt was nothing but his red

T-shirt. As carefully as possible, we pulled him out and carried him off the bridge, where we laid him on the grass verge next to the tracks. We prepared to attend to the suspect's wounds while one of my field rangers went back and retrieved a backpack containing the man's supplies as well as a loaded nine-millimetre pistol and a cell phone. Under the glare of our incident lights, we proceeded to stabilise him until the ambulance arrived. Why he hadn't dropped his pistol or, for that matter, his whole backpack into the river beats me.

We cut his trousers away from his legs to reveal the extent of his wounds, which also allowed us to dress and bandage them more easily. In so doing, we inadvertently exposed the rest of his physique, and it became immediately apparent to me why, when poachers ran from our rangers, they invariably got away ... The pathetic cripple lying shivering at our feet was built like an athlete. Although the man must have been in agony, he lay there without a whimper, shivering in shock and utterly helpless, yet none of us could help but look down on him with disdain. Most of us there were under no delusion as to the underlying brutality and senseless cruelty he was capable of. We had all seen too many murdered rhino to feel any sympathy.

For a few newly recruited field rangers from Protrack, there to gain experience, this was the first real live rhino poacher they'd seen. Until now, the only evidence they'd come across on patrol of our rhino being butchered by human beings, and not phantoms, was almost invisible: often only the odd faint shoe impression or bare footprint left in the sand – and of course the contrasting ghastly aftermath of their brutal forays if they killed a rhino.

It is impossible to predict where each pellet from a shotgun shell will hit. And there is so much I could say on the idiosyncrasies of scatter-guns, but this is not the forum. Suffice it to say, of the 18 pellets in the shell fired that day, only six hit the suspect in his lower extremities, breaking both legs. It was a textbook shot, one that only a man like January could have been trusted to pull off under those circumstances. In one leg the suspect's femur was broken and in the other the tibia, rendering him completely immobile.

The round lead pellets from a 12-gauge shotgun leave the barrel at a muzzle velocity of around 300 metres per second (compared to the high velocity of a streamlined bullet fired from a rifle – for example, a .223 Remington – which leaves the muzzle at over 1 000 metres per second). Furthermore, the drag coefficient of round shotgun pellets means their velocity diminishes rapidly over a short distance. SSG or buckshot pellets are slow and heavy, and although they will break bone and tear muscle tissue, they leave a much smaller wound channel than a high-velocity projectile from a rifle will. As far as firearms are concerned, I believe a shotgun used at field distances, with the correct cartridges, can be seen as employing 'minimum force'.

Months later, January informed me that he'd heard through the bush telegraph that the second man had received a stray pellet, which passed through the fleshy part of his calf muscle ... A few millimetres to the right or left and his tibia would have been smashed. So was this pellet lucky number seven or unlucky? ... I guess that depends which side of the fence you are on.

Which brings me back to the question of January's integrity: was this the action of a man who colluded with poachers?

A MOLE IN OUR MIDST

Seven full moons had waxed and waned since last we lost a rhino on Olifants. In the context of what we're up against, and in terms of the intensifying rhino poaching onslaught, this is a long time. However, while the lull is always welcome, it's an uncomfortable respite as we are fully aware that the possibility of an incursion increases exponentially with time elapsed. We know the poachers haven't given up: they're just blending in with their surrounds among the rest of the bottom feeders, getting ready for the next kill and growing more tentacles.

A few days ago, I remember looking at my grab-bag and deciding to check on the equipment. It holds most of the kit I'll need instantly, without needing to waste time packing the essentials each time – this is a bag that is always packed and ready to load when we need to respond to an incursion or poaching incident. A spare radio and battery, a ground-to-air radio, a spare map with grids, a military-spec night-vision scope, a sheath knife, a .38 special handgun, two smoke grenades, binoculars, a comprehensive trauma first-aid kit, a small towel, one small LED flashlight and spare batteries, pepper spray, cable ties, a windbreaker, a spare shirt, a spare bush hat, sunblock, two litres of water, rehydrate, USN protein bars, day-glo vests, nylon cord and, of course, my Bialetti portable espresso maker. I placed the portable radios in their chargers, just in case one was a little low. Then I mumbled something to Meagan to the effect that things had been too quiet for too long.

Full moon is one of nature's countless complimentary gifts; an exhibition to look forward to and behold, it evokes our most primal romantic instincts, which even a spectacular sunset doesn't quite do. Apparently even the wolves of Yellowstone National Park are known to stop what they're doing, and (often on empty stomachs and in the bitter cold) howl in communicative worship and appreciation.

Initially, rhino poachers used the light of the moon to hunt down and kill our rhino and, in so doing, blighted one more of the joys of our lives. Needless to say, these days a full moon – now referred to as a 'poacher's moon' or 'blood moon' – does little but fill a warden's heart with trepidation. Nevertheless, there have been positive developments resulting from a notable anti-poaching success during a recent full-moon phase ... so much so that full-moon nights are now avoided by some experienced poachers, who are forced to hunt on the blackest nights using small LED flashlights.

Combining the knowledge of many poachers' preference for the full-moon phase, along with intelligence gleaned from reliable informants, a co-operative strategy between the warden, members of the SAPS and Protrack's task team was meticulously planned. This all came together and culminated in the arrest of three poachers at the Grietjie Gate one night. A weapon and ammunition, an axe, knives, cell phones and food provisions for a few days were also seized. One of the suspects was shot in the lower leg as he tried to escape. They could see we meant business. Later the drop-off and pick-up vehicle was given up through the questioning of one the suspects and, within an hour, was seized near Gravelotte, along with the driver and an accomplice. Further questioning revealed that their intention was to try this new route to slip in undetected by our field rangers. Once through the gate into Grietjie, they would cross the Olifants River at this relatively densely populated, but minimally patrolled, point – somehow the poachers knew our field rangers did not prioritise this section of river – and then head through our area, eastwards into Klaserie.

Less than 12 hours after the apprehension and arrest of the suspects at the Grietjie Gate, tracks were seen by Protrack's field rangers entering the Klaserie Nature Reserve from the south. Clearly a two-pronged incursion had been meticulously planned. The poachers knew we couldn't cover two fronts effectively at the same time. This was the first time incoming tracks were located in this region, where usually the tracking was done reactively, after a rhino carcass had been discovered. These incoming tracks were followed up by Klaserie's new field rangers under the leadership of Willem Pretorius, who was eager to prove a point and which he most certainly did. Later that morning, the nine armed field rangers tracked down three poachers who were huddled in a thorny clusterleaf thicket. There was only one way in and out of this almost impenetrable bush, a route that was covered by the field rangers. So when the poachers were challenged, they came out one by one with their hands in the air, knowing any false move at this point would be their last. The arrest was made deep in the reserve. Two weapons were recovered: a .458 Magnum rifle and a nine-millimetre handgun. An axe with the price tag still attached, two knives, cell phones and some marijuana were also seized.

On the same morning, a snare poacher's bushmeat camp on state-owned Doreen, just across the river, was raided by Protrack's field rangers, working alongside a newly trained team of female field rangers (known as the Black Mambas), under the command of regional warden Johan Grobbelaar. Here, two middle-aged suspects were found trying to hide away in the long grass, a futile exercise considering they were hauled out and promptly arrested by women young enough to be their daughters! Before being taken into custody, they were made to reveal the location of all the snares they had set in the area. Among the many newly laid snares removed were numerous neglected snares in which the rotting carcasses of animals such as buffalo, waterbuck and giraffe were found. Some had been in the bush for so long that only a few sun-bleached bones remained – reminders of the horrific, pointless death of innocent animals.

This camp had been spotted from the air a couple of days earlier when the Jabiru aeroplane had been searching for two rhino that were believed to have moved into the area from Balule. The timely intervention not only disrupted the meat and muti poachers' offensive, it also meant that no rhino had fallen foul of these deadly cable snares. It goes without saying that those suspects arrested were charged with every plausible offence and given no technical loopholes to squeeze through.

Had they actually killed a rhino, a conviction and sentence was just about assured. Failing this, they would be out of custody on a paltry bail that would be paid easily and quickly by fellow gang members. And as we have learned, suspects out on bail begin plying their evil trade again within days. How terrible it is when one becomes so desperate to see justice done that a rhino's life is even thought of, albeit fleetingly, in these terms! Such is my faith in the efficacy of the legal system.

Shortly after the arrest north of the Olifants River, the tracks of three poachers were detected entering Klaserie from the south. It was an obvious attempt to spread our teams of field rangers over a wide front to try and dilute their efficacy; we were being infiltrated and attacked from all sides, it seemed. Although these poachers were able to kill two rhino, they were tracked down, and with the aid of a helicopter flown by Bennie's father Zander, the Klaserie field rangers made a second significant arrest.

It was increasingly apparent that the private reserves were facing an escalation in poaching activity. We were now being targeted by syndicates with sophisticated plans. We needed to counteract this leaking of information, whether passively or purposefully revealed, and respond by increasing our intelligence-gathering network outside, while placing more field rangers strategically in the most vulnerable areas within.

The danger and threat from organised syndicates was becoming something far more ominous and decidedly dangerous. While less obvious, it was often far closer to home than we thought, as the following illustrates.

The poaching kingpins' tentacles were continually probing for any opportunity to exploit every weakness in order to minimise risks and maximise returns for their efforts. This determination culminated in a well-laid plan, which led them right in among our ranks. Their goal was to gather information about the numbers and whereabouts of the rhino but, more importantly, the routines, weaknesses and strengths of our field rangers. Finding and killing rhino was the easy part; getting in and out with the spoils posed the problem.

Owing to the 24/7 shifts being implemented, and the inevitable leave schedule overlaps, we needed to bolster our field ranger squad. But we also needed field rangers who were experienced in anti-poaching work, men who could think like poachers and could strategise. There was simply no time to train new recruits, so I asked my rangers to put the word out. It was also important that they trusted whomever we took on, as their lives would depend on it.

Thanks to social media, I was inundated with applications. Most candidates were well spoken, security trained and keen to get out of urban crime fighting situations and into the bush. But I needed men with bush savvy, tracking skill and experience that had preferably been honed since childhood. There was no time to teach greenhorns about working in among wild animals.

Within a week, a man named Phineas Dinda arrived to apply for the post. Phineas was a tall man and, although in his late thirties, was lean and muscular. He spoke with authority and confidence, attributes I would expect from someone who had seen action and arrested a poacher or three. His whole demeanour inspired confidence. He opened a satchel full of relevant certificates, which he proudly showed me; thumbing through the pile revealed he had passed every course with flying colours: a model candidate, it seemed. Besides the formality of certification, he had grown up in the bush and knew his way around big game and how to avoid dangerous situations. It became apparent, as I spoke to him, that he had been to the University of Life, such as it was in the bushveld.

I was told he had extensive experience in anti-poaching in the Kruger National Park, where he had worked for a number of years as a field ranger. I was already impressed with this fact alone, as there can be no better training ground for this kind of work than the Kruger. Also, Phineas had been highly recommended by one of our own team, so he appeared to tick all the boxes.

I couldn't help thinking that the Kruger would surely feel the loss of a man of this calibre. So naturally I wondered why he'd left a relatively secure position working for National Parks to move to a smaller private reserve. When I eventually asked him, he told me that he and his wife, who was still working in the park, had recently divorced, and the parting had been less than amicable. As a result, the two of them were unable to work together, and as the Kruger doesn't shift quarrelling couples around without good reason, he'd decided to rather move on and find work elsewhere.

Although I was not up to the military style approach that he had been trained in, and was used to, he did have some good suggestions to make – particularly regarding strategy and the deployment of our field rangers. My field rangers seemed to understand and were keen to learn from him. Without the usual malice, they accepted that this man was someone they could happily take direction from. Here, finally, was a team leader who thought like a rhino poacher and had years of hands-on experience. I must admit, I thought we'd landed a gem.

At that stage Balule had yet to implement the compulsory voice analysis or polygraph screening of all prospective candidates, and the regular testing of full-time candidates, which both our field rangers and Protrack's rangers are now required to undergo. However, as is standard HR practice, there was a three-month probationary period before Olifants River Game Reserve employed anyone permanently. As it turned out, this time frame was to be our saving: as time went by my interest in this man's background grew, and a few cracks began to appear as the plaster began to dry. First, I'd noticed that he never queried or tried to negotiate a higher starting salary relevant to his qualifications, which I'd expected he would. Second, he owned a late-model Toyota Double Cab – hardly the sort of vehicle a man with his means could afford or, at the very least, service and maintain. I should know, I owned one! Naturally, the alarm bells began to go ding-dong loudly in my head. I began to suspect this was a classic case of something being too good to be true.

In the meantime, I'd been trying to do some background checks on his references. The section ranger he had given as a reference was on leave at the time and only one of his other references in SANParks had come back to me with an unconfirmed report that still had to be verified their end. As I could not wait for the onerous red tape to be cut, I went straight to an old colleague from my ranger days at Mala Mala, who also happens to hold a senior security position in the Kruger National Park. I knew he had a huge load on his shoulders and was always busy, so I simply sent him an SMS asking for a one-word answer. My text to him read 'Phineas Dinda for field ranger position on Olifants, Yes or No?' … I got his reply in less than 15 seconds. 'No! He is suspected of rhino poaching!'

I put my phone in my pocket, walked over to my two-way radio and called Phineas, asking him to report to my office immediately. I then explained the situation to Meagan, and within half an hour she had worked out the exact amount of wages owing to him and had the envelope and his cash payslip ready for signing.

Initially my anger was embarrassingly overwhelming. I was fuming at being taken for a fool, allowing myself to rely purely on my judgement of character. Placing my dented ego and reputation aside, I was now acutely aware that I had exposed my field rangers and their routine to a suspected rhino poacher. Everything in me screamed for revenge, but without solid evidence there was little I could do except to try and do some damage control by changing our modus operandi.

Handing the cash over to Phineas, I quietly informed him that he'd not filled the required criteria for the position as a field ranger on Olifants River Game Reserve. Although he looked somewhat bemused, he did not utter a word as he signed his payslip, nor did he count the wad of money in the envelope. With that, I thanked him for his time and asked him to please leave the reserve that morning after handing in his uniform and equipment. He said he would leave everything at reception when he collected his exit permit. With a broad smile, he thanked me in Afrikaans, extending his arm to me, but I simply could not bring myself to shake his hand. Then he turned around and walked out of my office … I'm sure he knew then that I knew!

Six days later I received another text from my old friend. Phineas Dinda's vehicle had been stopped and searched in a routine roadblock on the Barberton–Mbombela road. He and two other occupants were found to be carrying three rhino horns from animals poached in the Kruger, a large amount of cash and a .375 Magnum silenced rifle. They were arrested on the spot. Two months later, Phineas and his two accomplices were sentenced to lengthy jail sentences.

We'd dodged a bullet! Thanks to a good friend.

Our field ranger who had recommended the man, bringing him deep into our inner circle, was genuinely shocked. Inadvertently, he had released this wily jackal among the hens, and by compromising our security irreparable damage had been done. He has not stopped apologising to me. He attended the sentencing of Phineas and his accomplices of his own volition and at his own cost, as he felt he needed to report back to me on the details. I suspect he felt really bad and was trying everything to sweeten the bad taste that this near miss had left in my mouth.

This is the kind of subterfuge that is only supposed to happen in spy movies or, indeed, has been shown in real life to occur in fanatical terrorist cells. We agonise about how much information he has given out, how much is already being applied against us and our rhino. This is something that still haunts me: the poaching incidents that followed appeared to be blatantly area specific … as if the targets were known.

BLOOD AT RED PAN

Each and every rhino that gets killed in the neighbourhood is known to us. And despite assurances to the contrary, these losses are taken personally. Though there are man-made boundaries separating regions and reserves, the rhino populations are homogeneous: they move within the same greater open system, much as nature dictates. And so when one gets killed, it makes no difference on whose land it falls: it hurts us all. There is a strong connection, a sense of accusation as well as responsibility. The senseless murder of any rhino nags at the conscience of the most cynical pragmatist among us. It has a ripple effect, and although those closest to its centre will feel the disturbance more acutely than those on the periphery, the ever-widening ripples affect everyone to some degree.

On the night before Guy Fawkes Day, 2015, another rhino became a statistic. This latest incident, on a nearby landowner's property, brought to nine the number of rhino killed by poachers in his relatively small area over the last three years. Despite repeated requests to close a remote water point in his eastern section, known to our field rangers as 'Rooi Pan' (Red Pan), the landowner stubbornly refused. Its deep, ochre-red mud wallow, resulting from the overflow of the watering hole, was particularly attractive to the local rhino. Out of concern for their safety, it was thought prudent to have them utilise a water point closer to where they could be effectively monitored by our field ranger pickets. To compound our dilemma, it hadn't rained for months, and surface water began to get scarce; soon the concentration of rhino at this watering hole made it a focal point for poachers. Its vulnerability was highlighted when a patrol counted 12 rhino drinking there, the majority of them cows and calves. To poachers, this was a bank vault they knew the combination to and had all the time in the world to come and open. They were choosing the weapons, the venue and the time, which made this duel extremely difficult to win.

We had learned that the turnaround point for nocturnal forays by poachers was roughly 15 kilometres, placing this area comfortably within their killing zone. As this property fell into the region under my jurisdiction, I found the owner's short-sightedness extremely frustrating, not to mention a huge drain on our anti-poaching resources. I knew it would only be a question of time before poachers got through our defences to target our resident rhino as well as those coming in from Klaserie which, I should add, made up the majority of those individuals seen utilising this pan. (All the adult rhino in our reserves are easily identified by their ear-notch patterns, which are registered in a database at our respective headquarters, along with the microchip numbers for each individual. However, the responsibility for the horns, if found, and the criminal proceedings that follow in respect of a poached rhino, is determined by whose land the rhino falls on, irrespective of where it was ear-notched and microchipped.)

Desperate times called for desperate measures, so we 'checked' the wiring from the solar panel that drove the water pump and found it to be faulty. As none of us knew anything about electricity, we had little choice but to leave it in the state of disrepair we happened to find it in, albeit rather pleased that water was no longer being pumped. However, no sooner had the water hole dried up than the owner had the pump repaired, complaining that he'd lost an R800 battery as a result of the 'fault'. Clearly we were not going there again, so plan B was set in motion and a two-man observation-post-cum-patrol-base was established in the area. Concomitant disruptive tactics provided by the deployment of these strategic patrols, together with our team's early warning system on the river, enabled us to effectively thwart 12 known incursion attempts into this particular area over 19 months. But we knew it would only be a matter of time before relentless pressure and determination to get rhino would compel these killers to change their strategy, which they did.

The poachers became nocturnal; not only that, but knowing we were usually alert on moonlit nights they would often choose the darkest nights for their forays. In defence, we were forced to punch in the dark, which would prove to be most frustrating for our anti-poaching efforts. This was also to have tragic consequences for a number of resident and incoming rhino. They were being shot at in the dark, and if they did not fall, those badly wounded individuals that ran could not be followed; it was simply too dark for the poachers to track them. We came across a number of rhino that had died this way. Backtracking their blood spoor in the daylight revealed that one individual had run for nearly two kilometres, while others had wandered around for days before dying.

It was just after 7 pm when the call came through from our anti-poaching rangers on the river to say they'd heard two gunshots. At their best reckoning, the shots sounded as if they'd come from an area known as Dundee in Klaserie. The team based inland at the patrol post had also heard the shots. By triangulating the points given, we placed the shots at a known map reference. Upon investigation, and painstaking night tracking, we were able to pick up faint All Star shoe prints, clear enough to determine that a group of three suspected poachers were now moving out of the area and heading in a north-westerly direction. Evidently they intended escaping across the Olifants River. As there'd be no point stumbling around in the dark trying to follow them, our best chance was to leapfrog the bastards. We needed to anticipate possible exit points on the river and the main road, where ambush teams would be lying in wait for them.

Well-armed stopper groups, equipped with night-vision binoculars, were deployed to cover two of the most frequently used crossing points on the river. Even so, we knew it would be a gamble; the poachers held all the aces and always dealt from the bottom of the deck. Not only that, but we were in the grip of a serious drought – the driest season in nearly 13 years – and as a result, the river was no more than ankle-deep in most places; one could cross anywhere along the 20-kilometre wide river front. Deploying the second stopper group stacked the odds ever so slightly in our favour. Split into two teams, they took up positions on the R40 road between Phalaborwa and Hoedspruit at known drop-off and rendezvous points.

Close to midnight, a vehicle was observed moving suspiciously slowly along the R40. As the timeline was right, and it was cruising in the vicinity of a known pick-up point, the stopper group moved in. However, when they tried to intercept the vehicle, it sped away from the rangers, who wasted no time and were soon in hot pursuit. The ensuing chase reached speeds of nearly 160 kilometres per hour, and so, realising the sedan would quickly outpace their 4x4, reinforcements were called in ahead. The vehicle was eventually stopped at the crossroads in Hoedspruit, where the driver was found to be the only occupant. With the assistance of the local authorities the car was searched and details taken, but no incriminating evidence was found. There was nothing to do but to let the man go.

As soon as first light allowed, our rangers began backtracking the poachers' exit spoor. Weather conditions had improved. On any other day this could have been described as a beautiful morning; what wind had been gusting the night before had died down completely, and the faint glow of dawn on the cloudless horizon was fast changing to a deep salmon pink. In the distance I could hear the faint *whirr* of the Jabiru's Rotax motor approaching, I turned and looked west as the sun broke free and reflected off the little aircraft. Less than 10 minutes later the call I was hoping not to receive, but in truth expected, came through from the pilot. He'd located the carcass of a rhino.

'Please let it be only the one,' I prayed.

Flying the little fixed-wing in ever-widening circles over the area, to check for any other carcasses, the pilot located three live rhino moving deeper into Klaserie. Their proximity to the carcass, which lay less than 50 metres from the boundary, suggested that they were part of the same group from which the hapless rhino had been selected and killed. Later, on his way back, the pilot reported another seven rhino about four kilometres further west of our location. Swooping in low over them, he was able to confirm that they too appeared to be fine.

Once the area was 'taped', we sat and waited for the authorities to arrive. Shortly after 10.30 am, the last of the officials arrived on the scene. We were now able to move in closer to the carcass and confirm it was indeed a cow: a lactating mother, at that. It was also determined from her ear notches that this particular rhino had emanated from Klaserie. Their warden verified our suspicion that the cow had been nursing a very young calf. Those tiny rhino tracks found earlier by our rangers were now confirmed to be those of her orphaned baby.

Rooi Pan was now responsible for two more rhino lost!

An already dreadfully depressing situation had suddenly got worse: somewhere out there was a vulnerable baby rhino, and it had been without milk for over 20 hours. There was not a moment to lose: we needed to find this calf as soon as possible, before the complications associated with dehydration set in. In order to maximise our chances, we brought in a helicopter, which, in situations like this, is able to do a more thorough search than a fixed-wing aircraft can. Soon the search began, with four pairs of experienced eyes peering through the perspex bubble of Big Game Heli's Robinson R44. This indispensable machine had become a familiar sight in the skies over Balule and is as synonymous with the rhino poaching scourge as our resident vultures and short-tailed eagles are. Needless to say, it wasn't long before the little waif, not much bigger than a warthog, was located deep inside Klaserie and immobilised.

As we'd expected, given the time elapsed without nourishment, she was found to be in poor condition. Fortunately for this calf, however, she was in the hands of the most experienced rhino vet in the world today, Dr Peter Rogers, and she was quickly stabilised and prepared for evacuation. She was then gently bundled into the helicopter for a short flight directly to an orphanage run by Rhino Revolution in Hoedspruit ... their second orphan from us in as many months.

I returned to the carcass to find the autopsy team already hard at work. We exchanged a few cursory nods and wry smiles of sympathy, accompanied by some appropriate profanity. Nothing else needed to be said: we each knew what the other was thinking. Bloody-gloved hands meant that handshakes and hugs were out of place. Quietly, with neither banter nor discussion, everyone went about the macabre task as they had done more than a hundred times before. Not the smallest detail would be overlooked or tampered with as the team resumed their investigative work. Systematically, they began searching for needles of evidence in haystacks of flesh. Primarily, the search was for bullet heads; even a single projectile found could help tie the killer's weapon to this carcass, or indeed others.

Initially, thin steel rods were used to probe the wound channels to determine the angle of the shot, the path of the bullet into the body, and the depth of penetration. Most importantly, this allowed the team to narrow down our search for bullets within the carcass itself. Once that was determined, the dissection began. What had only the day before been a rhino cow weighing the better part of two tons, nourishing and protecting her tiny calf, was now reduced to neatly piled chunks of flesh. Off to one side lay a row of the rhino's hide cut into squares, each piece not much bigger than a tablemat. Muscle tissue was then cut off the main skeleton and placed on the skin as though portioned for distribution or sale; to the unknowing observer the scene would have resembled a rudimentary bushmeat kitchen. These smaller pieces were then carefully run over with a metal detector in order to find and recover any bullets or bullet fragments.

Within a couple of hours, six soft-nosed .375 H&H Magnum bullets had been retrieved from the carcass this way. This was a first for the team: it was a significant deviation; usually full metal jacket or solid monolithic bullets are used. All these clues were pieced together in order to try and visualise the rhino's last moments of life, her position in relation to the killers and where they'd fired from; this also gave us a smaller area on which to focus and search more effectively for possible expended cartridge cases. As a result, three of the six cases were found and collected as evidence. As usual, DNA samples of the toenails, skin and soft tissue were taken, while microchip scanners were used to positively identify the individual rhino. (On rare occasions the actual chip, not much bigger than a match-head, is found.)

This was the 19th rhino autopsy I'd attended. Each one gets progressively more difficult to process in my mind. Unlike those forensic pathologists in Hollywood movie studios who are known to munch a hamburger while conducting an autopsy, I've never let it become simply a routinely methodical job.

I suspect that, like most chronic pain, one is able to bear it while in a state of analgesic numbness, but to see the pointless waste of the precious lives of these innocent animals is not only heartbreaking, it's nauseating and doesn't get easier on the psyche. The sick feeling in my gut is not from the smell of putrefying flesh, or having to tramp through coagulated blood and stomach contents, but from the bitter taste of intense hatred for those responsible. I am beginning to understand how people can be driven to murder someone in a fit of rage, and my mouth dries instantly with fear at this realisation ... I am all too aware that there is no calling back a bullet.

Up until recently, our response to poaching forays in daylight hours had proved most effective, resulting in nine out of ten incursions being disrupted and poachers turned around before any rhino could be killed. I believe that early detection and an increase in the use of anti-poaching canine units are effective deterrents, which all but eliminate attempts at daylight poaching. However, deep down we knew that none of this would deter poachers for long; their determination would show no respite. True to our worst fears, rhino poachers have mutated in response to our anti-poaching techniques and, increasingly, darkness is becoming their habitat. Now, like a virulent disease, they attack when we are at our weakest, when we can offer the least resistance. At night they take full advantage when we are least effective, when short-sighted rhino are at their most vulnerable and trailing dogs least effective.

Rhino poachers own the night – and it seems the darker the night, the more of it they're able to call their own. Hunting exclusively in the dark, their hunting technique changes: with visual tracking almost impossible, they wait up at strategic locations like middens, wallows or water holes from where the rhino themselves are kept in sight, followed and killed, usually just after sunset and onwards.

We have only lost one rhino in our area on a full-moon night but know of reserves that have lost many more. There is no pattern cast in stone with rhino poachers. As this latest incident revealed, despite our field rangers hearing the gunshots and getting to the scene in less than 40 minutes, the poachers had already hacked the horns off and were at least 20 minutes ahead of us. Although our eyes began to adjust to the dark, we could not see clearly enough to give chase. For that one needs direction: only spoor will give us that and only natural light or military-spec night-vision equipment will facilitate it. Chasing poachers in the dark after the fact is totally impractical; disrupting their hunt prior to the kill is the most effective tactic. The frustrating quiet that follows once the poachers are on the run is deceptively peaceful, broken only by Mozambique nightjars and the distant drone of Phalaborwa's Chinese-owned mine, where it's business as usual. Powerful illumination of the mine's workings, which creates a beacon in the northern sky on the darkest of nights, allows gigantic diesel-electric trucks to extract raw materials around the clock. Billions of tons of magnetite and phosphate are then loaded onto trains and railed through the centre of our reserve en route to Richard's Bay. From there it's on to China to fuel a growing economy, which, in turn, now stimulates the demand for rhino horn, the very horns on those very rhino that these trains run past each day ... There has to be some tragic irony in this scenario.

How utterly sad that the deceptively gentle giant, which only the day before had been an iconic member of Africa's 'Big Five', is now reduced to pieces of soon to be vulture, jackal and hyena food. More significantly, this was a white rhino, the progeny of fewer than 50 individuals, which were brought back from the brink of extinction a little more than 60 years ago!

Three weeks later, Rooi Pan claimed another two rhino: an adult cow and an 18-month-old juvenile male. Both had been shot, but the horns of the juvenile were not taken. Evidently he was shot for being a nuisance, for trying to protect his mother from the poachers who were hacking her horns off. Poachers subsequently arrested at Thornybush Game Reserve were irrefutably linked by forensics to this incident in Balule. They will be in jail for a long time.

As wardens, we are custodians of the environment in which our rhino live and die. And, at the moment, this is what occupies our daily thoughts and focus. However, we feel no less responsible for those lesser-known rare and endangered animals that occur in the area – for example pangolins, which are killed for the muti trade and are also under serious threat as a species. Although these rather shy nocturnal creatures are relatively small and rarely seen, their demise is no less important. In contrast, rhino are huge, long-lived animals; they take a lot of killing and are often gruesomely maimed. It is no wonder their deaths do not go unnoticed: we take each incident personally and question ourselves each time the brutal death of a rhino occurs on our watch. Sadly, pangolins are disappearing while the wider world is focused on trying to save the rhino: we know this, and inwardly cringe at the thought, but we simply cannot spread our resources to cover all bases.

I sometimes wake at night thinking I've been dreaming and that this was all just a nightmare ... but unfortunately the pain-free respite lasts all of two seconds. Wide-eyed now as the reality hits home, I check my cell phone for messages from the camera traps. Although the infra-red images are invariably grainy and ghostlike, these pictures instantly deliver a crystal-clear picture of intent; with experience, I have been able to interpret much more from them than we used to. Though the beeping makes my heart skip a beat every time, it is not always bad news. I am fortunate tonight: scrolling down reveals a beautiful civet on the one image and the back end of an elephant on another. Relieved, I put the phone down and go through to the kitchen. I know that's my sleep quota for the night; it's espresso time, one of life's small pleasures.

THE LEGEND OF MARY

A proactive initiative to collect DNA from as many of our rhino as possible was being planned, yet another of the numerous essential control measures that form part of a nationwide campaign to help stem the tide of the onslaught against our rhino. All the data is collated at a central point so that each rhino will have an incorruptible identity. From the outset, Balule Nature Reserve took this one step further, and all the rhino we darted were also microchipped and ear notched; in addition to this, selected individuals were fitted with GPS and telemetric tracking devices ... And of course, they were all given names rather than numbers.

As undignified and risky as these procedures are for the rhino, we needed to get this done as soon as was practical. The operation started with adult bulls, then the younger bulls, with the heifers as our prime candidates. This was done in order to minimise the risk of abandonment or injury for very young rhino. So, all the adult cows with juvenile calves were left until their youngsters were weaned. We continued whenever the opportunity and weather conditions permitted, and within a few months most of those rhino stipulated in the former categories had been done. It was now time to focus on the adult cows.

Out in the helicopter one morning, searching for rhino, we located a cow and yearling calf shortly after takeoff. Going in closer, I recognised this particular rhino as the cow we all knew as Mary. I was pleased we'd located her so early in the day, as already it was beginning to warm up.

Mary was already a mature cow when I started working on Olifants;

she was one of the original five white rhino that were brought onto the reserve by the developers over 25 years ago. Even when the fences were dropped between Klaserie and Balule, back in 2005, Mary remained 'loyal' to her reserve; in fact, she moved in closer to the core of Olifants and was one of a few white rhino cows who remained on the cusp between black and white rhino habitat, where the distinctive shape of her horn made her instantly recognisable, even at a distance. She was the oldest pioneer rhino on our reserve and had produced many healthy offspring. Besides being a doting and often overprotective mother, she was now also a grandmother and, needless to say, a well-known and valued member of our rhino community.

A number of the reserve's shareholders had gathered a safe distance away and watched as the proceedings unfolded. A palpable mixture of trepidation and excitement prevailed; they'd come to see their favourite rhino up close and, if conditions allowed, to even get to touch her. For most it was a first-time experience.

The pre-loaded dart was expertly placed from the helicopter by Dr Peter Rogers. Mary's calf stuck close to her side in support, as if sensing mom was about to topple over; she was not in front and leading as the calves usually do. It was clear the young rhino could sense something was not quite right with her mother long before we were able to notice any signs of the tranquilliser taking effect. After a few minutes Mary slowed to a walk, then she began to stagger, lifting her front legs in the high-stepping gait typical of an animal about to succumb to effects of M99.

'Where should I set her down?' Bennie asked over the ground-to-air radio.

'Preferably somewhere shady and soft – after all, she is an old lady,' I answered.

The helicopter pilot par excellence that he was, Bennie then manoeuvred Mary into the shade of a huge knobthorn tree; there he gently held her until the effect of the tranquilliser took control, her hind-quarters gave way and she slowly sank down into a sitting position. Using the helicopter again, he gently manoeuvred the very anxious calf away towards a shady copse of thick bush close by. That done, the technical team began moving in to start stabilising Mary. Not only is exceptional piloting skill necessary for this work, but empathy and a thorough knowledge of the animal you are working with are vital ... Bennie had heaps of both.

Once the necessary blood was drawn, DNA samples collected and microchips implanted, it was time to reverse the M99 and reunite the two rhino. We didn't notch Mary's ears for identification, as her huge straight horn was so distinctive that she was instantly recognisable in the field. The M5050 reversed the tranquilliser within seconds, and the old rhino was soon up on her feet and moving in the direction of her calf. Bennie and I lifted up into the air to search for more rhino and were able to confirm that Mary and her calf had joined up again.

Less than nine months later, true to Pete's prediction from analysing her blood sample, Mary gave birth to a new calf. Soon after that, her teenage daughter 'left home'. Moving to a quieter area of the reserve, Mary and her calf were often seen in the late afternoon sharing a wallow with one of our black rhino at a water hole known as Wild Dog Pan. Her 'new' bull calf, although nearly nine months old now, still took great pride in leading his mother around. He knew she would always be there following close behind: it is the way of white rhino cows to follow their calves from the very earliest age, whereas young black rhino walk behind their mothers.

At the time of the incident two of the reserve's members, Doug and Bo Acheson, were quietly sitting in their vehicle sipping sundowners while facing Wild Dog Pan. A perfect spot, where the Drakensberg in the distance usually makes for a dramatic background silhouette as the sun slips out of sight. But today cloud covered most of this vista when the sun set, and with much of the peripheral afterglow now obscured, darkness quickly descended and the prevailing wind began to increase in intensity. Not to intrude on those animals wanting to quench their thirst, Doug and Bo had positioned themselves a good 50 metres away from the water's edge where they sat quietly and waited.

It was time for the crepuscular creatures to venture out of their burrows, hollow tree trunks and rock crevices and begin their activities with a thirst-quenching drink of water. A pair of black-backed jackals and a white-tailed mongoose moved in and drank almost side by side. Then, as abruptly as they'd arrived, they slunk away, spooked by much larger animals not renowned for their eyesight inadvertently invading their space. Since it was much cooler and windier than usual that day, the two-ton rhino did not linger to wallow as usual; after 10 minutes, she slowly followed her young calf into the bush and disappeared into the night.

Minutes later the otherwise peaceful scene was abruptly shattered.

It had just got dark and Meagan and I were sitting down to our supper when I received the frantic radio call from Doug, to say they'd heard a single gunshot south-west of Wild Dog Pan. I responded, telling him I was on my way. A minute later, he called again to say he'd then heard some crashing of tree branches, followed by two more shots. This was too much detail; it was too ghastly for Doug to be describing anything else. My God! I thought, How many people were actually listening as a rhino was being shot to death by poachers?

Raising the alarm at the Rhino Pens Protrack base camp, I then arranged to meet the unit's team leader at Wild Dog Pan. I loaded my rifle and grab-bag, plus an extra torch, and set off. Although only 30 minutes had elapsed since the radio call, by the time I got to the scene there was no one there. Doug and Bo had decided that flight was better than fight, in this case wisely, so they started their vehicle and left the area soon after hearing the last two shots.

Unbeknown to us at the time, but clearly revealed in detail the following morning when our trackers were able to backtrack the spoor, the whole ghastly story unfolded. It was clear that the hornless, bloody carcass was that of Mary, the founder mother of so many of our white rhino; it was also apparent she had been specifically targeted for her unusual horn: this was no chance encounter by opportunistic poachers. At the shots, her nine-month-old calf ran ahead, in all probability squealing in terror hoping his mother would follow, unaware that she'd been shot and now lay dying in a pool of blood while her iconic horn was callously hacked off. The little calf kept on running, hoping his mother would catch up soon. But with the wind blowing hard, he couldn't hear what was happening behind him, so instinctively he continued to run. He ran for nearly a kilometre then stopped and waited ...

Still dripping with blood, the horns were dumped into the poachers' backpacks to start their journey from Olifants to the Far East. With a head start of 30 minutes, the poachers ran into the night they owned. They must have heard my vehicle approaching.

Climbing out of my vehicle at Wild Dog Pan, I stood there looking into the bush and listening. Being overcast, there was not even starlight to work with, and the wind was still blowing, so what little I might have been able to glean would be drowned out or obscured. I searched with what little I could see, while my eyes adjusted to the dark, hoping to get any peripheral clues. And as hard as I concentrated to make out a shape or movement, a speck of light, anything at all, the night's inky blackness would give up nothing. Standing there peering into a wall of seemingly impenetrable bush, it felt as if a huge gate had been slammed shut in my face.

Somewhere in the quiet darkness that enveloped me lay the bloody carcass of a huge animal, its screams now silenced, while I stood screaming inside. I knew what had just happened and in my mind's eye could clearly see the killers scurrying away in the dark. But at the same time I felt completely and utterly helpless, like a blind man whose cane has been ripped out of his hands at a busy train station. Protrack's team leader arrived and I briefed him and all his field rangers on the situation and suggested stopper groups be set up in the south. But our standard operating procedure meant this was the team leader's call from now on, so I left the strategy up to him and his men.

Searching the area with a spotlight was the best we could do under the circumstances. My mind was racing, hoping for a reflection of light off a horn, an axe blade, a silver-worn rifle barrel, or even the brass of a spent cartridge case carelessly dropped – anything at all. But this was not the movies, where the good guys get a break; this was reality; this was where evil prevails.

I left the area to go home at around 10 pm, while the rangers continued with an all-night vehicle patrol. We hoped that maintaining a presence would disrupt the poachers, causing them to flee and keep running, hopefully looking over their shoulders, into the ambushes set up on the railroad near our southern cutline. But we knew that they had 360 degrees, like a roulette wheel, from which to choose an exit route. We did not even have a 50–50 chance at black or red, odds or evens; all we could do was place a single bet on one of the numbers and lie in wait as the wheel was spun. At this point we still had no idea if there was a carcass, or where it lay.

Restless and unable to sleep, I got up at 2.30 am and prepared to head out to the area for another look. I had just brewed some coffee when Protrack's team leader called me to say his rangers had located the spoor of three suspects walking on the railroad heading south. This meant the poachers were hours ahead of us – and still we had not located a carcass!

Despite searching the area around Wild Dog Pan again, using a hand-held spotlight, nothing could be located. At first light I took Olifants' field rangers off bridge duty and brought them to the area where, from Doug's description, the incident was most likely to have occurred. The men spread out, searching for any evidence. A short while later one of them called to say they had located a carcass. Approaching closer, but not so close as to compromise the crime scene, I saw the perfect ears and knew without any doubt that it was Mary. My heart sank even lower, as I knew she had a small suckling calf – and despite a thorough search by our field rangers, the little rhino was nowhere to be found.

Finding and saving the calf now took priority, so I agreed to call in a helicopter and a vet. The local rhino orphanage and rehabilitation centre run by Rhino Revolution was contacted and warned to be prepared for the calf's arrival should we manage to locate it. The helicopter duly arrived and, within 30 minutes of flying, the little rhino was located, wandering alone about 800 metres from where his mother had been killed. He was then immobilised and bundled onto the back of my Land Cruiser. We drove out along the railroad to meet the specialised transport trailer that would complete his journey to Hoedspruit.

How poignant the irony of this scenario, I thought, as we drove along the same road the poachers had used only hours before to escape. With Mary's bloody horns safely in their backpacks, the only thing on their minds would be reward. The arrogant bastards had left clear shoe prints in the sandy surface as if in defiant mockery. It was unavoidable that my vehicle, now carrying Mary's calf, would drive over and obliterate most of the tracks left by his mother's killers. Their footprints were being inadvertently fragmented into billions of dust particles. I glanced in the rear-view mirror and could see the sombre face of Balule's rhino monitor, Zala Hajdinjak, as she comforted the calf. Beyond them, billowing in the slipstream of my vehicle, was the last visible evidence of the killers.

Gathering every grain of dust again, and putting them together to form the footprints of those killers, perhaps best describes the futility of the situation. Utter helplessness and frustration suddenly overwhelmed me; this was the final straw. It was done, and I cried in grim surrender. Then, seeing the little shape lying in the back, I realised there was something positive we could still do: I sniffed hard and focused on the well-being of Mary's calf.

Happily, the calf arrived safely at Rhino Revolution's orphanage, which is dedicated to dealing with orphans of poaching. Incredibly the little rhino settled in quickly and, at the time of writing, appears to be in good health under the loving care of Jade Aldridge. However, being a male, his chances of being rehabilitated into a wild system once he matures are sadly quite slim. Then again, given the prevailing situation, would you want to send him back into a war zone to end up like his mother? Although officially dubbed Balu, to me and the Olifants shareholders Mary's calf will always be known as 'Zanie' after Leonie Hofstra and Zala Hajdinjak, arguably two of Balule's most dedicated rhino researchers. Leonie and Zala monitor these animals out in the field almost every day, under trying conditions, collecting valuable data from which they compile detailed rhino distribution maps to help our security efforts. Originally from the cloistered environment of the Netherlands and Eastern Europe respectively, these young women have been exposed to some of the worst of this war and are now, under the auspices of Transfrontier Africa, dedicated veterans of the cause.

Expert backtracking determined that the poachers entered from the south along the Klaserie/Balule boundary using the route along the four pylon power lines. They then moved directly into the vicinity of Wild Dog Pan where they waited until dark to kill Mary. Due to the windy conditions, the poachers were unaware of the vehicle parked near the Pan, only 300 metres away! Then, after cutting the horns off in just a few minutes (apparently experienced poachers can remove both horns in less than 12), they began making their way back to the railway-line road, where they missed the field rangers' stake-out post by a mere 400 metres!

Once on the wide, bush-verged road they headed south under the cover of darkness. One hundred metres before our entrance gate, they crossed the railway tracks, hugging the opposite fence line until they reached Hoedspruit.

It was clear that the poachers were disturbed when they heard my vehicle arriving, but they had already removed the horns by then and were heading out. In their haste to get away, they dropped valuable clues such as clothing items, tools and muti, which we located the following morning – dregs, sure, but if these poachers are apprehended any time in the future, for any other crime or routine investigation, DNA and fingerprint evidence alone will link them directly to Mary's killing.

Now came the hardest part of my job. I knew that what I was about to announce would cause grief to hundreds, possibly thousands, of people. But somebody had to do it, and there was no easy way to say it. That same day I sent out a bulletin to all my shareholders: 'Mary has been killed by poachers!' ... Then, in consolation, knowing they all knew she had a baby, I followed with, 'But, we have managed to save her calf ...'

The moment the 'send' button was pressed, a shock wave reverberated through the ether. I felt the blows as each recipient of that bulletin was punched in the stomach. It was as if a member of our family had just been killed at home, Mary's home, her nursing area and sanctuary. In relative terms, this was not only the epitome of wildlife conservation terror; it was Olifants River Game Reserve's conservation equivalent of 9/11.

We could not have been hit any more unexpectedly, or any harder. This rhino was killed after only 21 incident-free months on our reserve and right in the heart of our reserve. If this was an indication of the poachers' intentions from here on, they could not have opened their despicable game with a display of more arrogant brutality and callousness. Although Mary was estimated to be about 35 years old at the time of her death and in terms of a rhino's lifespan had lived an almost-full life, this didn't in any way mitigate the way she died.

Having made sure Mary's calf was in good hands I returned to help with the autopsy. The blazing sun soon had my head splitting with a migraine, but this was a pain I could manage. I got home that night and told Meagan that if it were not for the plight of our rhino I'd have been long gone. But while I am able to make a modicum of difference, I will continue for as long as I can to do whatever it takes.

Within a month, no visible trace of Mary's carcass could be found. The system that had given her life, and nurtured her young for 25 years, had reabsorbed the energy and soul of this much-loved rhino. In a fitting mark of respect to her spirit, nothing tangible was left as a reminder of the brutal horror that was her death. Instead, new shoots began to break through the soil where she last lay. Life-giving grasses, herbs and forbs now dominated the patch of earth that was so recently a trampled and bloody crime scene.

A couple of months after the incident, I was nearing the end of a routine patrol that happened to include the water hole close by, and though the wound of Mary's killing was still smarting I was learning to live with the pain. I accepted the reality that life and death in this process is inevitable, that I was inescapably a player on one side of this deadly game. I'd come to terms with the fact that although one or two balls would get past me to the back of the net, the goalmouth still needed to be defended. There were other rhino in the area that were just as vulnerable as Mary was, and I needed to be strong for them.

Sundown is to a rhino pursued by poachers what sunrise is to a convict facing the gallows. For us it's a time for sharpened senses and extra vigilance, and today was no different. In contrast to that dreadful night, it was quiet and the wind was still. Typical of the ambiance in the afterglow of a sun that had already set, dusk's ephemeral, soft light lingered long enough to set the mood for reflection at the end of this beautiful day. Seemingly in a hurry, shadows lengthened and silhouettes took prominence as it began to get darker but not before leaving enough light for me to see the familiar shapes of a white rhino and her calf making their way across the open plain.

Unhurried, the two rhino made their way towards a small river bed then crossed through and up onto the other side, a familiar sight at this time of day in the vicinity of wallows and water holes. And although the rear ends of a couple of rhino slowly disappearing into the afterglow don't exactly make for an Agfa moment, when the rhino stopped and the cow turned her head slightly my blood ran cold! Even at that distance there was no mistaking the silhouette of that unique horn: it was an iconic shape that will forever be etched in my mind. And although I do not believe in ghosts or reincarnation, I was looking at a rhino with a strikingly familiar straight horn ... Mary's horn! Knowing that light and shadows can and do play tricks on the human mind, particularly one clouded with emotion and melancholy, it was all I could do to keep from screaming out aloud as I reached for my binoculars ... did we make the wrong call; could I be looking at Mary?

Gathered light through the 50-millimetre objective lenses added half an hour onto the day, which allowed me to see what made the hair on my neck stand up and my heart thump against my ribs. I was shaking so much I needed to steady the 10x binoculars on the steering wheel. Then, as I adjusted the focus ring and the picture crisped into detail, the rhino turned broadside on, confirming what I'd suspected but thought impossible. There was no mistaking it: this was no mirage, no illusion; the image was crystal clear. This rhino had a long straight horn, and to the best of my knowledge there was only one cow on our reserve with that distinctive feature – and she was dead! Or so we had surmised. Naturally my immediate thought was that the rhino that had been poached at Wild Dog Pan may not have been Mary but indeed another old cow without ear notches, a 'new' mature cow that may have moved into the area. We'd all assumed it was Mary that had been killed; in fact, we were all so sure that nobody thought it necessary to run a scanner across her carcass to locate the two microchips that had been inserted in her withers and at the root of her tail when we collected her DNA all those months before.

Only when the rhino and her calf had moved up onto a clearing on the other side of the dry river bed was I able to move in closer and get a very grainy image on my cell phone, which I immediately beamed through to Neil Hulett, who used to see Mary almost every day. His blood also ran cold, as did Olifants' chairman Quentin Sussman's. We all thought we were seeing a ghost.

A mixture of speculation and excitement prevailed until a few days later when a strategically placed camera trap took pictures of the same two rhino at one of our monitored water holes. These pictures were clear daylight images revealing an adult rhino cow and calf. The cow had a horn that conformed to the unique shape and angle of Mary's, but, when enlarged, closer examination revealed this rhino was clearly a younger cow and with a slightly shorter, but in all other respects identical, horn to Mary's. This rhino could be none other than Mary's progeny; she was indeed her eldest daughter! So, in spite of all, the legend of Mary lives on in her legacy and her unique horn shape, which will be passed down the generations. If it is allowed to.

THE EFFECT OF RHINO
POACHING ON GAME RANGERS

Mary was a Rubicon moment for me. I would be lying if I said the focus on combating rhino poaching hasn't changed me. The fulfilment of a lifelong dream to live and work in the bush, the enjoyment and satisfaction of reaching each small conservation milestone, is lost in anguish with every faceless rhino carcass we discover. Every moment of joy I have had in the bush is sucked out and spat in the sand each time I attend an autopsy. Circling vultures, which used to signal excited anticipation of predators on a kill, now bring dry-mouthed fear. I jump at the sound of my cell phone ringing, and when my field rangers call in on the radio I assume the worst, until I hear their report that all is OK. When I phone Klaserie warden Colin Rowles for whatever reason, as with Quentin Sussman, I always preface the conversation with 'No shit' – just in case they feel the same anxiety when their phones ring and my name pops up on their screens.

Rhino poachers are not only killing thousands of rhino, they are catalytic in destroying the souls of people who have dedicated their lives to conservation. A career once motivated by passionate commitment and selfless devotion is now governed by circumstances beyond our control. Working as a game ranger in rhino country is no longer the most sought after, envied career of millions. Some of the best men and woman in the field of conservation have left their passion and life's work for less bloody pastures. Many have left Africa, taking their special skills with them, and who can blame them? At home, so much of the education, energy and commitment channelled into a career in wildlife management is now being set aside, while conservationists apply their minds and resources to the protection of two species of rhino. Practical nature conservation in the broader sense has made way for a focus on combating rhino poaching, which has necessitated a dramatic shift in our mind-set and our daily lives. There can be no question: we are their first line of defence. And unlike conventional comrades in arms, rhino have nothing but a piece of compact hair and poor eyesight to defend themselves against the determination, drugs and bullets of their enemy.

Many game rangers in southern Africa's Big Five reserves find themselves switching between running their reserves and moonlighting as man-hunters. Therein lies one of this conundrum's greatest challenges. To be an effective hunter of men you cannot do it part-time; you need to be focused, determined and, most importantly, that way inclined. Successful detectives, policemen and military strategists seem to be born with that bent, and most of them have trained as criminologists, whereas the majority of reserve managers and ecologists I know are not inherently man-hunters. Necessity has dictated that the majority of game rangers working in Big Five reserves have to make tough choices every day. Essentially, combating rhino poaching requires a military-style security approach that takes priority over ecological management. Ever resourceful and determined, poachers change tactics continually; in turn, our adaptive strategy becomes the focus. Needless to say, the vast majority of us have willingly adapted our lives to these changing circumstances in order to fight the good fight with whatever we can muster and consoled by the fact that rhino are, after all, an intrinsically important component of the ecosystem – not to mention needing all the help we can give them.

Offices once filled with interesting ecological paraphernalia, where enthusiastic ideas on innovative conservation strategy and management plans were pinned up, studied and discussed, have now become little more than pseudo war rooms. They're not unlike those found in underground bunkers during the world wars, where pretty young women in ugly uniforms pushed replica toys of war around on scaled-down renditions of battlefields. These days our 'war rooms' are a whole lot more sophisticated: shelves and bookcases filled with years of selfless research and meticulously gathered data, pertaining to the fauna and flora of our precious wilderness, now gather dust while we study detailed maps perforated with red-backed pins marking the GPS co-ordinates of all the known rhino carcasses. Far fewer are the green pins that indicate our field ranger pickets, and even fewer than these are the yellow pins showing where arrests were made or poachers shot. In among the plethora of pins, bold arrows vie for space, pointing to incursion and exit points used by poachers. But all this graphic efficiency really reveals is the possible emergence of trends – trends that may result in more effective strategic action plans being implemented. At the same time, it serves as a colourful reminder of how little we have learned about the enemy and how much we are losing. Although necessary, it is inescapably demoralising.

Artefacts and interesting bits and bobs collected from the veld over the years have been packed away. Conservation conversation pieces that used to festoon our office walls, and other more delicate or rare specimens that were neatly labelled in glass-covered cabinets, have had to make space for tactical, purpose-specific tools and gadgets, computer monitors, the latest two-way radios, infra-red camera traps, weapons and ammunition, as well as tracking and surveillance equipment. The burly men in sweat-stained fatigues discussing strategy with field rangers, giving them new patrol orders and replenishing their equipment for another day's fight, are now also managing technical kit costing more than the building itself, kit that clinically dominates the interior décor and surface space. Bullet-proof vests, too hot and heavy for practical use in the bush, are draped uselessly on the backs of chairs. Donated by well-meaning and concerned shareholders, most are worn once, and then discarded. Nevertheless, they remain in full view as reminders of the level of preparedness needed and the escalating threat from poachers, who have no regard for life and will stop at nothing to get what they want.

An ever-present reminder of how the poachers' ruthless persistence

pays off lies outside in the sun, on the baking sand: dozens of bleached
rhino skulls packed in neat rows for all to see. Clearly evident are the
characteristic chop marks from the poachers' brutal and hurried axe
blows in removing the horns – in some instances, while the poor beast
was still alive. Like a huge open-air evidence depot, each of the various
skulls bears identifiable signature cuts in the bone, like a handwriting
style that is unique to the axe man. Conclusive evidence gleaned from
this fact reveals that some of the horns were hacked off by the same
poacher, using the same axe. Like macabre prehistoric trophies in an
open-air catacomb, these skulls also serve as constant reminders of this
war's brutality – and as if that were not enough, some of those collected
more recently still exude the unmistakable stench of death.

These are just some of the sights and smells that have become integral to our new working environment ... and I, for one, am beginning
to hate what they stand for. I have learned what it is to hate. Mostly,
I have learned that my hatred is primarily born of fear, the fear of
what effect this will have on my psyche and what I may become. The
realisation of what an unguarded moment, a minuscule lapse in concentration, control or judgement, will mean for me and my family is
the stuff nightmares are made of. I am frightened of myself and what I
may do to a poacher I find busy hacking the horns off a rhino. My emotional self-control could be lost in a hate-filled spur-of-the-moment's
reflexive action.

Like all parents who have children studying at universities far from
home, our family's primary contact with each other is through cell
phones. So when my phone rings or tweets at some ungodly hour, my
thoughts should automatically be of my loved ones far away, that one of
them may be in need of something, right? ... Wrong! When my phone
rings, all my immediate thoughts are focused on the rhino poaching
scourge, and the scary part is that this psychological conditioning is
totally involuntary.

Besides the many phone calls I make and receive in a day, none are as important as when my field rangers call – usually twice. I wait for these telephonic situation reports with trepidation, but it doesn't matter where I am or what I'm doing at the time, I want to hear them. Occasionally when I am out of cell-signal range, the rangers will call in on the two-way radio. Although the messages are routinely benign, the expectation of what I have come to fear is enough to cause my stomach to turn every time my phone rings at dawn and dusk, or when I hear, '*Zutini, Zutini, ngena*' (Mario, Mario, come in) over the two-way radio. Most of the time, the single most beautiful word, and the one I most fervently anticipate, is *lungile* (all right). Then, as in 'Lion King'-speak, there's *hakuna matata* (no problems). But on those thankfully much rarer occasions when, minus the prefix, only the word *matata* is uttered, my heart is filled with dread, mingled with a sense of utter failure and frustration. I prepare myself for the worst; my mind instantly conjures the worst-case scenario, just in case we've lost a rhino or need to search for a carcass. Anything else, anything less, is sheer relief.

Wardens don't openly cry; they keep that display of emotion for when they are alone. The sense of failure is undoubtedly the overriding sentiment common to us all and, depending on the person, manifests in various ways, mostly as a profound sense of helplessness that develops into seething hatred and anger. More often than not, the display of emotion results in a knee-jerk reaction as we desperately try to find an outlet for our frustration, something to ease the pain. Like shouting 'Fuck!' when the hammer misses the nail and finds your thumb instead. We find ourselves looking for fault in our midst, according blame, somewhere to throw the hammer down with as much noise and force as possible. There is the analysis of the incursion, a report to compile and the autopsy to attend. However, despite these routine physical inconveniences, the lasting heartache lies in the breakdown of faith in our fellow man as we search for responsibility in those we used to trust.

Then of course there are the ever-present, patronising specialists in hindsight who live among us and reign supreme. You will know and recognise them instantly, these are the would-haves, could-haves and should-haves of the world … and they're a dime a dozen.

Worst of all, veiled conjecture begins to run rife. This is human nature and inevitably the responsibility climbs to the next tier, and the next, and so on ... until the 'buck stops'. As a result of increasing pressure, paranoia is manifest, the inescapable feeling that perhaps you are being held accountable to some degree or other begins to take its toll. Incidents of poaching, numbers of incursions relative to rhino lost, and other pertinent details have become some of the most guarded information among the various wardens. And this creeping insular perspective has become more noticeable with each incident. The sense of relief when a warden learns that the rhino carcass was found lying on his neighbour's side of the road is palpable. Some hide the feeling of relief better than others, but they are one on this. Even if the rhino was shot on your side and then ran over the boundary to die! You thank God this incident, this statistic, is not yours to report. Technically *you* didn't lose a rhino! Every warden I know feels this way, even though most won't admit to it.

However, it is the unenviable task of the head warden to compile a detailed report on every poaching incident on the reserve as it occurs. Contained in this report are the forensic results of the autopsy, the field rangers' report, the exact location of the carcass, as well as the identification of the particular rhino – or rhinos – and any other pertinent information regarding the poacher's entry and exit routes, et cetera. In short, it is a comprehensive account of events which is then distributed to all the regional wardens for their perusal. From there lips are sealed, the hardcopy is filed away and the bare essentials disseminated in newsletters and updates.

'Never judge your warden's efficacy in fighting this war by the numbers of rhino they lose.' This was the advice I gave to the chairman of a well-known private game reserve that was losing an embarrassing number of rhino at the time. He contacted me desperately searching for an answer, possibly even a hint as to a weakness within their ranks. Like most of those in positions of authority, who understand little of what we go through, he was looking for anyone 'real' to pin some of the responsibility on – anyone, it seemed, other than the phantom poachers themselves.

There is no 'silver bullet' or magic formula, and no conventional strategy to adopt. We constantly need to adapt to the ever-changing tactics employed by rhino poachers, as even the state-run Kruger National Park, which has some of the best tactical minds heading its anti-poaching operation, will tell you. Notwithstanding an arsenal comprising state-of-the-art technology and military expertise, SAPS's Special Forces assistance and, of course, their own highly trained and well-armed field rangers, they are still losing the most rhino in the country. However, to put this in context, we also need to understand a little about the ecology of white rhino. For example, at the time of writing, in one area of the Kruger and the adjacent Manyeleti Game Reserve more than 200 rhino have been poached on an area which, at most, could only ever comfortably carry around that number of rhino. The simple explanation is that this region comprises some of the best habitat for white rhino in the Lowveld: each time a rhino is killed by poachers, another simply moves in from the surrounding reserves to fill the vacuum. It happens on our reserve as well. Prime white rhino habitat is no longer viewed as an asset; rather it has become a liability. Consequently, there are regions in Balule where no poaching incidents have occurred, and not because of superior anti-poaching efforts but simply because their regions are insignificantly small or are not suitable habitat for white rhino. Poachers seldom waste time hunting where there's a low density of rhino, rather they focus on those areas with relatively high numbers. Even though anti-poaching efforts may be proportionately higher, their minds are focused on the kill.

The modern-day game ranger's most closely guarded secret is how many rhino have been lost to poachers in his or her particular reserve or region of responsibility. To illustrate the prevailing sensitivity and mind-set of those on whose area a particular incident took place, one needs to see how quickly there is a demand from the regional warden directly concerned to have the report corrected, particularly if the location of the carcass is a hair's breadth off actual co-ordinates, or if there is any hint of less-than-perfect efficacy regarding those field rangers in whose area the incident happened. Denial has become an involuntary response among some wardens. And, like the ostrich head-in-the-sand scenario, even when confronted with remnants of a stinking carcass, often the claim is that the wounded rhino was from another region and simply ended up dying on theirs. Some wardens I have spoken to wish there were no more rhino in their area of responsibility to worry about. Others have become cynical and look at the healthy, happy rhino as dead rhino walking, an imminent statistic to report on and another potential blot on their copybook.

And as if this depressing state of mind was not enough to face each day with, no amount of technical assistance will ever compensate for the lack of trust engendered, a perpetual vicious circle that can drive you nuts at times. When trust begins to break down, it can lead to an 'every man for himself' scenario. In defence of one's reputation and integrity, a natural response can be to become more insular. Unfortunately this leads to knowledgeable people becoming withdrawn and circumspect with information they fear may be twisted against them. This simply perpetuates conjecture, as men and woman previously beyond reproach, trusted as custodians of the reserve's wildlife, are now being suspected of being incompetent – or worse, complicit.

We all understand and need to accept that in such a high-stakes game no one is above suspicion and this speculation is only stifled when we are subjected to polygraph tests. Although the results invariably reveal nothing untoward, or in rare instances when 'some deception' is indicated, a sense of deep betrayal prevails; whatever the results, the damage is done. The bad taste this leaves in one's mouth will never be sweetened again. And indirectly, as a result of this spin-off of negativity and withdrawal, our defences are divided, we become less formidable opponents and rhino poaching claims another victim.

Considering the vast amounts of quick cash associated with illegally trading rhino horn, even the straightest men can be bent; even when it comes to indirect complicity, the tentacles of doubt can reach into and probe every crevice, and understandably so.

I experienced this undercurrent of mistrust first-hand when I was suspected to have known that a certain building contractor on the reserve was related to a high-profile rhino poacher, and to have withheld this knowledge with questionable intent. This spurious speculation emanated from a prominent shareholder of a neighbouring reserve at the time, who instead of confronting me with the allegation, bandied it about carelessly and disseminated it to all but myself over the course of nearly two weeks. Had I been aware of this earlier, we could have acted on this information and possibly put some of the intelligence he'd gathered to some good anti-poaching use. This was a lack of judgement of the worst kind and which was later proved to be completely without foundation. But why did he hold onto the information about my apparent knowledge or suspected complicity for so long? ... Scary? You bet!

My integrity was once again brought into question when I was suspected of removing the horns of a dead rhino and not informing the landowner on whose property we had located the carcass. It was a white rhino bull that had been shot and wounded in the dark. Unable to follow the spoor, the poachers had simply left it to die. The horns in question were, in fact, locked away in police custody as evidence in the criminal case subsequently opened, and which is still under investigation as I write. Fortunately, all the associated documentation, microchip numbers and DNA data on record were scanned and emailed to him for his red-faced perusal and subsequent trite acknowledgement of the fact. But the breakdown in trust was palpable.

Then, as if there wasn't enough against you in your own backyard, so to speak, the law of our land is also out to nab you. If not strictly applied, it works against the 'good guys' to constitutionally protect the rights of criminals. So in effect we go to 'war' every day anyway, knowing we might as well be carrying wooden guns and plastic bullets. And we are judged on our efforts to combat the scourge with hopelessly inadequate support. This is a recipe for frustration and bad judgement calls, the consequences of which could be life changing, to say the least. This was reiterated by the country's best lawyer in these matters, Coert

Jordaan, when on two separate occasions he held workshops where he addressed all the wardens and field rangers in the APNR with the same message: 'One cannot simply take out your frustration by shooting and killing poachers ... unless of course your life is in immediate and imminent danger.' He went on to say that when the chips are down and you have killed a poacher, in the eyes of the law at that moment you have killed a fellow human being. The difference between hero and zero is an unstoppable bullet leaving your weapon and finding the right or wrong human target. As a result you will be challenged by irate police officials and prosecutors baying for your imprisonment as they hover over the dead poacher with the same concern they'd give the innocent victim of a hit-and-run!

According to a senior SANParks security official, relentless statistics from intelligence gathering reveal that at any one time there are at least 30 groups of poachers hunting in the Kruger Park. However, on the rare, hard-won occasion that an arrest is made and the suspects handed over to the SAPS for due processing, all the millions spent to get to that point of success are nullified. The morale of the anti-poaching units is dealt a further blow as they find themselves hamstrung by the apathy and inefficiency that is the judicial system with respect to processing arrested rhino poachers. To illustrate this point, at the time of writing there are well over 200 cases pending in the Kruger, of which only 13 have proceeded to prosecution!

SAPS personnel arrive on the scene, as they have to by law, often without the basics such as a pen and paper to take statements, water or evidence bags! But they never leave their handcuffs or cell phones at home ... ever. In one instance I witnessed as officials from the LEDET visited the scene of a poached rhino. They showed absolutely no interest in the carcass, apart from the required collection of a piece of the rhino's toenail for DNA. After that, they wandered around collecting vulture feathers, which I suspected would be sold to a sangoma. I didn't ask for confirmation – they would have given me a bullshit story anyway – and so I spared myself any further anger.

To illustrate the level of frustration and tolerance we need to bear for the law, which still protects the rights of rhino poachers, the following brief anecdote is a classic case in point. It involves the well-known son of a game ranger in the Kruger National Park, a man who had grown up with the locals, learning their culture and speaking the Tsonga language fluently. Most importantly, when he followed in his father's footsteps and became a game ranger, he was one of only a few white men who could call themselves master trackers. Having learned this tracking skill since childhood, and having been taught by the best Shangaan master trackers in the park, he was soon able to put these skills to effective use in combating rhino poaching there.

As it happened, a rhino was poached close to the park's western boundary with the local community. And it appeared from the poacher's tracks at the scene that they came from, and were heading back to, a village about 10 kilometres distant. The spoor was immediately followed by the game ranger and his team of field rangers. Despite every attempt by the poachers to conceal their tracks, within a matter of hours they'd been tracked to a dwelling by this man and his team. Upon investigation, a search of the small hut revealed the still-wet rhino horns, which were recovered and the suspects duly arrested.

In court the accused claimed the horns had been placed in their dwelling by the poachers, whom they did not know, adding that they were told to look after the horns until the poachers returned. The accused insisted they had nothing to do with actually killing the rhino. With this, the defence turned to the game ranger and asked how he could be so sure these were the men who had poached the rhino.

'I was able to track their specific spoor from the carcass in the Kruger Park to the door of that particular house in the village,' was the ranger's confident reply.

This must have immediately raised an eyebrow with the defence. Here was a white man professing to be an expert at what is predominantly the domain of local master trackers. Black men can't swim and white men can't track … Right? But as spurious as this perception is, I suspect it was enough to help this clever defence attorney drop a bombshell …

'Do you have any certification to show that you are qualified as a tracker?'

'No, I don't,' replied the game ranger.

The rhino poaching charge was dropped. And although the suspects walked free of this serious charge, they were nabbed on the much lesser possession charge. For this dedicated, highly skilled game ranger and his team it was a demoralisingly small consolation prize for such a huge bust.

Certified tracking courses are now being conducted in the Kruger (for what they're worth). This has become a formality, a prerequisite for trackers to be able to offer evidence in court – even though, as is true of gifted artists, master trackers are born with this ability, which is then honed with experience. Schooling and pretty certificates do not a tracker make. But in compliance, this is yet another hoop the good guys need to jump through in order to secure the conviction of suspects. Which makes me wonder: what next? Will trailing dogs be required to pass an olfactory assessment examination as well?!

There is an increasing trend to pay handsomely for reliable, verifiable information and then to focus resources accordingly to help achieve the objective. This is money well spent. For every rhino poacher arrested or killed in the field by routine patrols using risky military-type responses and confrontation, dozens more arrests are made miles away from the killing fields, using informants and intelligence gathered through payment. However, like the rhino that simply move in and fill the vacuum in Manyeleti, so too do aspirant poachers stand in line to 'have a go' at the spot where they know they stand a good chance of killing a rhino.

By and large, poachers are not easily deterred by hardship. Integrating with the environment, they use natural phenomena to their advantage; whether a pitch dark night or a full-moon night, both scenarios are exploited. They will walk through areas where large populations of elephant, buffalo and lions occur and wade through rivers infested with crocodiles with apparent impunity. Of all the incursions we have recorded, there are only three confirmed instances I am aware of where rhino poachers are known to have been killed by wild animals.

One incident occurred on a game farm in the Gravelotte area, not far from Mica, where poachers were killed and eaten by a pride of lions. And in an example of the sweetest poetic justice imaginable, a white rhino is known to have killed a poacher in the Kruger National Park. Unfortunately, regarding the third event, I have only limited anecdotal information of the incident, which occurred on a neighbouring private game reserve. However, I will relate what was told to me by the security chief in charge of anti-poaching for this particular reserve (whose word, by the way, I trust implicitly).

One morning on a routine patrol he came across a rusted rifle lying in the road. It appeared to have been kicked into the road by an elephant; otherwise it might never have been seen. Closer examination revealed it was a .375 Magnum with thread tapped on the barrel to accommodate a silencer which was not recovered. It was undoubtedly a weapon that once belonged to a poacher. Given the rusted condition of the rifle, it was thought to have been lying in the bush for at least two months. Backtracking and a subsequent thorough search of the area recovered the remnants of a backpack, a shredded jacket, a chewed-up running shoe, bits of clothing and an axe. Essentially this is the kind of paraphernalia usually associated with rhino poachers. What was of interest was that the backpack and bits of clothing appeared to have been torn to pieces by predators. On the inside of the shoe and on the backpack evidence of what appeared to be dried blood was found. This could have been from the freshly hacked horn of a poached rhino. However, the relatively clean axe quickly dispelled this theory. Knowing that the last thing a poacher would ever leave behind was his rifle, and given the spread of the clothing, popular conjecture was that these poachers were attacked and killed by elephant, then over time their bodies dragged off by various predators and scavengers and eaten.

Discouragingly, the ratio is one poacher killed by a wild animal per thousand rhino poached! ... Give or take a few.

Recently, however, five elephant poachers were killed and eaten by a pride of 22 lions in Zimbabwe. Three poachers were badly mauled and a few escaped injury. This occurred in the region where Cecil the lion was shot by the US dentist ... are the tables turning?

Laying an ambush that culminates in a confrontation with poachers is a rare event. So rare, in fact, that in the last four years on Olifants River Game Reserve our outsourced anti-poaching field rangers have only managed to assist in one successful arrest. Almost all the successful arrests we have made have been as a result of efforts by Olifants' own field rangers. Their years of experience and dedication have also thwarted hundreds of incursion attempts. Nevertheless, it remains a most demoralising, frustrating affair where, more often than not, there's little or nothing to show for all the effort and sacrifices made in extremely difficult and dangerous conditions. Anti-poaching rangers are inhibited by the law, which in turn fosters hesitation, and these split seconds spent in indecision are all a poacher needs to escape.

By focusing on one suspect, we are sometimes able to make an arrest, knowing the other killers will scatter into the night and escape. These are 'let go' most reluctantly because we know they will regroup and return, and that they will better equipped, more alert and more educated in our ways on their next nocturnal foray. We also know there are hundreds of wannabe poachers waiting for their chance at the Klondike; so an 'eye for an eye and a tooth for a tooth' approach will simply create a vacuum and make space for the next gang.

Security organisations all have shortcomings, but we are further knee-haltered from the get-go against rhino poachers, who enjoy full protection under the constitution. In a conventional war a soldier is allowed to kill the enemy if he is damaging state property or attempting to damage state property, whether the enemy is armed or not. So even though 'state-owned' rhino occur in the entire Greater Kruger Park area, including Balule, South Africa still falls short of an official declaration of war on rhino poachers. Had this been so, the killers of our rhino, who are mostly foreign nationals, would have been shot and not simply shot at. At the moment the few who get arrested are soon released on bail; most skip the country never to be seen again … or, as has been found to occur, they equip themselves with other weapons and return to poach again, sometimes within a week of being released on bail!

Maybe we need leaders like the president of Botswana, Ian Khama, whose approach when dealing with poachers is so effective that there is virtually no poaching in his country. As far as I know, it is the only country in Africa that can proudly boast this achievement. It appears Kenya has been pushed to the point where it too has begun to adopt a hardline take-no-prisoners approach to rhino poachers; lately, ivory poachers have been added to the list. Their northern race of white rhino is down to a few hundred individuals, and this important subspecies has little time left on the planet.

However, it is abundantly clear that our government hasn't allocated the resources needed, nor does it demonstrate the political will to fight this war with the dedicated resources and support required. Until our field rangers are protected by legislation that backs a 'shoot-to-kill' policy, the poachers' rights under the law will prevail, giving them the upper hand – where they need to shoot first for us to respond. I know what Wyatt Earp would have said if told to wait for the baddies to shoot before he drew his gun! But this is not the Wild West: mechanisms to effectively combat rhino poaching are well within our country's capability and, most importantly, enshrined in the constitution. No longer should wildlife conservation, particularly that of rhino, be relegated to stand in the queue of political priority; rather, patriotism, pride and priority of the highest order must prevail. Though South Africa still manages some of the largest populations of wild rhino left in the world, though their conservation started in this country, tragically it seems it will all end here too, unless drastic action is taken now. When the last one is killed, no power on earth will be able to replace them.

COMBATING RHINO POACHING:
THE FUTURE

The festive season was upon us once again and the reserve began to fill with visitors young and old. Pulling off to one side of the narrow road as a vehicle approached, I recognised the driver as one of our long-standing shareholders; he stopped alongside to chat. Of course there were the usual topics of common interest to discuss, then he changed the subject, saying he'd seen many 'new people' driving on the reserve, including a number of young faces he did not recognise. Had there been an influx of new shareholders? I thought about this for a minute, reflecting on how our staff's visiting children have grown, mine included. I explained that these new faces were most likely those of the children who had grown with the reserve, a reserve that many of their parents helped establish more than 25 years ago, and that what he was seeing was simply the baton being passed from one generation to the next ... along with the game-viewing vehicle's keys, of course.

But it doesn't end there.

I remain convinced that the long-term future of Africa's wildlife and wilderness areas will depend on a broader buy-in from its people. Education will prove to be the most powerful measure we can employ. From the earliest age we need to instil a sense of pride and nurture a culture of responsibility towards nature – and in every school the curriculum must include environmental education as an entrenched subject, like mathematics, without which you will not be considered properly educated. Having said all that, my question is: do our rhino, and other threatened species being targeted by muti and bushmeat poachers, have enough time?

One morning, while standing in the parking area near my office, I watched as four teenage children made their way down from the main staff village, heading to the smaller accommodation block behind the administration complex. Passing the woodpile between the two, they slowed down and stopped. They'd heard a vehicle approaching and waited for it to pass before crossing the road. Smiling broadly, they waved at the people in the game viewer that rolled past them. The occupants were shareholders heading out on an early-morning game drive, who cheerfully waved back in greeting as their vehicle crested the steep hill and disappeared in a faint cloud of dust. Direction: Palm Loop; lion country – where else would anyone on a game drive be headed? Their heads turned in the direction of the vehicle, which was now out of sight, the kids were still waving. I couldn't help wondering what they were thinking ... Which got me thinking.

On a hunch, I summoned our black rhino monitor, Sinhle Mathebula, to my office. Sinhle was a natural communicator, and I needed an important message to be conveyed. So I asked him if he'd be interested in helping with educating young children on the basics of nature conservation, expanding on this to share his knowledge of rhino conservation in more detail. Sinhle had never hidden his wish to branch out from monitoring and become a field guide one day: he jumped at the idea of guiding a responsive audience in a game drive scenario. So I asked him to make a list of all the children of school-going age who were visiting their parents in our staff village and to divide them into groups of seven. As it turned out, there were five groups of youngsters between the ages of six and sixteen!

Over the next few days, instead of taking a siesta after his monitoring duties, Sinhle started up an old but reliable Land Rover, donated years ago by one of the reserve's shareholders, and took each group on a game drive. Conveyed in their native Tsonga, the impact of the environmental education absorbed by the wide-eyed children was clearly evident. Needless to say, the enthusiastic kids came away having learned something meaningful about the conservation of their environment, particularly this reserve, the one their parents worked in. And I'm sure they got more out of it, knowing this was also part of their environment and their heritage. Whatever rubbed off, it would have been so much more than they would have learned traipsing aimlessly between the two staff villages over the December holidays ... And then, of course, there's next year and the years after that.

Although Sinhle did an excellent job, sadly he is no longer with us. However, all is not lost, as in the following chapter I intend to talk about another long-term anti-poaching and environmental education programme. It is unique in that it comprises the establishment and deployment of the first team of women field rangers, known as the Black Mambas. Besides being effective eyes and ears, these 'bobbies on the beat' are a constant presence – and poachers don't like people watching over their shoulders. More importantly, these women are instilling a culture of pride in conservation, which rubs off on the children in their village each time they go home ... where they deliver the all-important message that wild animals, particularly rhino, are not the 'pets' of the wealthy elite, but in fact belong to, and are the responsibility of, everyone.

How often it is the simplest solution to an immediate problem that stares us all in the face, and yet owing to its simplicity makes us suspiciously find reasons to complicate the issue. (Never ask a committee to design a horse from scratch: you will end up with something resembling a giraffe!) Everyone concerned about the escalating killing of rhino has a proposal, an idea, an angle or a solution to try. It is entirely possible that among a myriad of e-mails, and endless personal conversations with fellow conservationists or shareholders, I have been approached with a concept that may just lead somewhere positive.

Concerned people inundate me with streams of suggestions, innovative ideas (as well as contact numbers and names), most of which deal with how to apprehend the poachers – that is, reactive measures. I have tested drones in the night sky with thermal-imaging cameras and infra-red cameras, sat up night after night with night vision until everyone appeared green to me for days. I have been introduced to the most sophisticated anti-poaching equipment and technology available, most of which requires monitoring and focus. However, no proactive measure anyone has employed to date has proved to be as effective as dehorning. Though this is not a long-term solution, and is fraught with controversy, it would nevertheless buy some desperately needed time for these animals.

The APNR and SANParks are vehemently against dehorning. To the purist, this drastic measure degrades the rhino's stature, which is totally understandable. Nobody wants to see a wild rhino with its most iconic feature amputated. But then again, rather a live rhino with that scenario, which is temporary, than a putrefied, hornless carcass, which is a permanent state of affairs. The average rhino's horn grows back completely in three to four years; therefore multiple amputations may be required in the average lifetime of a rhino. Hopefully this would only need to be done until we are able to stop the poaching, at best, or exercise a modicum of control, at worst ... but importantly, in the meantime, many of the dehorned rhino that undoubtedly would have been killed, will have been passed up and left to live.

Although poachers are paid per kilogram for rhino horn, an intact horn is worth much more than ground-up horn or pieces of the same weight. Ground rhino horn or small pieces of horn very closely resemble the keratin component parts of many common animals like water buffalo or African buffalo. So while they have a choice, poachers will target large-horned, healthy rhino and will invariably pass up a dehorned rhino.

Since canine units have been successfully deployed to track poachers during the day, incursions into our region are now predominantly carried out in the dark. Though scent trails are easier to follow at night, the dogs are not. Trying to keep up with dogs on a scent trail at running speed can result in serious injuries as thorns rip at flesh and clothing, and unseen branches can knock the handler unconscious! Instead, we have strategically deployed pickets and river patrols around the clock, so poachers now have an even smaller window of opportunity to enter the reserve, kill a rhino and get away in the dark. They now have to get in at night, hunt a rhino in the dark, shoot them in the dark and escape before light. Their usual modus operandi is to cross the river at about 10 pm, hunt until 4 am and then exit, with or without success. Of all the recent incidents, only two have occurred on full-moon nights: importantly, however, all the rhino were shot in relatively thick bush.

From all the evidence we glean post mortem, it appears the poachers are shooting the rhino at close range, aiming for the heart–lung area. In other words, they are mostly shooting at shapes and silhouettes, so there is every chance its horns will be obscured or partially obscured from the shooter. It is in these situations that a dehorned rhino may very well be killed in error and its stump of horn taken as consolation for the effort. Naturally this will lead some people to believe they have specifically targeted the dehorned rhino. The last thing any poacher wants to do is advertise his position. Shooting a dehorned rhino just so that they don't make the mistake again is codswallop; it is simply too much of a risk they do not want to take. Some of the rhino carcasses we found had their spines cut through or their hamstrings severed to prevent the animal from getting up for whatever reason. A second shot would be quicker and more efficient, but the poachers would rather hack and sever, because it's quieter.

Further support of the argument for dehorning is that a neighbouring reserve, without any field rangers in its employ, has not lost a single dehorned rhino in eight years! In fact, the reserve is a popular route used by poachers to access Balule's southern regions from the R40 road. And another reserve situated a stone's throw from Hoedspruit that comprises relatively dense bush habitat, thereby providing ideal poaching conditions, has only lost two dehorned rhino in five years.

The ecological implications of dehorning – particularly its effect on social interaction – are not fully understood at this stage. Some believe that cows need their horns to defend their young against predators or fend off the occasional over-amorous bull, and that bulls need theirs to hold their territory against belligerent competitors, which is where

I lean. All of these scenarios are seen to be easier if you have a sharp horn. But if there were no horns in play, dominance and defence would still be possible, in my view.

Two tons of rhino behind even a blunt stump at 30 kilometres per hour will send anything backwards or indeed skywards. Penetrating wounds are not always necessary to show who is more powerful or dominant. A lucky thrust from an inferior bull, or indeed a cow, could – and does – kill even the most powerful rhino bull. It would be safe to say a rhino's horn is used more as a fighting tool than anything else, so it goes without saying that if all rhino were dehorned they would not need these weapons at all. Yet they would still be able to assert dominance by using their stumps, like boxers in a ring use gloved fists to determine a winner. In more than 35 years in conservation, I have never seen a rhino defend itself or its young against predators by using its horn, nor have I found evidence of a single predator gored by a rhino. However, I have seen white rhino using their horns to fight each other, causing serious penetrating wounds, and at times they fight to the death.

Though I have never seen a rhino actually kill or pierce a predator, I know of five instances where calves have been taken by lions or hyenas. All of these incidents occurred at night and despite their mothers' gallant attempts the calves were taken. Furthermore, if indeed it happens that the occasional dehorned rhino is killed by another with horn, the overall numbers lost will nevertheless be significantly lower than if we left the rhino to the mercy of poachers – of this I have no doubt.

However, dehorning should prevail only until the day sanity triumphs and those people using rhino horn find out it is as effective as eating toenail clippings! At which juncture, poaching will cease and we can allow the surviving rhino to simply grow back their iconic horns and go about their business as nature intended.

… And now for something completely different.

Late one Friday afternoon I was parked on the mowed verge of the

Timbavati/Eastgate airport turn-off on the R40. This was our rendez-vous point for the school lift club from White River to Hoedspruit. It had been a particularly warm day, and being a few minutes early I stood outside the vehicle, leaning against the fender, taking in the distant mountains and bush sounds as the day began winding down.

About 50 metres away from me, a flock of helmeted guinea fowl were running up and down Kapama Game Reserve's fence line trying to get in from the wide grass border between the road and the reserve. There was no apparent panic among the birds, who probably knew exactly where they wanted to roost that night, but somehow it seemed that this afternoon they were finding it difficult to get there. Their unsuccessful efforts went on for at least 10 minutes, until one of them moved away from the fence. Standing back a couple of metres from the rest of its flock, it seemed to make a quick, jerky-necked calculation; then, as if spooked by a gun dog, it launched itself into the air and sailed over the fence effortlessly. Moments later, the rest of the guinea fowl followed suit, although with somewhat less graceful flapping and screeching, and all managed to get over the fence quite easily. It had taken that one bird's slightly different approach to show the others another simple way to tackle the obstacle. Otherwise who knows how long they would have run up and down poking their heads through the bottom strands like chickens in a run ...

Sometimes a solution only needs the action of someone with a radical approach, someone who is able to step back and offer a basic resolution to a complex problem, to guide us through what often seems an insurmountable obstacle, someone whose thoughts are focused and crisp. Usually it's the application of a mind that is able to focus, unclut-tered and free of clouding pessimism, that bears the most fruit. To put it in a nutshell, it's unlike the desperate mind-set that characterises many of our strategic thoughts, which are unavoidably influenced and shaped by the graphic detail of what we face in the killing fields every day, leaving little room for lateral thought. Much as I suspect that it wasn't the foot soldiers trying to survive from one minute to the next in the mud-filled trenches of Western Europe who discovered radar and cracked the Nazi codes, rather it was those whose minds – though equally focused on survival and winning – were able to approach the problem from clean, quiet studies or laboratories.

At this time, heated controversy surrounding the overturning or upholding of the CITES ban on trade in rhino horn was on every reserve's agenda. This was a particularly hot potato, so we needed to be very discreet – even when expressing an opinion. Within the APNR itself, reserves sit on both sides of the divide. Those against trade believe that legalising the trade will simply open the market for illegal horns – as was the case with elephant ivory, where poaching is on the increase as a result. Understandably, the fear is that more rhino will be killed owing to the growing middle-class market in the East and the escalating demand fuelled by affordable horn. The fear is well founded but for one exception: rhino horn differs from ivory in that rhino horn can be produced.

Rhino horn is renewable and harvestable, without harming the animal. Therefore it can be seen by some as a sustainably tradable commodity, like sheep's wool, where, although a little discomfort is experienced now and then by the animal, there is no need to kill them to keep supplying the market. A large white rhino's anterior horn can grow as much as a kilogram per year. In other words, a rhino can produce at least 35 kilograms of horn in its lifetime and still die a natural death from old age at around 40 years. In terms of the money earned at today's market value, theoretically a rhino could earn over R6 million in its lifetime. No other animal on earth is capable of producing that return sustainably.

On the other hand, elephant tusks grow at a much slower rate, and even if it were feasible to harvest some of their ivory, this would create a problem, particularly in the drier regions where, besides the social dominance the tusks assist with, elephant also use their tusks as tools to help them access certain foods.

The other side of this logic, and another controversial hot potato, is to promote the flooding of the market with 'farmed rhino horn', theoretically to control supply and demand and to control the price as is done with the lucrative international diamond market. And yet one idea goes even further than that, an innovation that intends to flood the market with rhino horn that is mass-produced, biotechnically, in laboratories! Crucially, there can be no risk of a 'blood diamonds'-type scenario in the following ground-breaking proposal, which presents a viable alternative to supplying rhino horn to the market, whether the trade ban is lifted or not.

I am always open to investigating any innovative ideas, however technically complex and 'out there' they may seem, so when Meagan and I were given a brief background on a company looking into the possibility of 3D-printing technology being used to help solve the demand and supply issue of rhino horn, we jumped at the opportunity to learn more. We agreed to host Matthew Markus, the CEO of an innovative company called Pembient, and his PR person, Juliette Marquis, for three days on the reserve. This was to give them a basic insight into the situation and to actually show them a few 'dead rhino walking' – the rhino they would be trying so hard to conserve with their ground-breaking proposal. Besides one or two directors of Olifants and close friends, no one knew what was being proposed and what we'd be doing, when, why and with whom.

In a nutshell, Pembient is the creation of Matthew Markus and George Bonaci, who are from Seattle in the USA. Matthew holds a BSc in Mathematics and Computer Science and a Master's in Engineering Management as well as in Genetic Epidemiology. George has a BSc in Biochemistry. Essentially they believe that rhino horn's obscenely high price incentivises poaching and corruption, which they aim to undermine by using biotechnology to fabricate rhino horn and to make it available at a fraction of the cost. In response to the demand for rhino horn in the East, where it has been used for centuries, and in all likelihood will continue to be used, the primary aim is to substitute the illegal trade currently running at around US $20 billion.

Pembient are currently juggling with the irony of combining state-of-the-art technology and innovation with an eye on supplying the lucrative Eastern market with artificial rhino horn – made up of calcium and melanin embedded in a keratin matrix – and in so doing, to create a business and help save our precious rhino at the same time. Using 3D-printing technology they are able to 'grow' rhino horn, to the point where they are mass-producing artificial horn that is microscopically and molecularly indistinguishable from the real thing.

Ultimately Pembient will move towards engineering completely animal-free rhino horn, a product that will contain rhino-specific keratins produced by microorganisms. Once the keratins are purified and dried, they can be combined with rhino DNA and other biomolecules to form an ink for a novel 3D-printing process. *Non posso!* Impossible! That's exactly what the world exclaimed to Leonardo da Vinci when he sketched the rudimentary design of a concept helicopter!

After a number of swapped e-mails, Matthew and Juliette hired a 4x4 and drove in from Johannesburg. They found us easily enough. Matthew was almost as I had imagined: a lanky American, extremely intelligent and, needless to say, a computer fundi with far more brains than brawn. Juliette, of Ukrainian descent, painted a breathtakingly gorgeous picture as she got out of the vehicle to greet us. It was as if she had stepped off the cover of *Vogue* magazine, not out of a dusty 4x4. But this was an exterior that, we were soon to find, hid a focused and professional efficiency. Both were beautiful people with a beautiful idea, we thought.

Early the following morning the three of us were on the airstrip sipping coffee while we waited for Big Game Heli's R44 helicopter. I detected some apprehension from Matthew and soon found out why. This was going to be his first time! Nevertheless, he made no fuss as I helped him with the headset and belted him in, and was brave throughout the two hours we spent in the air looking for rhino and then going in to photograph them. I sat in the back with him while Juliet used the relative space in front for her equipment and to focus on her photography. Despite the relatively smooth flying, when we landed a couple of hours later I noticed that the inside of Matthew's left hand was black. We both burst out laughing when he told me why. He'd gripped the bar between the two front seats so tightly for two hours that the paint had rubbed off onto his sweaty palm! Matthew later admitted the flight was one of the most exhilarating experiences of his life.

We spent a fruitful few days swapping ideas. Mostly I listened or answered direct questions pertaining to our poaching problems, including showing them the remnants of poached carcasses. This was an outside-laboratory sensory perception for Matthew, and he appreciated it. Juliette accompanied my field rangers on a routine river patrol, which they do every morning, checking for insurgents. Although she had slightly underestimated the African sun, she pushed through to the end without a whimper, having gained a healthy tan in the process. Above all, she went away with an appreciation of what we are up against.

In a day or so Matthew and Juliette would fly to Vietnam to continue researching rhino horn and the traditional medicine markets, including those who control the distribution network. Both were fully aware that black market racketeering and corruption characterises, and controls, these Eastern dealers and suppliers' markets. However, Matthew realised that in order to gain a meaningful insight there would be no room for a sanctimonious attitude … they needed to start at the end.

THE BLACK MAMBAS

It's arguably the best known and most feared snake in the world. Utter the words 'black mamba' wherever you are, in any language you care to name, and there will be an immediate response. I suspect that Inuit hunters huddled in an igloo, surrounded by pack ice and snow, in an Arctic white winter, will have heard of a black mamba. Among the peoples of its native Africa, this snake is revered for its mythological connotations, legendary speed and, of course, the death sentence it delivers with each bite, also known as the 'kiss of death'.

Depending on which end of this enigmatic snake you find yourself – coming or going, that is – black mambas can also be described as intelligent and beautiful. In terms of serpentine criteria they're long and slender, supremely athletic and dexterous; even the males have effeminately delicate features, and all mambas wear a permanent smile, which is definitely not to be confused with friendliness. Like true natural beauties, they need no lurid make-up, no stripes, no spots and no tattoo-like patterns. Black mambas wear subtle shades of slate grey with a pale-turquoise underbelly … and concealed at their business end is a pitch-black mouth. This 'close-kept' secret of their identity is the last feature you will remember of this snake before your death, as it is only when their mouth is agape in the act of striking that its inky-black interior is revealed. (As an aside, the female black mamba is invariably bigger and deadlier than the male.)

Imagine having these deadly beauties on our side in the war against rhino poachers! … One man did.

From the outset there was much scepticism surrounding this project, as the physical challenges of working in the bush meant this was essentially a task for young, fit men who had been through rigorous training. To train and deploy women in the bush against poaching would be an innovation, to say the least! I guess that's the word that best describes it, although it must be said that there were a number of other comments bandied about at the proposal. However, undaunted and flying in the face of traditional culture, a man by the name of Craig Spencer was up for it.

As head warden of Balule Nature Reserve (since 2014), and with his commitments as CEO of Transfrontier Africa, Craig already had his hands full; nevertheless, he knew that if he did not throw his full weight and influence behind this potentially ground-breaking project, it would fizzle out and die. Primarily, he needed to gain the respect and support of those who sat around the 'testosterone table', at which matters pertaining to conservation security were discussed. He needed to convince the predominantly ex-military men who trained most of the field rangers that there was a place for women in the war against rhino poaching – not an easy task in this neck of this woods, where male chauvinism is known to unabashedly spread its hood from time to time.

Amid the odd snigger and cynical remark thrown around in good humour, the concept was approved on a trial basis. All eyes were now on Craig, who must, in truth, have had some trepidations of his own. This was a huge paradigm shift in the war on rhino poaching. How would he set about making an initial impression and gain the momentum to quell the veiled cynicism? In a moment of inspiration, fuelled by desperation and lubricated by a dram or two of Captain Morgan, Craig had a eureka moment; he knew these young women would need their efficacy in the field to be taken seriously from the outset. They needed an identity synonymous with fear and respect. Needless to say, the 'Black Mambas', as they are now formally known, hit the spot. What better name to give a team of anti-poaching field rangers, comprising 26 young women from the local community, who are fast becoming as feared?

It all started in 2013 with a concept project of six young female recruits who were put through their paces for a year on the Olifants West region of Balule Nature Reserve. Against all odds, Craig remained committed; he believed that this could work. However, despite heaps of enthusiasm, these new recruits gave the term 'baby steps' a whole new meaning. The wardens watched with sceptical interest, and I am embarrassed to admit I was one of them. I knew how tough the training programme was going to be and was poised to be among those to tell Craig that I could have told him so!

These women had never been exposed to communal or group discipline: none had been to boarding school, for example, or ever been on a camping outing. However, all were from rural backgrounds so, needless to say, their lives had been no cakewalk. Sharing this common thread, most understood hardship and frugality, and this resilience was to stand them in good stead in the months to come. In terms of formal basic training, a radical approach was needed – a huge challenge, to say the least, in what was previously a male-dominated arena. All the known criteria were related to men. In spite of this, all went well for the initial 12-month trial, and the experiment produced encouraging results.

Though most of these women grew up within an hour's drive of the Kruger National Park, their knowledge and understanding of wildlife, particularly big game, was virtually non-existent. However, any thoughts of a gradual introduction were allayed when, in a baptism of fire on one of their first training patrols, the young women stumbled upon a pride of lions eating a kudu bull that they'd killed minutes before. Despite all their training to date, the survival instinct kicked in. As one, the six young women did what every human in a similar situation has done since hominids were considered part of these big cats' diet: they ran away! And while they were running, and looking for suitable trees to climb, they got on the two-way radio. Incoherent jabber, punctuated by panicked squeals and huffing and puffing, filled the airwaves. Months of expensive radio-procedure training were thrown out the window in a single panic-stricken moment. Ever the optimist,

Craig's initial thoughts were pragmatic.

'At least they can now use the two-way radio,' he reflected.

After that gem, he couldn't help himself; what followed was possibly not the most prudent response, but knowing his wicked sense of humour, it was not surprising at all. Needless to say, his loud laughter over the two-way radio did not go down well with the six terrified women whose shoulders had just been touched by death!

Try to picture the scene, as I believe Craig would have in that instance: six wide-eyed Black Mamba trainees running in one direction, five terrified lions in the other, and a dead kudu in the middle. The faint cloud of dust kicked up in panic now gently settling as the grunts and growls from the lions and shrieks and squeals from the young women fade away, swallowed by the bush.

Given his experience with wildlife, Craig knew the ladies were relatively safe; there'd be no real danger to them. As long as the lions had a huge kudu to eat, they would be intent on their meal, with little interest in attacking anyone. In fact the lions' initial reaction was to run away in the opposite direction, as wild lions invariably do in surprise confrontations with human beings. Then, with the ladies having left the scene, the lions would undoubtedly have returned to their kill the moment everything had settled ... but clearly not everyone there understood lion ecology.

Craig simply couldn't help himself. To the Mambas, however, his laughter on the radio signified a lack of caring or not taking their safety seriously. They were so shaken and upset; their fear had now turned to anger, and it was directed at him. Tears flowed down their dusty cheeks for the second time that day as they openly cried on parade that afternoon. But they showed their commitment once again and reported for duty the next day, on time and parade-ready. Most importantly for Craig, they even made a little play about the lion incident, which I suspect was much funnier than the real experience.

Being natural born recitalists, the Mambas took the few weeks of training they'd had on the search, seizure and arrest of a suspect one step further. Acting the likely scenarios out, they were able to bring out the humour in what was essentially a serious and dangerous part of their job. Basic courtroom procedure was also turned into a soap opera where each took their part seriously, rehearsing their lines well. No doubt little was forgotten this way.

Eager to put all this theory and playacting into meaningful action, the Mambas couldn't wait to start with their advanced bushcraft and tactical training. This was the paramilitary aspect of the training programme, and there could be no compromises or concessions made for the fairer sex. Physically it would prove to be the most difficult part of the course, and they expected nothing less. The course took place in the heart of Big Five country and included full-moon foot patrols, living in the bush without washing for 12 days, sitting up in ambush positions quietly for hours on end, and sleeping under the stars. Dry, military-style rations (rat packs) and bottled borehole water was all they had for sustenance. When on patrol and the water they carried ran out, there was little option but to drink from the water holes utilised by game. (The cornucopia of aromas surrounding these water holes and the muddy flavour of the water are secondary considerations when you are hot and thirsty.) And though a few trainees fainted from the exertion, not a single one became ill or dropped out.

A particularly poignant example of fortitude sticks in Craig's mind. Despite having attained a remarkable level of fitness, one young Mamba fainted on their last *opvok* (fuck-up) run. This was a gruelling 17-kilometre run in the heat of the day, a final test of endurance and willpower before qualifying. The careful monitoring, constant roadside assistance and regular offers to quit at any time, simply made this particular candidate more determined not to quit. Helping her up and cooling her down with cold water, Craig offered to take her back. She refused and adamantly told him to go away before the others thought she was softer than them. She continued and finished the run in the time allotted.

Their passing-out parade was a happy occasion, and many tears of pride and joy were shed amid ululating and impromptu harmonious singing that sent goose bumps down our spines. They humbled Craig almost to tears himself – or was he simply using his shirtsleeve to wipe a couple of those irritating little mopane flies out of his eyes, as he told everyone? When the time came to say a word or two about the Mambas, he congratulated them all on their determination and commitment, then in conclusion made a point of singling out this young cadet and giving her a deserved accolade. When he'd finished, the young lady stepped forward and gave a speech that Craig told me would forever burn in his brain.

She said: 'When I finished 12 years of school, I thought I was going places. Then after some years of waiting and never getting any jobs, I felt let down and thought my whole life I would be in the village carrying firewood and water cans. Today, I am special. I am part of a serious thing!'

With that, and not a mopane fly in sight, she started to cry, unable to speak any more. Today, having literally earned her stripes, she runs the operations room and is the Black Mamba Unit's Staff Sergeant. Little could she, or anyone else there at the time, have known just how serious this 'thing' would become ... but the rest of the world would let the Mambas know soon enough.

Having an extensive boundary with the R40 roadway, Olifants West had always been plagued by bushmeat poachers and petty theft. It was just so easy for them to hit and run before anything could be done, and as a result the incidents appeared to be escalating. However, the first six Mambas proved to be so effective in chasing the poachers out and disrupting their treacherous trade with early detection of incursions that Craig decided to roll out and recruit another 20 young women. Advertising was done by word of mouth, literally. The first six Mambas were sent out to canvass for cadets in their respective villages. Less than 24 hours later, Craig had a sea of keen young black women standing at his headquarters. His Mambas had been 'sent forth to multiply', and indeed they had done just that. There were so many prospective candidates that he couldn't count them all. His work now cut out for him, Craig began the lengthy task of interviewing each one. To assist him, he had the six Mambas set up the most relevant questions. Having been through the training, they could help with the process of elimination by explaining the subtle nuances to the applicants in their native Tsonga. This oiled the process no end and, in so doing, helped Craig select the most likely 20 trainees in far less time than he'd anticipated.

The Mambas helped with the basic induction training of the new recruits for the first fortnight. This was an all-important preparation phase prior to the survival course and tactical field ranger training, which now included basic firearm training. Although they were primarily employed in non-combatant roles, musketry training was necessary in order that the Mambas understood and respected firearms. None of the women had ever used a gun. Some quite literally did not know which way the rifles needed to be pointed. As this was proving to be quite a shenanigans, safety training was made a priority. Persistence paid off, and their musketry skills have improved to a point where most are proficient, and others are pretty skilled, markswomen now!

Next to learning how to operate a two-way radio and the associated radio procedure, teaching the Mambas to drive in the bush proved to be one of the most difficult aspects of their training. Despite Craig's perseverance, patience and neutral attitude, after three years of trying, he still can't find the Mamba who is able to drive a 4x4 through the bush without using it as a paint marker for trees!

The Black Mambas are primarily non-combatant; they are not trained to use lethal force and, as is true of their namesake, will only strike when provoked. Essentially, these women are not trained to be man-hunters: while catching poachers is certainly high on their list of aspirations, it is not the main thrust of the programme. Rather, the intention has always been to use Balule Private Nature Reserve as a platform to develop a sense of responsibility and pride towards wildlife among the local tribal folk and communities. Having the Mambas working on the reserve for 21 days at a time gave us a captive audience that could be motivated and moulded. There was no script or mission statement to subscribe to. It was a dogma they developed of their own volition, like a set of values, a talent and sense of worth that has lain dormant and has only now been discovered. This ethic is entrenched in their personas, and they have become staunch ambassadors for the wilderness and its wildlife. This mind-set is taken home with them, infecting their children, extended family and friends.

Imagine a little further down the line, when in two generations' time the Mambas are the elders in their respective villages, looking after their children's children. Never mind the technology, television and social media, nothing will ever replace a one-on-one bedtime story from Grandma. Anecdotal accounts involving wildlife – of when they were charged by black rhino, elephant and buffalo, and how these animals were merely doing what nature decreed; how fear and ignorance were replaced with respect and love, which culminated in an empathy and desire to conserve nature in all its forms – this is what will be related and passed down daily, something even David Attenborough's excellence could not do as effectively.

Under the guidance of the late Jason Sherwood and Johan Grobbelaar, who were their training officer and regional warden respectively, the Mambas continued to impress by making significant inroads into the poaching gangs that appeared to have free rein on the notorious state-owned Doreen. Here they thwarted meat and muti poachers, who were either sent packing or arrested, and removed hundreds of their deadly cable and wire snares. News of these achievements, and with it the Mambas' reputation, began to spread and get noticed beyond our immediate environs. As to their achievements to date, the list briefly reads as follows:

- Southern African Rhino Awards 2015: The Black Mambas received three nominations in various categories and won in the category of 'Best Rhino Practitioner'. They received their prize from Prince Albert of Monaco at a ceremony in Johannesburg.
- New York City, 2015: The Black Mambas were awarded the honour of 'Champions of the Earth' by the United Nations Environmental Program (UNEP). Ban Ki-moon (UN Secretary General) personally congratulated each one and handed them their prize.

- The Black Mambas were invited to lunch with, and to form a guard of honour for, President Jacob Zuma at Skukuza in 2015.
- London, 2016: Overseas again, the jet-setting Black Mambas were given an award by an NGO called Helping Rhinos.
- March 2016: The Black Mambas were invited to attend a conference in The Hague, where issues surrounding the illegal trade in wildlife and wildlife products were discussed. The Mambas spoke on the topic of community and National Park co-operation.
- Toward the end of 2016 it was announced that a Hollywood production company plans to turn their story into a feature film.

Sky News planned to give the Black Mambas a two-minute slot on 21 January 2016. So fascinated was the interviewer that protocol was disregarded and Craig Spencer, speaking on behalf of the Mambas, was not cut short; instead he was allowed to talk for more than nine minutes! Apparently this was unheard of.

Apart from these world travels, the Mambas have been mentioned in several presidential and parliamentary speeches in South Africa and were invited to meet with Sally Jewell (US Secretary for the Interior), which unfortunately they could not accept owing to logistics. They have dined with the Prince of Monaco; with Graça Machel, wife of Nelson Mandela; with Ban Ki-moon of the United Nations, and a few other dignitaries … a long haul from sweat-soaked bush fatigues, dry rations and drinking from water holes!

RHINO RESCUE PROJECT

There is no need to elaborate on the already thought-provoking state of affairs regarding what is happening to our country's rhino. However, there is a need to share with the reader some of what we, as a reserve, have tried to do in order to become more proactive in waging this war against poaching. Rather than always responding reactively, desperately trying to close the door when the horse has already bolted, we started to pursue some of the innovative ideas that came to the fore. And just when we thought we'd considered everything, gone down every avenue, new side streets lit up, begging to be explored.

There was a time when people – I believe Leonardo da Vinci was one – hid incredible scientific discoveries from the world for fear of religious retribution. Today there are some who use science instead of religion as a screen to prevent sticking their necks out, for fear of failure and criticism from their peers. Sheep-like, they are unaware that an integral part of science, particularly the natural sciences, involves delving into the unknown and testing the untried.

Enter a young *boeremeisie* (farm girl) who, impassioned by the brutal slaughter of rhino on her father's farm, put her slender shoulders behind the wheel of rhino conservation. Lorinda Hern managed to put into practice what many had only thought about, had only uttered in hushed tones, behind closed doors and in dark, secret places. Her Rhino Rescue Project (RRP) pioneered the treating of rhino horn with non-lethal toxins and an indelible dye. Basically, the idea was to contaminate the horn and render the material unfit for its intended end users but without any adverse effect on the rhino.

Many rhino owners were sceptical, and most remained vehemently against tampering with rhino horn in their stockpiles, or on their living animals for that matter. I suspect this is driven primarily by prospects of profit. Many rhino owners and ranchers – and the government, with its valuable stockpile of rhino horn from the Kruger National Park – were concerned that if the trade in rhino horn was to become legal there would be dire financial implications for their uncontaminated stockpiles, which they are hoping to sell. Any sign or rumour of poisoned horns would kill the market, so in some respects it is understandable they remained negative. Then, to add to the critics' ammunition, the first televised demonstration to promote RRP's treatment went tragically wrong when the subject rhino being worked on died on camera. The old rhino bull was later found to have had a heart defect, something no one could have foreseen.

Despite this huge PR setback on national television, Lorinda remained committed: in fact, she was more determined than before. At the same time, I was more aware than ever of the need to look at the bigger picture in terms of anti-poaching measures: we had to do something a little out of the box. An unfortunate mishap could not be allowed to deter our optimism about the concept. Armed, military-type anti-poaching patrols were not enough, we knew, while being part of the greater Kruger system and under their policy regarding dehorning meant this was not an option either. Sacrifices in another sphere needed to be made. This was ground-breaking technology, which was not fully understood, and trials were in their infancy. Understandably there were many cynics and critics at the outset, and there are those who will remain sceptical. But with the extinction of a species at stake there was no time to bother with protocol: we were aware that there were – and still are – many unknowns regarding this treatment in terms of its efficacy and longevity. Needless to say, it was always going to be a huge leap of faith, in spite of which the board of Olifants Game Reserve put their trust and support behind the proposal, as did Sabi

Sands Game Reserve and Hoedspruit Air Force Base. It was given the unequivocal go-ahead, and a proposal was tabled. This was presented to the committee and received unanimous acceptance. RRP would treat at least 20 of Balule's rhino.

However, the Kruger National Park watched with only casual interest and were sceptically against the concept from the get-go. In my experience, if an idea does not originate with them, or comply with their draconian methodology or protocol, they are not really interested. They have always thought of themselves as the benchmark of conservation innovation ... and ironically, more recently, regard themselves as leaders in the field of combating rhino poaching. The following disparaging words of a good friend, who also happens to be one of the heads of security for SANParks, still resound with alarming clarity: 'Mario, Kruger Park has thrown every conceivable resource at this problem, we have everything except a frigate on the Sabi River at our disposal to combat rhino poaching, and still we are losing at least three rhino a day!'

Three rhino per day that the Kruger knows about, I thought to myself: how many more carcasses are out there that they miss and never find? From my limited experience in a comparatively small area, I know how easily fresh carcasses are missed, and indeed how, in less than a week, scavengers can reduce a carcass to virtually nothing but a scattered bone here and there. In the dry season some carcasses semi-mummify as they retain much of their shape when the skin dries out stretched over the skeleton. But this is the exception rather than the rule. Within days you could fly over the scene of a rhino massacre without being any the wiser.

We intended to treat the rhino during a relatively quiet time on the reserve, which was to coincide with cooler ambient temperatures. So we chose early autumn, in the week before the Easter holidays. The Hoedspruit Air Force Base Reserve was doing its rhino around the same time, so overall costs could be kept lower. There would also be minimal disturbance to shareholders as only a few units would be occupied during this period.

Unfortunately, as is often the case when dealing with wildlife and the plethora of logistics required to co-ordinate this kind of operation, it had to be extended by a few days. As it turned out, there were a couple of unforeseeable situations, for example when emergency surgery was needed in Hammanskraal for a juvenile rhino whose tongue had been severed. This meant veterinarian Charles van Niekerk, who does the horn treatment, couldn't come out until he'd operated on and stabilised the little rhino. Then the air force base couldn't locate a particular rhino ... and so on. Eventually we had no option but to reschedule for the following week ... smack bang in the middle of the first busy weekend on Olifants.

Back in Hammanskraal, after stabilising the injured rhino, Charles loaded up his Land Cruiser and drove through the night to Olifants. I met him at Palm Loop station, on the railroad, at 1.30 am, and took him to my house. I could see he was utterly exhausted. Without much more than a handshake and a cursory goodnight, he took his overnight bag to the room and climbed into bed.

Tomorrow was going to be a big day and Charles was going to need all the sleep he could get. Assistant vet Shaun Beverley, who had arrived earlier, was already fast asleep. Now it was my turn, I thought, snuggling into the cool cotton cover of the pillow. But my mind was racing, filled with trepidation about the huge task and the risks that lay ahead. I agonised about the unknown, every possible scenario that Murphy's Law dictates, and any counter-measures I could prepare for. We'd be conducting a new procedure, and I'd be working with people I didn't know. What were we letting ourselves in for? I didn't sleep a wink, quite literally.

Getting up just before 5 am, I felt a little like I sometimes do on a New Year's morning. Only this time there was not going to be a lazy sleep-in after a plate of scrambled eggs, this time I'd be in a helicopter at 6 am searching for rhino with a pair of eyes that hadn't been shut for 24 hours. At least Bennie would be flying, a comforting thought.

Although we could have diverted some of the activity to the fringes of our region in order to minimise any disruption, I'd had another thought … why not involve as many people as possible, including shareholders, to observe the process? In consultation with Vince Ryan, the reserve's director in charge of the rhino anti-poaching donations, from which the funding for this operation was derived, we decided it would be good for those people who were on the reserve at the time to see how some of their funds were being used, and join in on the experience. It proved to be an excellent idea.

An announcement was made over the reserve's radio network that those shareholders who wanted to watch the proceedings were to meet on the airstrip at around 6 am for a briefing. This was to ensure that everyone knew what the procedure entailed and what was to be expected of them as spectators. Well, I'm sure some eager beavers must have camped out all night, or were there before first light, because when I arrived to meet the helicopter, the airstrip was already abuzz with members sipping coffee and dunking rusks. The atmosphere was electric with enthusiasm and expectation.

I could go into so much more detail here, but suffice it to say as it turned out my apprehension was for naught. Everything went smoothly and soon everyone was standing around watching as the treatment was applied to the first rhino's horns, microchips inserted and one of its ears notched. All the while, during the 40-minute procedure, the rhino was monitored by two veterinarians, a comforting protocol as this is a relatively long time for an animal to be tranquillised and naturally all possible risks needed to be minimised.

Given the complexity of such an operation, I would have been happy with three or four rhino getting done that morning. However, again and again, the co-ordinated efforts of the team had everyone gaping in awe, as Bennie's expert flying and the professionalism of the capture team and veterinarians gelled, culminating in five rhino being treated, marked and released by the time the ambient temperature had began to climb.

By nine the following morning, the last rhino had been done. The entire operation from start to finish was a success, one of those high-five moments to be shared with all who were there. We had treated 20 rhino, plus another one in a neighbouring region. Most of the infusions were attended by busloads of local schoolchildren, as well as staff members from the neighbouring reserves. Signboards were posted along the fences of the reserve, and at all the entrance gates, warning of the 'poisoned' horns.

Stifling and negative bureaucracy in the National Parks could not contemplate this treatment without routine, time-consuming and conclusive testing. As a result, bound by their peers and protocol, not to mention that it was not *their* innovative idea, certain ecologists in the Kruger did not give the concept a chance. Nor did they allow for any research into furthering the efficacy of the concept. Had Natal Parks Board's rangers followed the same protocol back in the 1960s, there would have been no problem today – the Kruger wouldn't have had the white rhino that were saved from extinction by being brought up from Natal using the untried, risky but innovative M99!

Why, I ask with real tears in my eyes, could these narrow-minded egotists not look at the woods rather than focusing on the bloody trees? Next, a popular television programme, famous for exposing criminal activity and corruption every Sunday evening, broadcast a one-sided 'investigative exposé', which promoted the interests of SANParks and horn stockpile-holders, cynically undermining RRP's efforts and those of the reserves that had put their hearts into devaluing the market for rhino horn.

Naturally, this message would also have reached all the rhino poachers, whether by word of mouth or beamed to those now rich enough from the proceeds of poaching to watch the programme in their lavish homes – from Massingir and Maputo, to Beijing, Bangkok and Ho Chi Minh City. There can be no doubt that rhino poachers would have interpreted from this ill-considered exposé that they could now effectively expand their killing field and target any rhino they pleased. It was business as usual: it showed that Rhino Rescue Project's attempt to dupe the killers and end users had failed ... and all confirmed on television by 'scientists' working in the Kruger National Park!

No matter the backpedalling attempt a couple of weeks later by the investigative journalist, the damage had been done. And the biggest irony of all ... since the programme's exposé of RRP, the Kruger National Park has lost nearly 2 000 rhino to poaching, known carcasses and counting! Add to this the private reserve losses and the figure creeps up to nearly 2 500 rhino killed between 2013 and 2016.

How sad that investigative journalism and the egos associated with exposing the facts at all costs can take precedence over a vulnerable species' very existence! Ultimately there can be no doubt that there will be many treated rhino killed, rhino that might otherwise have been passed up because their horns were believed to be 'contaminated'.

The concept of RRP's infusion was primarily aimed at spreading the word among the local population, from where the message would reach the poachers and end users that treated horns were contaminated, rendering their mythical healing properties questionable and the horns unfit for consumption. The degree or efficacy of contamination was never the issue. Essentially it was largely a 'smoke and mirrors' campaign and those of us desperate to save the rhino from extinction all knew this from the outset. Unfortunately now the poachers, and the end users perpetuating the demand, know it too!

Most people would have curled up and died after the criticisms and allegations made concerning RRP, but not Lorinda. She is the quintessential example of fortitude and conservation commitment to a specific end goal – to save rhino from going extinct in the wild. And the latest developments look promising indeed.

The other day I received an e-mail from her outlining the basics of RRP's ongoing research. For the last 18 months they have been working with a nuclear physicist and oncologist who has helped refine a technique whereby rhino horns are devalued through the introduction of radioactive isotopes similar to those commonly used in human nuclear medicine. The horns are thus detectable by law enforcement – even inside a fully packed, 40-foot container. They have also partnered with a UK-based university and the manufacturer of a DNA product that forms a permanent bond with horn on a cellular level, and illuminates under a UV light.

With Lorinda's never-say-die attitude, RRP is still committed to achieving what it sets out to do. Technical details and proof of efficacy aside, their concept of rhino horn infusion remains one of the most proactive innovations attempted by anyone to date. Hats off to them for their noble effort.

SABA, MY BLACK-FACED DOG

In *The Man with the Black Dog* I paid tribute to Shilo, the canine love of my life. 'A man will have one dog in his lifetime, only one he will share that special bond with,' I wrote. Although this was a number of years ago, I still mean every word of it, though I must admit that it owes something to a linguistic sleight of hand: the new dog in my life is not a 'dog', as Shilo was, but is in fact a 'dam', the polite description of a breeding Belgian Malinois female.

Her name is Saba.

OK, OK, I love her just as much; there, I said it!

Saba, it has to be said, came into my life some 18 years late. Had I known all those years ago what I do now, I would have been less accepting of a life in the bushveld devoid of canine companionship.

Nearly two decades had passed since I'd buried Shilo, during which time I'd simply moved on without challenging company policy, even though I was probably the only game ranger in Africa who was not allowed to own a dog. But it was stipulated clearly in my contract: 'After Shilo, no dogs allowed!' So, my life went on without a dog, and I busied myself with building the reserve. There was a lot to do. My children grew up without the pleasure of being around dogs and instead made do with inconsistent but exciting interactions with wildlife. Being weekly boarders, they had limited time at home on weekends, which were usually spent grinding through heavy homework loads anyway, so it was never a priority to have a 'weekend' dog. Looking back, I have no regrets on that score.

However, the changing priorities of nature conservation prompted an about-turn in the directors' attitude towards dogs on the reserve. The escalation in rhino poaching was an ideal opportunity to revisit the dog ownership issue and rescind a rather draconian policy.

Whatever ulterior motives lay behind this decision, I grabbed the opportunity with both hands. I knew that my choice of a dog hinged on a quid pro quo: there was a modicum of obligation, a certain degree of expectation. Sure, I could have a dog, but I was under no illusion: it could not be any random breed ... it should at least be seen to be a deterrent to rhino poachers, hardly the job for a Yorkie or a Maltese poodle.

Suddenly, from nothing for all these years, it was all in front of me now. Not only could I get a dog, but I could get two or three dogs if I wished! I felt like a starving child let loose in a candy store – I didn't know which to choose. The only thing I knew from the start was that I would only be getting one dog. As exciting as this was, I knew this man–dog relationship also needed to meet certain criteria for me personally. I knew it was not a relationship to be entered into lightly. I'd owned and loved a dog before; I had a pretty good idea of what lay ahead of me, and at 57 years of age I was also well aware of my limitations. Was I up to the task?

I was keenly aware of my responsibility to meet the committee's expectations. However, first and foremost, the choice of dog would be my decision: this would go beyond simply acquiring and owning a pet. Once I'd picked a dog, it would be my life for the next 12 to 14 years; I had to be sure. Importantly, I also knew it would not be a purely dog–handler working relationship. I was determined to break the mould and prove that a dog can be just as effective when coaxed off a comfy couch into action as one that is loaded into a crate from the concrete floor of a kennel and deployed to task; I knew this could be done. I was clear from the outset that if acquiring an anti-poaching dog meant keeping it at arm's length to be treated and cared for purely as a working dog, as a living tool, then there was no question: I'd rather not have a dog at all; I'd rather make use of professional K9 units as and when we needed.

Primarily I needed a dog that would be able to cope physically with the challenges of living in the hot bushveld. Some breeds of dogs are more tolerant of the heat than others, but these variances are so minimal that it would be safe to say that those breeds favoured as trailing dogs will invariably be heat intolerant. I researched what I thought would be suitable breeds, I spoke to many trainers, breeders and owners, read extensively and of course visited 'Dr Google', and sought the sage advice of Dr 'Slang' Viljoen, among others. Eventually I'd narrowed the search down to four breeds. Then I managed to eliminate two close contenders, namely the Rhodesian ridgeback and German short-haired pointer. The ridgeback was too big for me to handle: I needed a dog I could pick up easily at my age. The pointer, although the ideal size, was ruled out as I was warned that gun dogs may pose a problem and require firm training to keep them off game scent. I had now narrowed the choice down to two breeds, and even further down to two reputable breeders. It was going to be either an AfriCanis from Edith and Johan Gallant, which they would source from rural Zululand, or a Belgian Malinois from Antwerpen Kennels near Johannesburg.

The AfriCanis has evolved from a long line of sight hounds, dogs that were used on the savannah and deserts of Africa to work in small packs and run down quarry for their masters. Although their noses are as good as that of any medium-sized dog, it is their keen eyesight and ability to focus on the quarry that comes to the fore in this breed. Speed and stamina are what make the AfriCanis stand out as a hunting dog. However, I needed an all-rounder: essentially I was looking for an intelligent dog with a maintenance-free coat and a good trailing nose; being a good hunter was of secondary importance.

Initially my inclination was towards the AfriCanis, as this is an all-African dog, a hardy strain which through natural selection has become well adapted to this continent's people, climate and parasites. Importantly, they are also lightly built, gregarious, highly intelligent and loyal to the extreme: everything one could wish for in a bush dog. However, in the end it all came down to timing and scent-trailing ability – the latter attribute needed more thought and was of more importance when considering my specific requirements on the anti-poaching front. It is interesting to note that the much revered 'lion dog' or Rhodesian ridgeback was originally bred from AfriCanis lines.

The second breed I researched in depth was the Belgian Malinois (pronounced *Mal-in-wah*). The history of this dog goes back to 1891 when Belgian veterinarian Adolphe Reul established the strain. In 1900 the Belgian shepherd was recognised by the Société Royale Saint-Hubert as one breed with four varieties, namely the Malinois, Groenendael, Laekenois and Tervuren. Belgian shepherds are extremely versatile dogs, and the Malinois, named after its city of origin, Malines, was originally used as a herding, scout, border patrol and Red Cross dog. As far as the American Kennel Club was concerned, from 1950 to 1965 there was still uncertainty as to what the Malinois' classification would be, and then in 1965 it gained full recognition as a separate working breed. I believe it was only officially brought into South Africa as late as 1978.

To simply say 'Belgian shepherd' is misleading, as although they share the same general attributes it is remarkable how different from each other they are in outward appearance. However, of the four varieties I suspect it was primarily the much shorter coat of the Malinois that proved most practical for working in warmer climes and which has made them more suited to Africa. For me this was of pre-eminent importance; the other incredible traits intrinsic in this breed simply made the choice that much easier.

I'd first heard of the Belgian Malinois from a Belgian-born neighbour by the name of Stefan van den Borre, who owned a property in Balule. We met at the train bridge shortly after my field rangers had their first fire fight with rhino poachers. Naturally we began to talk of additional means and tactics to combat poaching, and the subject of dogs came up. He mentioned a breed of dog that the US and UN military forces were using in the Middle East with a good measure of success. My ears pricked up instantly: a breed that could work in hot desert environments ... Well now, I thought, that is very interesting. Although he told me the name, I could never remember the correct pronunciation, and it soon faded from my memory, as did any thoughts of motivating my committee to allow for me to have a dog at the time.

There was no further prompting to jog my memory; no one else around spoke about dogs, and nobody I knew used dogs specifically for rhino anti-poaching work in the Lowveld at the time. However, I do recall an occasion a few months later when Stefan was invited to attend one of our wardens' security meetings, and he asked if he could bring his dog along with him. Reluctantly I had to inform him of our committee's policy regarding dogs. He obliged and left it at home. In hindsight, a short-sighted decision, one that I possibly could have waived on that occasion.

A year later I was in Gerrit's surgery in Phalaborwa shooting the breeze and mostly talking about fishing in Mozambique. He'd just completed spaying a beautiful tabby cat, but not before showing me how delicately intricate this operation was. We wandered off the subject of fishing momentarily and got onto chatting about working dogs, and Gerrit mentioned a dog that had recently chased a snare poacher to the banks of the Groot Letaba River. The poacher dived into the river and began swimming across, confident he'd get away. Without hesitation or encouragement the dog jumped in and swam after him. The man was caught as he clambered out the other side, where the dog held him until he could be arrested. It was Stefan's Malinois! ... Fast forward four years.

Having weighed up everything, I finally made up my mind. The deal was sealed and I was comfortable with my decision. When Belgian-born breeder Agnes Jiroflee heard what I needed the dog for, she placed my name at the top of her long waiting list for puppies. Even then, before Malinois were sought after as anti-poaching dogs, they were a relatively new breed in this country, and with only a few registered breeders at the time good puppies were difficult to source, so I was humbled by her commitment to the greater cause.

Another deciding factor was that Antwerpens' Malinois pups would be born 12 weeks ahead of a litter of AfriCanis pups that Edith had lined up for me in rural KwaZulu-Natal, so the timing went against the African dogs. I admit having had sleepless nights wondering if I was simply being impatient. Did the urgency of the escalating rhino poaching crisis lead me to choose the Malinois? Or was this kismet? Only time would tell as I began to count the sleeps before my pup could be collected.

I had no idea of what lay in store for me, but Edith enlightened me a little in advance. She understood the reasons for my change of heart and was an absolute honey about my decision to opt for the Malinois. Having bred them in the past she knew the breed well ... but she did have this to say to me: 'Mario, Malinois will do the job you require, but they will drive you crazy.' Needless to say, Edith's words still ring true, but for all the right reasons.

I visited Saba's parents a month before her birth, and despite the Malinois' reputation for being aloof and distant I found these to be a couple of affectionate and energetic dogs. They appeared to be profoundly alert, with a sense of duty to protect on a level I had not seen in other dogs before. I could see from their temperament and demeanour that this breed thrives on work: a Malinois would not be happy on your lap all day; they need a purpose in life. I fell in love with these 'up-eared dogs' immediately.

Without so much as a whimper, Saba was taken from her siblings and brought home with us. And at the tender age of eight weeks, her training began. With the help of professional trainer Jonathan Swartz we began with the baby steps of trailing, which quickly stimulated her inherent skill. Jonathan spent a few days teaching me how to train Saba, then left me with a comprehensive homework sheet to follow.

Primarily Saba was trained in trailing human scent in order to assist our anti-poaching rangers to track down elusive rhino poachers, a far cry indeed from what Malinois were originally bred to do, which was to herd and protect sheep in Northern Europe. Later, as these herding dogs stole the hearts of their owners, they were bred to protect man and his property, becoming a popular choice as military and police dogs, and latterly as anti-poaching dogs ... I now know why. As each day passes and another anti-poaching canine gets that little bit sharper, stories of their successful contribution in this war reach and touch us all – and Saba is right up there with the best.

A growing number of reserves are now using dogs to assist their anti-poaching units in the fight against rhino poaching. Although a number of other breeds are being used with success, the Belgian Malinois is rapidly gaining popularity as the breed of choice. Many are being trained primarily as trailing and attack dogs, where ideally a minimum of three dogs need to be deployed. Without exception, all the dogs in this type of deployment need to wear GPS tracking collars, as no one will ever keep up with them once they are released. I know of one section ranger in the Kruger National Park who has needed to use a helicopter to keep pace with his pack. If all goes well, both the dogs and the poachers will be located at the same point ... invariably the only place safe for poachers being hounded by a pack of Malinois would be up a tree.

Belgian Malinois do not make ideal pets. Besides being highly intelligent and athletic (the latter being particularly important in our bushveld heat), they are instinctively guard dogs, protectors and herders by nature. Attacking any threat would come naturally to them, so needless to say being trained specifically to capture and attack rhino killers would be a huge incentive for them. However, keeping this breed focused on the scent trail and tempering their impatience would be where the all-important training and discipline comes in. The Belgian Malinois wants to work: physically and mentally they need regular exercise and stimulation. Some may even require professional training to realise their full potential, and all Malinois need to have an assertive 'pack leader'.

Depending on the light, a typical day in Saba's life starts around 4.30 am, a little later in winter. Of course she sleeps in the house, on her couch! Where else? After a quick check with a flashlight that there are no hippo or other creatures patrolling the lawn, she is taken outside to answer the call of nature. This routine is closely followed by a small bowl of watered-down milk, a token amount which is lapped up in seconds while Meagan and I attempt to drink our first cup of coffee. However, in order to keep up with Saba's demands of imminent duty, this ritual has been reduced to a caffeine infusion. No longer am I able to savour my favourite blend of arabica while birdsong and the distant roar of a lion herald the beginning of another day in the bush. Instead I gulp my coffee down while being subjected to an increasingly persistent wet-nosed nudge against my bare legs accompanied by the *squeak-squeak* of those irritating rubber balls. (I now drill the whistle out as they are taken from the package.)

Like their distant cousins the border collie and Australian kelpie, Malinois need regular exercise and constant stimulation. Before feed-lots and paddocks, this would have come from running flat out for hours herding obstinate sheep in open country. But as these woolly targets are in short supply in the Lowveld, we've had to improvise with fast ground-rolling frisbees and rubber balls (the latter recently limited because chewing on the balls wears down her teeth).

Her comfy, chewy-strewn bed and couch now all but forgotten, her tail wagging and her pink tongue lolling, Saba is now ready for the day, full of unremitting, pent-up energy. Tired rarely happens, and exhausted is not in the Malinois vocabulary. Needless to say, most of the ball-play and frisbee-throwing that Meagan and I do at this time is in dressing gown and slippers and underpants and unlaced boots respectively; we're simply given no time to get dressed. What a sight we must make. Thank goodness this is not suburbia, and the only specta-tors are our resident Natal spurfowl or the occasional bemused nyala on the other side of the fence. The red-headed weavers with their unti-diest of all weavers' nests under the eaves near the back door have seen this all before and go about the duties of parenthood with the same lack of interest as do the tawny-flanked prinias nesting in the shrub-bery next to the carport.

Although perfectly suited to many occupations as a versatile working dog, Saba will not be employed to herd sheep or sniff for contraband

and narcotics, nor will she be trained as an attack dog for use in a law enforcement K9 unit, or by the military. Her work will focus primarily on trailing the scent of people. More specifically, she is being trained to assist our field rangers and trackers in those rare circumstances when 'hot' tracks are lost or when in hot pursuit. Her nose will pick up invisible trails, those covering rocky terrain, for example, where the best eye fails and footfalls can only be followed by keen scenting. This is probably one of the most difficult tasks one can expect of a dog: even the best of bloodhounds are known to lose a trail more often than not. No dog can be expected to perform with infallible consistency and reliability; there are simply too many variables at play. Nevertheless this is the one task to which most of our canine friends are naturally best suited ... and one that no machine can emulate.

High ambient temperatures have a limiting effect on working a trailing dog: the hotter it is and the longer your dog has to work, the less efficient it will become. This means that training is always best done in the early morning or late afternoon. With my routine as it is, late afternoons seem to work best. Initially I'd go out every day, but as Saba matured the sessions were reduced in frequency. I would usually prepare a new trail on my own, but on occasion, to change the scent, I would use one of the staff or contract labourers as a trail layer. The trail would then be given time to 'age' (depending on ambient temperature and humidity this could vary from 10 minutes to an hour). Location, time of day and distance of trail were varied whenever practical, to cover as many as possible of the various situations, veld types and terrain she would be required to work in when she was needed to trail the scent of a poacher.

When she senses the routine Saba eagerly awaits my return. She is then harnessed and given a certain command unique to the task, one that will remain constant throughout her life and is used when I need her to trail the real thing. When the harness goes on, she already knows what's coming and her whole demeanour changes. Incredibly, even at the tender age of 16 weeks her drive was such that if I did not use a chest harness – padded at the front throat area with 10-millimetre felt to make it more comfortable – she would choke on her collar.

As much as I would have liked to temper Saba's extreme drive, I always thought it was better to give her her lead, rather than restrict her too much. This is one time when the 'nose knows', so I followed this awesome miracle of nature at a run, puffing and panting as I was dragged through the bush on the end of a 10-metre leash. As much as I was overjoyed when she tracked a flawless trail, I also loved it when she lost the scent momentarily in her impatience to anticipate, as is the way of the Malinois. When the scent was lost she would stop abruptly, drop her nose to the ground and backtrack a little way, then momentarily running side-to-side she would range until the scent trail was picked up once more, and then she would hurtle off again ... Fantastic!

Having started at just over eight weeks of age, Saba underwent progressive training until it reached a point when at a little over three months old she was tracking trails of more than 500 metres! There appeared to be no end to her drive; it seemed like she could go much further and wanted to go further. I was half-inclined to worry that she might burn herself out!

I nevertheless decided it was time to consult another expert tracking/ trailing dog trainer, Warwick Wragg. Sadly, since writing this piece, Warwick has passed away. He understood the Malinois impatience and determination like few others did, so I was grateful for his time and advice. Warwick suggested I cut right back and slow down, not only from the physical aspect, but more because the methodology – the 'why' – needed to be understood by the dog. Then as a parting shot he reminded me of something I suspect both Saba and I were becoming oblivious to in our enthusiasm and sheer enjoyment of working together. He reminded me that although Saba had the incredible drive and determination typical of the Malinois, I would need to be the adult, take charge and rein her in a little; after all, she was still a baby!

Although Saba has become everyone's overzealous friend, it is not by chance. Since a puppy her social skills were emphasised, and any sign of aggression, even in play, was discouraged. I knew from the outset that Saba would never be used as both a trailing and attack dog. She would be taught to focus on trailing human scent only, and at the point of locating poachers, or in very close proximity to them, encouraged to bark and not attack. To have physical contact with poachers would be to risk injury or worse. Therefore, as a backup method of control, Saba would always be joined to me by that 10-metre leather tracking line.

At a little over a year old, her trailing had progressed in close parallel with her blossoming into maturity, which manifested itself in increasingly measured and decidedly deliberate behaviour. I believed she now knew exactly what was expected of her and that the balance between working dog and loving companion had been achieved. However, this kind of relationship does not suit all situations and requirements. Saba could 'ride the bicycle'; now all she needed was to enter a race and hopefully get to wear the *maillot jaune*. But even champions have to train hard, and at five months old, she would find herself trailing the 'real thing'.

You may recall when I wrote about the first black rhino poached on Olifants and how we were close behind the poachers. Their tracks were so fresh, in fact, that some of the grass bent by their feet was springing back up as the rising sun drank the dew. Although we already had some of the best men ready to take up and follow the poachers' tracks, I thought this would also be a good opportunity to bring Saba in behind the trackers for a training exercise. So I radioed Meagan and asked that she bring her to the airfield. (This would take at least 30 minutes, and I couldn't allow the trackers to waste even a moment, so they began on the spoor immediately while I waited.)

I knew the poachers' tracks would now be contaminated with the scent of the trackers; nevertheless, I thought this would be excellent practice for Saba. The thought, preposterous as it was, did cross my mind … imagine a five-month-old dog tracking down armed poachers at her first attempt – wow! Needless to say Saba had no such delusions of grandeur, just the drive and focus typical of the breed. Fearlessly and like a seasoned professional she took to the tracks immediately, with as much enthusiasm as she had done since she was eight weeks old.

Despite an inordinate amount of zigzagging, Saba located the field rangers and trackers within minutes. What had taken three men more than 30 minutes to accomplish, she had done in two! That was more than good enough for me ... it was fantastic! This was the longest 'natural' trail Saba had followed to date: about 900 metres, with all the 'false trails'. A little while later, after checking the Palm Loop River bed for any tracks crossing the soft sand and finding none, I proudly led my happy pup back to the vehicle. After a good drink of water Saba went home with Meagan while I returned to the carcass and the autopsy team.

The reason for the unusual zigzag line created by the tracking team, which Saba trailed as they walked it, was that they too were coursing, checking each game trail in an effort to locate the poachers' spoor. Crafty as always, the bastards were doing everything they could to throw us off the track. But Saba was not easily fooled: she had led us to the railway line, and at least we now had a rough idea of which direction the poachers were taking.

We later determined that the poachers had climbed onto the railway track close by and used it in the same way that escaped felons pursued by dogs are known to use a stream or river; this anti-tracking measure slowed us down considerably. I then got prepared to face the practicality of the desperate situation that now confronted the Balule regional wardens and field rangers: it was as though there was a haystack right in front of us with two needles moving through a relatively narrow area of the stack. All we had to try and do was anticipate where they were most likely to emerge and when.

My elation with Saba's ability may have been a little premature ... I needed to return to the reality that she was only a puppy. This was as far as she would go for now.

A TAIL OF PLUCK AND PERIL

I can understand why the pioneer hunters never visited the Lowveld in the wet season. If malaria and nagana didn't kill you and your livestock respectively, then there'd be a host of other creatures determined to find their way into your boots or your bed as routinely as if it was part of their natural life cycle. To this day, summer time in Africa's Big Game country is not for barefoot children or the un-gloved hand, nor is it the ideal place for domestic dogs. I am always a little on edge at this time of the year when I am out with Saba.

At night the big cats rule. A dog that wanders from its master or too far from the fireside will be taken by a leopard as quickly as a fox takes a rabbit. A brave dog will have its skull crushed by a lion before it can utter a scream, and a curious one will have its eyes spat in by a Mozambique spitting cobra before its first birthday. 'Ratters' that don't listen and constantly nose around for rodents in hollow logs and under rocks will be killed by a venomous snake sooner or later. Overprotective dogs will meet their nemesis when they square up to baboons which have canines longer than a lion's. Nowhere is safe in the true sense of the word, and even taking your dog onto the lawn of your home at night can be a perilous excursion.

Saba was less than five months old, and Meagan had just taken her out to have a last widdle before bed. On the way back to the house, less than a couple of metres from our back door, Saba uttered a howling scream so loud and relentless that my knees went wobbly. I rushed out to find Meagan holding Saba and looking at her foot with a flashlight.

Initially I thought my puppy may have stepped awkwardly and injured her leg, but a quick examination revealed nothing obvious. It could only be one of two things, I thought: a puff adder or a scorpion. Taking a flashlight, I traced the route to and from the spot where Saba had relieved herself and noticed something small and black, about as thick as a pencil, sticking out of the grass. Closer examination revealed it was the business end of a thick-tailed scorpion, *Parabuthus transvaalicus*, but it was motionless. Saba must have stood on it, crushing the creature to death, but not before it reflexively delivered some of the most potent scorpion venom in the world into her little body.

At that time there was no antivenom serum for scorpion stings. The pain, particularly from a thick-tailed scorpion sting, is indescribable, and nothing is known to block the pain receptors. In the past the best treatment for humans involved immersing the site in the hottest water bearable. This apparently helps by breaking down and partially cooking the protein in the venom cocktail that is responsible for the pain. But how was I going to get my little pup to understand that the pain of the near-boiling water was for the best and would be short-lived? Instead I telephoned Gerrit's colleague, Dr Sampie Ras, who advised me to give Saba a valium and then bring her to the clinic as soon as possible.

Travelling through Olifants North, a journey of well over an hour, is still the shortest route by road to Phalaborwa. Being late at night, this was an unusual time to exit, so I explained the situation to the gate guard who then tried to lean into the window to look at Saba out of curiosity and offer sympathy. Instead of a whimpering puppy, he was met with a defensive growl. Well, I thought, that's a good sign: Saba is still alert and on guard, so she can't be dying!

At the clinic, Sampie took charge and immediately tranquillised Saba. While she was still groggy, and the pain easing, as part of the treatment he injected a huge subcutaneous dose of calcium into her shoulder area. He explained that as there was no known pain blocker, he would keep her in a semi-tranquillised state until her body had dissipated much of the venom, which usually took a day or so. It was the only thing to do to relieve the pain.

Once Saba was comfortable and out of conscious pain, Sampie showed me two of his other patients that had been stung by the same species of scorpion and were busy recovering. The little Maltese poodle appeared to be in better shape than the much larger Ridgeback cross. At that time of the year Sampie dealt with up to three dogs a day stung by scorpions! And as the thick-tailed scorpion is a nocturnal species, all the serious incidents occurred at night, mostly on summer nights, and more often than not after a thunderstorm.

I gave Sampie the bottle of 2008 Backsberg Merlot that Meagan had conjured up as I left home. How the hell does she think of these things at a time like this, I wondered. Anyway, I thanked the good doctor once again and wished him a good morning. It was already way past midnight and I needed to get back.

After a sleepless few hours filled with trepidation, I phoned Sampie at around 8 am as he'd suggested. Maybe it was a little earlier than he said, but what the heck. Waving my apology aside, he told me Saba had responded well: she had eaten, which was a very good sign, and although she was still in a little pain, I could come and collect her that afternoon around 2 pm. A typical symptom of a dog recovering from a scorpion sting is a gagging cough repeated a few times a day, as if they are trying to bring up bile but don't have any to expel, he explained. Apparently this can last for up to a week, and the best part of this reaction is that it is a good sign: it means all is OK.

A couple of months later Saba had completely recovered. The calcium lump on her shoulder, which had been the size of a cuttlefish bone, had been completely absorbed by her system. She was now nearly seven months old, and I needed to take her in to the clinic for routine jabs. Afterwards, when I let Saba out on the lawn to sniff and investigate all the strange smells outside the clinic, a beaming Sampie took me around to his surgery where he opened his dispensary and proudly thrust a small vial into my hand. 'This is scorpion antivenom, from the first batch ever produced!' he said. He had ordered more, but at a cost of nearly R2 000 per vial he couldn't keep too much in stock. Cheap at the price, I thought, as I remembered Saba's agony. I would have paid any price for the antivenom had it been available at the time. What a relief to know that it was now available; I commissioned a vial to be on perpetual standby.

But this was not the end of the scorpion saga, not by a long shot; I had more anguish to endure. Venom was about to be unleashed into my ear for which there is no known antivenom! A couple of days after the incident my telephone rang: Agnes Jiroflee, Saba's breeder, had heard of Saba's ordeal. Expecting a polite enquiry about Saba's recovery and some words of commiseration for my 'pain and suffering', instead I was subjected to a tirade of patronising advice.

'Haven't you heard of ultraviolet scorpion flashlights?' she spat. 'You of all people should know about them: now go and buy a few, then make sure there are no scorpions around to sting my baby again!'

Well, I guess that message sank right in ... I now have five ultraviolet 'scorpion torches': one for each room and two spares!

About four months later, in the early autumn, we had another close encounter. It was late afternoon and shadows were lengthening as the autumn sun sank lower on the horizon. The incessant *zizz* of a billion cicadas began to fade as they handed the baton to coveys of crested spurfowl that were signalling the onset of roosting time: familiar sights and sounds at day's end in the South African bush. And like a hundred others that characterised the last summer, it was also hot and dry. Perfect conditions for a quick dip in the pool, I thought, as I called Saba outside to our carport. Before I'd clicked my fingers a second time she'd already leaped into the back of my Land Cruiser.

I drove down the familiar route to the Olifants River floodplain, a road Saba and I take every day to the office. While wending our way down the hill in the early morning we often come across herds of impala, waterbuck and zebra as they head up into the bushlands after spending the night on the relatively sparse river floodplain. Usually by mid-morning things have quietened down, and the sunbaked plains appear relatively desolate until late afternoon when the animals return there to sleep. Troops of baboons cross the open grassland, heading back to roost in the safety of the huge ebony and boer-bean trees that line the banks of the Olifants River.

Glancing in the rear-view mirror I could see Saba panting, and though her spoon-shaped tongue was doing a good job of regulating her body temperature, the excited wag in her tail told me she was anticipating a much more enjoyable way of cooling down. There was no surprising Saba: no amount of subtle suggestion or hidden hint could fool her; she knew exactly where we were headed. But I would try not to hype her up unduly, as this could lead to disappointment when on occasion the pool was occupied by shareholders and we'd need to give it a miss. At least then she'd have a mini game-viewing drive, going there and heading back home again. Saba always showed a keen interest in the game we drove past, particularly the herds of impala, which must have triggered some latent sheep-herding instinct in her. Though less woolly and a lot more agile, these were nevertheless flighty herd animals.

Having recently embarked on some routine thatch maintenance on a small cottage near the pool area, I thought I'd check on progress and give Saba a quick dip at the same time. She loves swimming, and since she was a tiny pup it has always been huge treat for her, particularly in a climate where she needs to be able to utilise any available water hole or wallow in the bush as a cooling aid. Being a Saturday meant that the thatchers would have finished at midday, and hopefully those few shareholders in residence had already headed out on an afternoon game drive, so we'd be disturbing no one and have the pool to ourselves for a while. However, we arrived to find things were not as quiet as we expected.

Approaching the parking area, I could see there were baboons on the lawn surrounding the pool. It was clear the lack of activity had also been an open invitation for our resident troop to make use of the facilities. I entered the clubhouse with Saba on a lead as I knew the sight of these primates so close to home would trigger her prey drive. As usual, the baboons had taken full advantage; they'd completely ignored the clearly marked 'His' and 'Hers' WCs and used the poolside paving instead. Needless to say, when they saw us they dropped a few more 'calling cards' in surprise as they vaulted over the fence and ran down the river bank barking and screaming. I waited until they were a good distance away before tossing a ball into the pool for Saba to retrieve.

Being somewhat distracted cleaning up the baboon poop on the poolside paving, I was caught completely off-guard when Saba climbed out, dropped the ball onto the lawn and made for the fence. Unbeknown to me, a huge baboon, which had hung back until now, had sauntered past in full view on the outside of the fence. The baboon's arrogant swagger and sideways glance was too much for Saba, and she gave chase before I could respond. Even so, I thought the electrified fence would stop her, as it usually did; ever since inadvertently getting shocked as a puppy she had been wary of its 'bite'. Unfortunately, the thatchers had forgotten to turn the power back on when they left for the day. Saba .must have sensed this and went through the strands chasing after the baboon, which was now hellbent on catching up with the rest of its screaming troop.

By the time I had jumped into the vehicle and driven around to the river floodplain some 300 metres away, it was all over. A huge donga blocked the vehicle's way, and despite my state of desperation I knew this one would be too much, even for the Land Cruiser. Unable to drive any further, I ground to a halt in a cloud of dust, quickly switched the motor off and climbed out. Other than the cacophony of the baboons fading into the distance, there was not a sound. Dry-mouthed I called out to Saba, desperately hoping to get a response while deep down expecting none. Fearing the worst, I unzipped the gun bag and shouldered my rifle. Stooping, I made my way along the floodplain trying to locate tracks in the fading light. I hadn't got too far when a movement caught my eye: it was Saba running up a hippo path on the other side of the gully towards me. At a distance all looked OK; she appeared to be running easily. But as she got closer I could see blood streaming from a gash on her flank and other smaller wounds near her rear end.

Reflexively I clicked my fingers, and she leaped effortlessly into the back of the Land Cruiser, but there was blood dripping everywhere; I needed to get her home quickly and stop the bleeding.

Trying to get a vet late on a Saturday afternoon in our area is no easy task. The only one who could help me was Gerrit. At my call he dropped everything and opened his surgery in preparation for Saba. Within an hour and a half she was on an operating table getting treated by one of the best surgeons in this field, eagerly assisted by yours truly, possibly the worst assistant in the field. But, given the circumstances, I could not possibly have wished for more. Under anaesthesia, and with the aid of the powerful theatre light, a thorough examination of her wounds was done, revealing the full extent of her injuries. Gerrit did the surgery while I helped him by monitoring Saba's breathing, blood pressure and heart rate. I also made a conscious effort in my apprehensive state not to ask too many stupid questions but rather let him get on with the nitty gritty of patching my dog's wounds.

Although rather nasty looking, the deep fang wounds on Saba's rump were largely muscle damage, and according to Gerrit the prognosis was good. He then lifted Saba's leg and showed me the smaller, not so obvious wound inside her groin, which could have killed her. The baboon's canines had only just missed her femoral artery: a close call indeed. Saba had come within 10 millimetres of bleeding to death on that dusty floodplain that afternoon; she would have been 18 months old.

Even as I asked the question, I knew what the answer was going to be: 'Will she learn from this traumatic event, Gerrit?'

With a wry smile, he turned to me. 'No, my friend, only you will: protective dogs and dogs with a high prey drive will always chase baboons; it's in their DNA!'

In fact, though I would have been reluctant to confess it to Gerrit, Saba was on the trail of rhino poachers less than nine days after the incident, her stitches still in situ!

Some time later I was watching her as she loped next to my vehicle on the training run we do almost every day. As always, I kept one eye on her and one on the road and adjacent bush. I always marvelled at her pulling power and athleticism, her love for running, and sometimes I'd become a little mesmerised by her motion. Next to me, between the seats, is my rifle; God knows what I carry it for on these runs, but I guess it gives me a measure of assurance … in that I'd rather have it and not need it, than need it and not have it … And so far, touch on wood, I have not needed it. As we rounded a smooth, sandy corner my peripheral vision caught the briefest glimpse of something unusual in the road. I jerked my head round and glanced dead ahead of the vehicle, and there in the road, not 50 metres ahead, were two huge male lions ambling straight towards us! Saba hadn't seen them, or was pretending she hadn't. I ground the vehicle to a halt and jumped out in front of the bemused lions. Leaving the door open, I pulled Saba around to the back of the vehicle, clicked my fingers and gave the command 'Up' – which simply meant, 'Jump on the back of the Land Cruiser as quick as you can, my girl, before we both become lion food!' To my relief she did exactly as instructed. With Saba safely on the back, I then turned to look at the road: the lions were gone, and the rifle was still between the seats. Not that I would have needed it for anything more than a shot in the air … at worst.

I am often asked about the possible threat to Saba from armed poachers. At the risk of seeming flippant, I am beginning to suspect, going on statistics alone, that she is more at risk of getting injured at home …

TRUST YOUR DOG:
'THE NOSE KNOWS'

Relentlessly persecuted and driven to the brink of extinction by man, only a fraction of the world's wolves now enjoy protection. These wild ancestors of today's domestic dogs still depend on an acute sense of smell for their continued existence. This is particularly evident in wilderness areas such as Yellowstone National Park in the USA where wolves have been successfully reintroduced and are doing very well. Well-established packs are living wild, using their noses for finding small food items or carrion, receptive mates, and to form the social bonding necessary to structure effective hunting packs. However, despite their protected status, which is confined to the park boundaries, they are becoming more dependent than ever on having a superb nose for their survival, particularly in the face of another ominous threat to their lives each time they wander beyond the protected zone.

From time to time pack dynamics can dictate that some wolves may lose their status and get pushed beyond the boundaries of the park, which is surrounded by domestic stock farms. Until they become established or form packs of their own, these individuals often enter private land where they inevitably come across domestic animals. Being apex predators, wolves do not distinguish between wild or domestic prey, and these efficient killers can take a considerable toll on the relatively easy-to-catch farm animals, which naturally brings them into direct conflict with man. Farmers determined to protect their livelihood use every means at their disposal to combat this threat. Subsequently, these nomadic wolves' survival now hinges almost entirely on their olfactory acuity, and many of them have learned to use their noses to detect hidden traps and avoid meat laced with virtually odourless poisons. Alas, even among wolves there will be individuals with better noses than others, so some do fall victim to man's deadly ploys. On the upside, I suspect the survivors will return to breed even sharper-nosed pups.

The canine nose is one attribute that has changed very little with domestication. By way of example, surmising a Maltese poodle is about as far from a wolf as one would care to breed, I would wager that their sense of smell is still as keen as a jackal's. An average dog has about 200 million olfactory receptors. A bloodhound has more than 250 million! A Belgian Malinois like Saba has about 220 million. Humans, by comparison, have 5 million. It's no wonder then that dogs' scenting ability is legendary, so much so as to seem unbelievable or even miraculous at times. Little wonder that the sceptics among us often believe the dog is wrong.

Saba was 11 months old when Roxanne Brummer of GreenDogs Conservation visited Balule. Although Rox had scheduled this follow-up visit with the other regional wardens' dogs, which she had trained and brought into the area, I too was keen to meet the 'Barbara Woodhouse of the bush'. Having heard so much about her success with dogs, naturally I was keen to observe her training methods at first hand and possibly get some advice on training Saba. It was most encouraging to hear about the efficacy and progress of her anti-poaching dogs deployed in Zimbabwe, Zambia and even further afield in Africa. What I found particularly fascinating was that some dogs had been trained to detect wire and cable snares.

Although I gleaned from the presentation that her training technique differed slightly from what I'd been doing with Saba, the objective remained the same. So when the other dogs had been given a brief lesson and the wardens shown how to continue with their training programme, I arranged with Rox for a quick session with Saba.

Early the following morning we drove out to my usual training area, which is not too far from our house. It's a quiet vale comprising raisin bush thickets and sandy game trails with gentle curves rather than sharp corners, ideal terrain for trailing. But today of all days a breeding herd of elephant was in the valley; they were feeding peacefully, which meant they could be there a while. I suggested we leave them to their breakfast and move on to the riparian woodland near the Olifants River instead. We stopped at a given point along the road, Roxanne and regional warden Frikkie Kotze got out of their vehicle, and, as we'd arranged, from there they would simply wave and walk away from us. After 10 minutes or so I was to put Saba on their trail. Saba had taken to Rox the moment she met her, so with her tail wagging my doting puppy watched her new friend disappear from view as the bush closed in behind them. I then let her down off the vehicle and placed her into her trailing harness, waited the agreed 10 minutes and set her onto their trail.

Saba's trail seemed to angle down towards the river, but I had a feeling that Rox and Frikkie would have avoided the water because of hippo and crocodiles. So I gently pulled on the lead, encouraging her to sniff along the trail I thought they would most likely have taken, which ran parallel with the floodplain. Again after about 50 metres Saba inclined back towards the river, but with more persistence. This time I let her follow her nose until I saw she was making straight for some boulders on the river's edge. I knew Saba loved the water, and since it was a warm morning possibly the prospect of cooling off was attracting her. By my sceptical reckoning, the rocky outcrop, being the only cover on the plain, was too close to the river itself, too exposed and perhaps too obvious a place to hide away from us. So once again I pulled her away, and once again Saba obliged and ran on the game trail that I encouraged her to, incredibly jumping clean over the carcass of a baby impala, showing absolutely no interest in it at all. Again after a couple of hundred metres on 'my' trail she strained on the lead, and again inclined back towards the river. Suddenly the lightbulb in my stubborn brain lit up; this was too determined, even for a puppy,

I thought. But it was too late! Frikkie and Rox were already walking up from the floodplain with that ho-hum look on their faces. They had given up waiting for us, thinking we'd gone in the opposite direction (which we had), and told me they had been there all the time, hidden behind the boulders; in fact they'd heard me talking to Saba and pulling her away, only metres from where they huddled.

If only I had listened to my dog … Strike one!

Since an eight-week-old pup, Saba had not known anything other than the warm, dry bushveld of Olifants River Game Reserve. It was where she'd lived and trained; it was the only environment she'd known until 12 months later when we took her with us on a short holiday to a slice of heaven, high up in the Drakensberg Mountains of KwaZulu-Natal, called Rainbow Lakes.

Our hosts, Olifants shareholders Liz Castle and Dr Neville Howes, were keen to see a trailing dog at work, even though at this stage of Saba's training it was still a huge game for her. Scent trailing was fun; it was exciting and of course rewarding. However, this part of the country is wet and cool, essentially a treeless terrain of rolling hills and mist-covered grassland (the antithesis of her training ground), so although I was a little apprehensive as to what effect it might have on her scenting, I was keen to see how she worked in cold conditions.

Liz and Meagan set off into the cold, mist-shrouded hills to lay a trail while Saba, Neville and I lounged in front of the cosy fireplace of the fishing cottage. I'd asked them to leave a tissue on the fence at the end of the paddock to mark the start of their trail; Saba and I would give them a 45-minute head start.

Locating the marker and a few trodden blades of grass which were already beginning to straighten, I gave Saba the tissue to sniff followed by the command '*Soek soek*'. Trailing confidently, she bounded over fresh molehills and field mouse tunnels, dropping her nose only momentarily when the direction of scent changed. Saba appeared to love the cool, damp conditions; I suspect this weather was reminiscent of her bloodline's country of origin. For her ancestors this was the norm, and true to the nature of this dog she adapted immediately to the calling.

I clung onto the 10-metre leather lead as the mist closed in, reducing visibility to less than 30 metres. After nearly a kilometre of trailing, a lone figure loomed ahead of us; as we got closer I recognised the cottage's housekeeper who had taken a short cut and was heading home over the hill. I immediately assumed Saba had mistakenly been trailing her scent, so I exerted control and changed direction. Despite Saba trying to pull me back onto course, we headed back to start the trail from scratch.

Again at the start of the trail Saba took off, and again in the same direction as earlier, but before I could correct her once more we came across Meagan and Liz walking back towards us. When I told them about the housekeeper and why I'd turned back, they said they'd seen her pass right by them, but because they were well hidden, she'd not seen them. Then as time passed they'd become concerned that Saba and I may not find them either and so decided to head back. It was then that I realised my mistake: Saba had been right all along; had I allowed her to, she would have passed the housekeeper, focusing on the tissue scent, and found Liz and Meagan. Although this was embarrassing for me at the time, I once again learned a valuable lesson regarding my working relationship with my dog.

Strike two!

From that day on I trusted Saba's nose ... Implicitly!

Many people confuse tracking with trailing. There are fundamental differences, as I will briefly try and explain. 'Tracking' is following visible signs; human beings like the San Bushmen, Shangaans and Apache are among the best at this. 'Trailing' is following a scent trail, and here nothing in our context can compete with a good dog. What about truffle-sniffing pigs, I hear you ask. Well, that's another ball game entirely, but I suspect that trailing poachers with a plump porker on a lead is simply not a practical option in the African bush. Not to mention the handler's dented ego.

We are finding that the early detection of incursions and follow-up hot pursuit operations are key to keeping poachers on the back foot. However, a few do slip through from time to time, and it is at this point that a good trailing dog comes into its own. By assisting our tracker's eyes with her nose, Saba is able to save precious time, time that would otherwise be wasted when poachers employ anti-tracking techniques that are undetectable to the human eye but can be picked up by a trailing dog.

Early one morning, less than a month after Saba bagged her first rhino poacher, our field rangers made contact with three poachers who had waded across the river early one morning. When challenged by our rangers, the poachers fled, but in their haste to get away they dropped a small backpack containing a pair of boots, a knife and some food. It was all we had as proof of their existence as the early dawn light and the thick riparian vegetation simply closed in behind them, and they melted away.

It is not often we get a scent article as fresh as a smelly pair of boots or, indeed, a sweat-soaked pack, and this was as good as it gets! Unfortunately, in their eagerness to catch the fleeing poachers, much of the trail was contaminated when our rangers gave chase, inadvertently mixing the scent. Despite this, Saba took the trail, leading us through the bush along the floodplain. Then, as if being yanked by an invisible cord, she inexplicably slowed down and angled sharply back towards the river, taking us to the water's edge. Through the reeds I could see a steep drop-off into the deeper sections of the river. As Saba was unaware of the danger from the huge crocodiles that lurk in these pools, I held her back and guided her through to the relatively shallow section instead. Initially I thought she'd wanted to get to the water because she was feeling the heat or needed a drink, or simply because she'd lost interest in the trail and wanted to play in the water ... I was wrong on all counts. Trusting Saba, I followed as she led us all along the river bank into another thick reed bed, where once again she tried to get into the water. This time I held her back for fear of crocodiles; however, my faith in her was resolute, so I instructed the rangers to head back upriver, cross the train bridge and check the bank opposite our position for exit tracks.

I must confess this was based on more than a hunch. I knew Saba could detect scent over the span of the Olifants River, but the trust I increasingly placed in her nose was underpinned by an event that had occurred nearly 10 years before, not too far from where we stood now. I recalled the incident as vividly as if it had happened yesterday. At the time fences were still up between ourselves and the Klaserie Nature Reserve, and we were compelled to provide supplementary feed for our rhino and buffalo through the winter months.

As it happened back then, I watched as more than a hundred buffalo stood on the opposite bank of our reserve. They had waded through to state land, on an old familiar migration route, and spent the night in search of grass on the northern perimeter of the region. Finding little, they had returned to the river where young shoots of Lowveld reeds, which grew on the sandy banks, offered some nourishment. Several of the older buffalo were standing in the shallows, seemingly undecided on whether to return to equally poor grazing prospects or to turn around and go further north: a perilous journey into the mining properties and more state-owned land. Who knows what goes on in the mind of an African buffalo?

The Olifants River was at least 200 metres wide at that point, and I had no way of enticing them back across. Somehow I needed to convince them of the supplementary feeding on offer on our side. Fortunately, a faint – ever so faint – breeze was drifting across, which gave me an idea. I split one of the lucerne bales I was carrying in the back of my Land Cruiser, then, climbing onto the roof of the vehicle, threw pieces of it as high as I could into the air. Most of it fell back to the ground, but some of the finer dust drifted on the wind. It was a long shot, but it was clear from their jittery attitude that the buffalo knew we were there, so they must have picked up our scent ... And I surmised that if they could smell us, they would most certainly smell the lucerne. In times like these, hunger overruled caution – the need to eat was greater – and within minutes, more than 140 buffalo were in the water, wading across to our side. What a sight it made, wild African buffalo coming towards me like cattle in a cowboy movie being rustled across the Rio Grande. Though it had been years since they had been fed lucerne through winter, they knew exactly what that dry lucerne dust promised and somehow communicated this to those too young to know. It was a promise we kept at the rate of 40 bales per day until the rains came.

Less than an hour later we received confirmation that the poachers had indeed crossed the river, directly opposite to where Saba had indicated. I had been spot-on in trusting her ability: she could smell where the poachers had climbed out of the water; her gaze pointed to exactly where they had crossed, something no eye could ever have picked up over the span of the Olifants River. Only an exceptional nose could have done that!

At great risk to themselves, the poachers tried to fool us by wading through the deeper section of the river, no doubt thinking we'd be covering the shallower water where incursions and retreats usually took place. However, with Saba having done her job she had saved our field rangers hours of needless tracking and backtracking. Though the rangers could now easily track the poachers, who had thrown caution to the wind and were running hard, they'd had an adrenalin-fuelled head start of two hours and were able to reach the main road before we could catch up with them. There, on the side of the road in the sand, were all the signs, as clear as if a detailed note had been left for us; they indicated that the poachers were picked up by an accomplice's vehicle. However, this time it was on empty stomachs and empty handed.

Having reiterated that one of a dog handler's greatest failings when trailing scent is to not trust your dog's nose, it is also true that a relationship can develop between a handler and their dog that is so close they can read each other's body language. In such an enviably close relationship a dog can be pulled and assisted to get back on the trail it has lost temporarily, particularly one that you have been able to verify by visual means – or indeed if information allows you to leapfrog, thereby saving precious time and getting the dog onto a fresher scent.

In certain circumstances a combination of dogs can be used to maximum effect, particularly in rounding off a scenting dog's efforts. Ideally, trailing dogs, such as a pack of American foxhounds, are released on the fresh scent trail. The pack is then followed by helicopter to keep pace. On board are at least three fresh attack dogs, such as Belgian Malinois and Dutch shepherds. These dogs are a popular choice for 'finishing things off', because although both breeds are excellent trailing dogs, they are super athletes and can be extremely effective attack dogs as well. When the foxhounds locate the rhino poachers the attack dogs are then released to help rangers secure an arrest. Nobody can hide or get away from a pack of Malinois!

In conversation with Richard Sowry, one of the senior rangers in the Kruger National Park, I was pleased to hear that dogs are being used more and more to track and apprehend rhino poachers. Richard is undoubtedly the most experienced ranger on the ground in the war against rhino poaching in the Kruger. He was also one of the first rangers to recognise the efficacy of using packs of dogs. His commitment and his success with canines have led to an exciting development in this regard. Overseas interest and funding have assisted this project in getting off the ground in a big way. In fact, so much progress has been made that a large K9 academy has been built at the Wildlife College near the Kruger Park's Orpen Gate. I told Richard that if I were a younger man the challenge of training and working with dogs of the calibre they have at this centre is something I would have loved to become involved with.

Talking of dog-loving game rangers, this chapter would be incomplete without a brief mention of Craig Spencer's Malinois, Shaya. This well-trained sniffer dog was given to him by the Wildlife and Environment Society of South Africa (WESSA), a valuable donation indeed as a professionally trained Malinois can fetch upward of R200 000! Not quite within the range of a game ranger's accessories budget. Needless to say, this was the least of Craig's reasons for becoming terminally besotted with his handsome new dog.

A year or so before acquiring Saba, I met Shaya for the first time one dark, humid night. As it happened, Craig and two of his student rhino monitors were parked at one of our larger water holes on Olifants investigating a static signal from one of the GPS rhino collars. This signal either meant the wearer was dead or had thrown the collar, or that there was a technical hitch. In any event, we all needed to determine the reason, one way or the other.

Craig and I stood there in the dark, chatting quietly, while some calculations were being made to determine the direction and distance of the signal. All the while Shaya lay quietly on the back seat of Craig's Land Rover.

Craig explained that Shaya was specifically trained to detect contraband, such as drugs, but now the focus of his training had been shifted to detect bullets, spent casings, ivory and rhino horn at roadblocks, airports and border posts. This was intriguing for me as at that stage I had no idea of the differences between sniffer dogs, trailing dogs and tracking dogs.

'Let him out, Craig,' I said.

'No, shit, Mario, I can't, he bites!'

'Relax,' I said. 'I'll stand next to my vehicle, and if he looks like he wants to eat me, I'll jump in.'

With that Craig opened the door and let Shaya out. It was really dark, so I was unable to get any warning; I could see no expression or sign of aggression, just his wagging tail and total devotion to Craig as he lay down next to him with a single command: *'Platz!'*

'Watch this,' Craig said, now a little more relaxed since Shaya had not shown any interest in taking a chunk out of me. Taking charge, he put Shaya into work mode immediately and asked me to stand away from my vehicle but leave the door wide open.

Using the same command I now use for Saba to take a trail, *'Soek soek!'*, Craig showed Shaya my vehicle. He then pointed to the area of the chassis between the front and back wheels ... strange place to direct a dog, I thought.

I was sceptical to say the least and expected this to go badly. First, because whenever you want to show someone how well your dog performs, something unforeseen will cause the 'trained' pooch to become distracted and not quite step up to the plate. And second, because I'd shot a couple of impala that morning for staff rations and knew that despite thoroughly washing the blood out of the back there would always be a vestige stuck away in some crevice missed by the scrubbing brush. I assumed Shaya would focus on that or indeed be distracted by the two dog pellets caught between the running board and doorjamb that I'd accidentally dropped when feeding the mangy jackal that day.

Shaya sniffed the chassis under the vehicle, went past the bloody smells of the tailgate with only a cursory sniff, then around to the driver's side where I was sure the pellets would stop him. He stood up on the running board and craned his neck into the cab, his chest directly over the two dog pellets. His tail wagged and he 'spoke'. Craig pulled him back, and we both peered in to see what he'd picked up and barked at. I was absolutely dumbstruck: it was the two spent .223 cartridge casings from the bullets I'd used to shoot the impala that day, and which I'd dropped in the footwell. All caution to the wind, I immediately stroked and patted this incredible dog; being bitten by such an intelligent animal would have been a privilege! Scars to show my grandkids? Alas, to this day, Shaya has never bitten me.

Malinois are canine athletes; they don't know what it is to slow down or take it easy. Everything is done at a frenetic pace. Even in play, they give it their all. Only a month after our meeting, Craig phoned to tell me that Shaya had injured himself in a tragic accident. He lost his footing at full speed playing near a dam in the Timbavati Nature Reserve, where he slipped and fell onto jagged rocks. The bones in his front left leg were smashed beyond repair. Craig was given two options: to have Shaya humanely put down or to have the leg amputated and keep his dog with only three legs. Without hesitation, he opted for the latter.

Craig's decision to keep Shaya gained him my deep respect as a person. And though, as he rightly claims, Shaya is essentially a sniffer dog and so will not need all his legs to do the job he was trained for, I know this rationale was way down Craig's list for keeping his beloved dog.

Saba's next call to duty led us to a familiar spot on the southern bank of the Olifants River. Recent weeks had seen a spate of incursions by three poachers whose presence on the reserve was only ever confirmed when our field rangers came across their tracks crossing the river, heading out. On one occasion, with their ghastly mission accomplished, they'd carried the horns of a poached rhino to the river bank at around midnight. Throwing all caution to the wind they set the backpack containing the horns down in the soft sand. Still warm, the sinus passage tissue hacked off along with the horn bled through, pooling in the indentation left behind. Then the killers calmly took off their shoes, shouldered the backpack, their axe and the rifle, waded into the river and exited the reserve. Arrogantly, as if in mocking defiance, and spiked with the euphoria of success, they did not bother to conceal their tracks, knowing we would only find their point of exit at first light, by which time they'd be long gone.

We knew from the tread patterns of their shoes that it was most likely the same three poachers each time, but we remained completely at a loss as to how or where they were gaining entry without us seeing something. The tally to date was six incursions, with this latest having resulted in the loss of a huge white rhino bull, something we ascertained by backtracking the poachers and locating the carcass, from which vital forensic evidence was then collected.

One morning I received a call from our rhino monitor, Lisa Trueman, and her team to say they had seen suspicious footprints in the soft floodplain soil close to the CARE primate rehabilitation centre across the river, not far upstream from my office. Admittedly I was rather sceptical of this information as it was nearly eight kilometres upstream from where poachers usually crossed, an area our field rangers seldom patrolled as it was a fair distance from our reserve's core white rhino habitat. But having learned over the years that when dealing with rhino poachers anything is possible, we went to investigate as a matter of course.

January was quick to pick up the spoor on our side and confirmed the estimated time of entry. Three people had indeed crossed the river into our reserve in the early hours of that morning. They wore shoes with patterns that were consistent with those we had become chillingly familiar with. Two wore All Star running shoes and one wore combat boots. This was the breakthrough we'd been looking for; this was where the bastards were coming in, where they'd being entering with impunity for months – and it was virtually under our noses!

On the river bank, in among some huge boulders, January pointed out where the suspects had sat down out of sight and put their shoes back on after wading through the river. I looked around and suddenly recognised the outcrop: these were the same random boulders Rox and Frikkie had hidden behind when simulating a poacher's trail for young Saba to follow, nearly two years previously! Who would ever have guessed it was at this point, along 18 kilometres of Olifants River frontage, that the poachers had chosen to cross.

Yet more irony unfolded as this time Saba was put onto the trail of the real thing within metres of where I'd ignorantly pulled her back from Rox and Frikkie's scent trail when she was little more than a puppy.

Although we were well into autumn, it seemed the sun was reluctant to relinquish its grip on summer. It was already past midday at this point; our best estimation had the poachers more than eight hours ahead of us, which gave them an edge. Keeping Saba wet helped keep her cool and focused on the scant scent trail which led us high into rocky terrain. On a ridge in the shade of a shepherd's tree we discovered where the poachers had sat down, rested and eaten some maize meal. The most interesting clue they'd left behind, besides a few maize crumbs, was a fly switch, which one of them had plucked from a silver raisin bush, the leaves of which had only just begun to wilt. This was as close as we'd been to these bastards for months!

Until shortly before that point, it was apparent the poachers had no idea we were closing in. However, when they saw the Jabiru aircraft quietly circling overhead, giving us air support, the suspects must have known we were onto them. Any plans this gang had been hatching were summarily abandoned as they swallowed a last mouthful of maize meal, turned and fled. Within an hour they'd made it back across the river, some four kilometres upstream, and escaped our pursuit. Adrenalin-fuelled, carbohydrate-loaded and fitter than most of us, it was impossible to keep up with them. Letting Saba go on the scent never entered my mind; even the real prospect of her catching up with the poachers without our encumbrance was not worth the risk. Bennie was in a meeting and the other helicopter was out. It just wasn't our day, but at least the rhino were safe for the time being, and this gang's entry point was now exposed.

Happy that they were put to flight with a determined show of force, I couldn't help wishing they'd gone to ground and chanced their luck, hoping to stay hidden until nightfall, in which scenario I'm sure Saba would have flushed them. After all, she had a point to prove – she had some unfinished business from when I mistrusted her nose at those same boulders over two years ago.

A CHRISTMAS TO REMEMBER

As far back as I can remember, the festive season in the Lowveld region has been the polar opposite of weather conditions traditionally associated with Christmas. What little wind dares to blow simply circulates the hot air like a fan in a huge convection oven. However, in the days leading up to the end of 2014, any ambient discomfort we may have felt was the least of our concerns; we were already sweating about something that would show no respite, irrespective of any drop in temperature or humidity.

Instead of the airwaves carrying messages of goodwill to all men, nothing but tidings of ill intent came filtering through on Christmas Eve. The butterfly-shaped leaves of the mopane trees fluttered ominously as the 'bushveld telegraph' warned of three rhino poachers planning an incursion into the reserve later that night. Apparently they would be entering Olifants North and 'the two rhino that walk together' were their target. Needless to say, the intimacy of the reference to these specific rhino had us particularly worried. At the same time I was concerned that this informant-sourced intelligence was unusually specific and could well have been misinformation thrown 'out there' purposely to mislead us.

Anxious doesn't begin to describe the prevailing mood among the anti-poaching rangers. So acting purely on a hunch we decided to focus on our own 'front line' – just in case. What little rain we'd received for the season had fallen intermittently and far too gently to cause the run-off needed to raise the level of the Olifants River. We knew that low water meant wading would be easy, and the poachers were coming, but exactly when and where along this extensive river front they would cross was anyone's guess.

As might be expected over the holidays, a number of our staff were on leave, including members of our field ranger anti-poaching unit, which left us rather thin on the ground. Essentially we were operating with a skeleton force, something that in all likelihood was also known to the poachers.

Dawn broke on that Christmas Day typically clear and windless. Although I'd been awake since 3.30 am, I had waited a couple of hours before contacting our field rangers posted at the bridge, asking them to check the floodplain very carefully for tracks. Sure enough, less than an hour later they informed me they'd located the spoor of three suspects who had crossed the Olifants into our reserve the night before. This meant the poachers had a head start on us of at least 10 hours! My chest tightened; I knew that in this game of cat and mouse 10 hours can be a lifetime.

Our field rangers were immediately alerted and mobilised, and then tactically deployed. Two of the men took a vehicle and moved to the river floodplain where the spoor was first detected. They would stay with our team of master trackers and provide logistical support, vehicle mobility, communications and supplies, et cetera. We needed to ascertain the general direction the tracks were headed in, and I needed a reliable link between our field rangers on the river and those deployed inland. We scoured the boundary firebreak of the general area, comprising approximately 150 square kilometres, where our rhino were known to be targeted.

Even without anti-tracking subterfuge, the aptly-named Klipheuwel (Stone Hill) area makes for extremely difficult tracking conditions. Added to this, the temperature was fast approaching 40 degrees, and any moisture evident in the scuffed earth was burned off to blend in quickly with the surrounding soil. Then, as the sun climbed to its midday position, there was little or no shadow being cast to reveal any vestige of spoor. However, persistence paid off, and by leapfrogging on the trail the team were able to determine that the poachers had crossed under the four pylons heading south-east into prime white rhino area.

I'd called for a helicopter at 6 am but the only one available was being used to work on a rhino elsewhere early that morning. In the meantime we carried on with strategic ground operations and deployment tactics. At about 10 am the deafening cacophony of cicadas quickly faded to background noise as the distant sound of a helicopter's rotor blades took centre stage ... what a comforting sound in a crisis! Seconds later Gerry McDonald of Big Game Heli swooped in with his R44 and was soon flying grid search patterns over the area.

When we are sure there is an incursion, it becomes a hot-pursuit situation. All the available field rangers are deployed in a focused man-hunt. And, whenever possible, we call in for helicopter support. This combination has proved to be the most effective disruptive tactic to thwart daylight poaching forays. The helicopter is there primarily to keep the poachers' heads down while we buy time tracking them and, secondly, to locate rhino carcasses ... if there are any. Nothing discourages even the most determined poachers from following through with their intended hunt quite like a helicopter in the air.

Flying a grid search pattern for over an hour revealed no carcasses and no vulture activity; instead we saw eight healthy rhino, four sable bulls in the wash below one of the main water holes, and a few buffalo wallowing in the mud near a windmill-fed pan. But this wasn't a game-viewing flight, nor did we hold out any hope of even a glimpse of our target: we all knew it was virtually impossible to detect a hidden poacher from the air. However, when field rangers and master trackers are able to pinpoint an area where they know poachers are hiding, we call in the heli. And while it hovers like a hawk eagle waiting for a partridge to break cover, the poachers are challenged and told to come out or else. This had worked well on two occasions in the Klaserie Nature Reserve, and six arrests were made like this.

To the best of my knowledge, no one I knew at the time had used dogs to trail rhino poachers successfully in this kind of situation on scent alone. And I remember thinking what a huge asset it would be, never dreaming that in a few hours my Saba would make local history.

We were flying over prime white rhino country, focusing on the area where the poachers were most likely to be at this point in time, hoping to pick up any clue to their general location. Incidentally, in all the Kruger Park's patrols and hot-pursuit operations, only once have hidden poachers been detected from the air. In this instance an Agusta helicopter had flown low over the poachers without seeing them. Then, losing his nerve, one of the poachers had pulled his exposed lower leg into the bush the rest of his body was concealed in. That tiny movement was spotted by a casual backward glance from a sharp-eyed ranger – and the rest, as they say, is history.

Primarily we use a helicopter to let the poachers know we know they are there and are determined to thwart their plans: most importantly, that if they shot a rhino we'd be onto them; it would be a showdown in which they'd be taken down and shown no mercy. However, having come straight to us from its earlier charter, the helicopter needed to head back to refuel. At around 45 degrees in the shade hunting conditions would be more difficult, even for determined poachers, so we predicted that they would rest up and try to kill a rhino in the hour or two before last light. To counter this, we'd planned to keep the helicopter in the air until sundown, so I asked Gerry to return at 5 pm. Tactics aside, I simply did not want to lose a rhino that day. Gerry is a family man and on Christmas Day I felt for him. But he never skipped a beat. Come to think of it, I have never seen him without a smile on his face.

Keeping cool was on every living creature's mind at the time (including the poachers'). It was so hot that your eyelids cooled over your eyeballs when you blinked; neither a leaf shook nor a creature stirred. It didn't take rocket science to figure out that prime focal points for rhino and the bastards intent on killing them would be the well-used water holes and cool mud wallows. On a hunch, I suggested to the team leader that he place a two-man team at each of the four water points in the area and provide surveillance cover at all the known rhino middens and scratching posts close by.

So while the rest of the world sat down to Christmas lunch and pulled crackers in celebration, our reserve's field rangers settled into their positions and concealed themselves in whatever shade they could find. There they sat, quietly sipping blood-warm water, watching and waiting. Back at home I sat down with the family for lunch and underplayed what was happening. I didn't want to spoil the day for them. Only Meagan, who reads me like a book, guessed that something was about to go down when she noticed I hadn't touched a drop of wine or champagne and had only eaten some cold smoked trout (which I cannot resist); I had even ignored the tempting trifle and Christmas pudding. I knew to stay hydrated and only eat lightly today.

After lunch, I went back to the Land Cruiser and checked my gear again. I pulled the portable radios, now fully recharged, out of their chargers and repacked the cooler with ice. The thermometer under the carport measured 42 degrees! I thought about my field rangers out in the bush and sympathised with them.

Saba was lying in the shade outside on the lawn. Ears cocked and panting, she was watching my every move – well, until distracted by my daughter Eleana, who came out to play with her. Saba will leave her food to play with a ball or frisbee. Besides play, Eleana has been responsible for all Saba's 'party trick training', namely, high fives and lately, using both front paws, high tens! She has the uncanny knack of eliciting complete focus from Saba and is able to train her with minimum effort. Maybe one day I will headhunt her from her accounting firm and have her go into full-time dog training with me.

At about 3 pm, the two field rangers at the water hole known as Mbiri Dam saw one of the poachers, stripped to his waist, furtively approach the water's edge on the other side of the dam. Hearts pounded noisily in their chests as they watched an embodiment of the status these treacherous poachers had earned as apparitions crouched at the water's edge filling a water bottle. Here was a hot, thirsty man in plain sight, not a nocturnal phantom with the magical power of invisibility. Just then the radio, which had been silent up until that point, crackled into life, shattering the sticky silence. The poacher and his two comrades immediately took off, running through the bush in the direction of the four power lines.

Knowing the poachers were not superhuman, that they not only felt the heat but also the fear of being pursued and captured, the field rangers gave chase with renewed vigour. But with a head start of nearly 200 metres, the bush closed in behind the fleeing men, quickly absorbing them and any signs of their passage.

At least we had an immediate point of departure and a direction; most importantly, the poachers were on the run with escape rather than rhino poaching on their minds. Racing to a strategic point near an expansive open area known as Jackal Plains took just over 15 minutes in the Cruiser. Here I waited, commanding a 360-degree view and hoping to get a glimpse of the poachers as they made a run for the river – but no such luck. The thinking then was that the poachers had decided to keep to the thick bush, so I made my way to meet up with the team leader and some of his rangers. They had tried to leapfrog the poachers and were much further north along the four pylons, hoping to cut off their escape.

When I caught up to the team, I could see they were dangerously dehydrated. In the excitement of the chase they had focused on the job at hand and neglected to stay hydrated. Nevertheless a few litres of cold water, Coke, energy bars and Jubes from my grab-bag soon had them replenished. I radioed Olifants' base and asked to have more water and ice brought from the office, together with a spare ground-to-air radio for those teams following the poachers; no doubt they would need it to communicate to Gerry in his helicopter later on.

While everyone caught their breath, I decided to call the helicopter in earlier than scheduled. At 4 pm, Gerry and the team leader were circling over the Mbiri Dam area. The aerial search was supported by one of our neighbouring landowners in his fixed-wing Jabiru. Circling over the area where the first contact with the poachers was made, the helicopter crew spotted a day pack and some clothing on the ground. Those field rangers closest to that point were then quickly called in and directed to the location in order to secure it.

I'd also picked up this communication on my radio and raced along a short cut I knew of that would shave minutes off the usual route. I was more than just a little curious to get a look at the bag and its contents: at last here was something tangible at least, and sweaty and stinky at best. Arriving at the scene, I found the area swarming with field rangers, milling about like a pack of foxhounds waiting for the master of the hounds to finish his sherry, sound the bugle and commence the hunt. Needless to say the poachers' scent, or rather what was left of it, had been inadvertently contaminated by our own men's spoor. The wash from the helicopter rotors and the hot, dry conditions didn't help matters either. Nevertheless, I phoned Meagan and asked her to load Saba and meet me under the four pylons as soon as she could.

About 20 minutes later Saba was with me. Quickly slipping on her tracking harness, I took her to where the helicopter had first located the bag. Belgian Malinois have particularly expressive ears, and the attitude of hers spoke volumes. Saba had never seen so many field rangers at one location. The atmosphere was filled with expectation, and she could sense this was not a routine training exercise, particularly when I pulled a shirt belonging to one of the poachers from the pack and used it as a scent clue for her to sniff. Saba needed no more than a whiff for her brain to register the scent and memorise it. 'Soek soek,' I told her, and she set off at a run, with me trailing her on the end of the 10-metre tracking line. Following closely behind me were three armed field rangers, which was reassuring to say the least. Besides a two-way radio and my cell phone, all I carried was plenty of water for Saba: even though it was cumbersome and heavy, I knew it was essential. It was still sweltering hot, and I had no idea how long we would be on the poachers' trail.

After about a kilometre of confident trailing, Saba stopped and, turning hard to the right, stuck her nose into a dense thicket. Oh shit! I thought, hoping it wasn't a sounder of warthogs, which love to lie under just this type of dense thicket to get out of the heat. With hair bristling on her back and rump, she barked at what appeared to be a small, greenish bag wedged deep in the dense tangle of undergrowth. Gathering the slack on the tracking line, I moved in closer to investigate; it was then that the 'bag' moved! Saba could hardly contain herself: something in her prey drive registered that this was a potentially dangerous situation ... I'd never seen her like this before. As I strained to focus through sweat-filled eyes, I could see this 'bag' was in fact a greenish overall trouser leg, the wearer of which blended invisibly into the darkness of the undergrowth. This was all I could make out, until the form of a man began to emerge, half crawling, half wriggling, all the while trying to lift his hands in surrender. However, the bush was so thick it hampered his attempts to do much more than lie there while three rifles were trained on him and Saba 'held' onto his ankle. He begged for mercy and apologised profusely as the field rangers dragged him out into the open and placed him in handcuffs. Then, making him more comfortable on his knees, he was offered water and treated with a tad more empathy than he'd planned to show our rhino that day.

'A bird in the hand' was not worth the two still lurking in the bush as far as we were concerned. And now, motivated in no small measure by Saba's success, we all wanted to capture the other poachers as well. So while a team of field rangers focused on the arrested suspect, a pair of smelly trousers was pulled from his pack and shoved in Saba's face. Once again the magical words were uttered and again she took off at a run. We tracked with her for another kilometre or so, heading north on the trail of the other two suspects, and although Saba was tracking at a slower, more deliberate pace, we simply could not keep up with her. At this point everyone was absolutely exhausted. We needed to accept that our enthusiasm had exceeded our physical ability, so with the light fading, we reluctantly called it a day. I later found out that both the shirt and the pants belonged to the suspect who Saba had already located; what she was now trailing were merely the dregs of association and the rapidly dwindling scent left by the other two when they ran through the bush.

I looked at the suspect's ID book, did a quick calculation and realised just how old I was, but I was pleasantly surprised at how good I felt for 58. It is astonishing what adrenalin can do to a spent old body! Despite having run for a couple of kilometres behind a Belgian Malinois hellbent on catching rhino poachers, I felt light on my feet and swollen with pride at Saba's incredible achievement ... nothing else in the world mattered at that point.

The day's heat began to relent as the sun began to lose its brassy glare. I went over to the suspect and made sure the handcuffs were secure. Shortly afterwards, the team leader loaded him into the van and drove him to the police station in Hoesdpruit, where he was duly charged and processed.

There were a number of positives to take away from this incident. Most importantly, no rhino were lost that day, and the morale of our field rangers was lifted high as a result. Useful information was gleaned from the suspect while he was held in custody, and his cell phone provided a number of leads to further investigations. For me, one of the most important results of the day's success was the message about the suspect's experience on Olifants. This is a word-of-mouth message that will spread from tavern to tavern and from one beer hall to another. Inadvertently, he will become our greatest ambassador by instilling caution in the minds of any wannabe poachers contemplating giving us a go. Olifants River Game Reserve will become known as a place to avoid, where you are literally 'hounded down' and caught; where, despite the conditions, no quarter will be given and no expense spared in the effort to protect the rhino.

Last but not least was Saba's role in that day's success. For most K9s this result ranks up there with those 'once in a lifetime' achievements. Rhino poachers are elusive and unpredictable trail layers: they give nothing away; every tiny clue is hard won. Trailing elusive killers in the sweltering African bush, as Saba did that day, has to be the epitome of a tracking challenge for any dog. Countless hours of focused training since she was eight weeks old were brought to bear and, when combined with her inherent qualities, culminated in success. Saba came of age at just 17 months old!

I got home and celebrated, but not in the conventional sense, rather I gathered my family, including Saba, around me, poured myself an ice-cold Windhoek Light and relayed the afternoon's events in as much detail as I could remember. Obviously Saba will never know what she had achieved that day; to her I suspect this was not much more than a seriously fun but rather intense 'soek soek'. Her tail wagging and ears back, she now appeared to be more focused on the dish of roast turkey thrust in front of her ... gravy and all! Meagan had gone to considerable pains roasting the huge bird in a somewhat temperamental oven, but was quick to help carve off pieces to be chopped up and given to Saba. Each of us had sacrificed some of our turkey for her. After all, she was also one of the family, and it was Christmas Day.

I was overwhelmed with her achievement, and though I seldom post anything on social media, I thought to post the simple image taken on my cell phone of her success and to share it with those who visited my Facebook page. Accompanying the photo, which went viral, I wrote the following: 'Most of you woke on Christmas day to find Santa's boot prints in the snow after he'd filled your stockings with presents. I too found boot prints on Christmas morning, but these were not Santa's and they were not in the snow ... These were the footprints of rhino poachers left in the sand when they entered the reserve in order to kill rhino. Despite extremely difficult conditions, and at a little over 17 months, Saba rose to the occasion. On her first attempt at the real thing, she successfully trailed the suspects, resulting in an arrest and no rhino lost ... How could I possibly wish for more?'

To my utter amazement this post was viewed by nearly 1.3 million people, from every corner of the globe, in less than four days, and there were more than 5 000 'likes' posted! What this proved beyond any doubt was that as great as the world's love for our canine companions and their achievements was the universal abhorrence of rhino poachers. I hypothesise from this reaction that a lynch mob comprising 1 000 social media users, from all corners of the globe and from all walks of life, would be virtually unanimous in their selection of a candidate for the noose.

Recognition of excellence manifests in many ways: awards, medals, prizes and certificates of achievement. Saba needed none of these trappings as a measure of her ability. These days my grab-bag has a companion: a second smaller bag added to what I grab, which comprises a day pack containing all the spare equipment Saba may need out in the bush, including two litres of water, a spare harness and lead, a plastic bowl, tinned dog food, biscuits and a towel. And despite her achievement and a flood of congratulations, I was most humbled by a single compliment paid to Saba by her breeder. Agnes drove all the way from Johannesburg to visit Saba for a couple of days and, like a doting grandmother who just couldn't get enough of her granddaughter, I saw genuine pride and love for 'her' dog.

Recently I was contacted by Lente Roode who owns Kapama. This huge game reserve just outside Hoedspruit is home to a number of rhino that, needless to say, have also been targeted by poachers. In desperation, Lente turned to Jonathan Swartz who, as I said earlier, helped me with Saba's basic training when she was a puppy. Lente told me that Jonathan had suggested she contact me for some background on Saba as an example of what could be achieved: for practical advice and suggestions as to which canines and what training focus she would need in their particular situation.

What a compliment! However, before strutting around with my chest out, I had to ask myself whether this was as a result of Jonathan's faith in me as his protégé, or in the Malinois' ability. I strongly suspect it was the latter.

Like fishermen who don't give away a good fishing hole's location, the independent gangs of poachers clearly don't share information on rhino whereabouts or anti-poaching details. The result is that they unknowingly enter the reserve to risk it all for a chance to kill a rhino, as we found out when, exactly one month after the Christmas Day incident, another incursion occurred and the same area was targeted by rhino poachers. Again, early detection by our foot patrols and helicopter patrols, sponsored by shareholders of the reserve, were effective in letting the poachers know that we knew they were there and were now hunting *them*.

Frikkie Kotze brought his bloodhound, Ranger, in on the faint chance of getting a scent trail. His bloodhound 'sounded' as only these wonderful hounds can do. Any poacher crouched in hiding within a kilometre radius would have heard the baying and known someone had 'let the dogs out'. Saba joined Ranger on the trailing patrol, but with no scent clue to follow, we were simply hoping for the best. Neither dog picked up anything positive, but both appeared to be trailing a faint airborne scent that led in the same general northerly direction, indicating the poachers had done an about-turn and headed back to the river. Trusting the dogs' noses, as I have learned to do, this gave us a modicum of comfort that at least no poachers would be targeting our rhino that day.

It was now midday and the heat was beginning to exert its limiting role on K9 performance, so without anything strong to trail we called it quits. I got back to Olifants in time to drop off Saba, attend to a wounded zebra, take a quick shower and rendezvous with our reserve's chairman as together we drove off to attend a Balule Nature Reserve committee meeting.

Later that night one of the camera traps sent us a chilling image of the three poachers we had chased that day. All were leaving empty handed but were clearly armed and ready for any possible confrontation with our field rangers. We must have rattled them that morning, and as a result they appeared to be anticipating an ambush. Anyway, at the very least we could sleep easy ... for a while.

Until the new year's onslaught, which, thanks to Saba, we will be that much more ready to tackle.

... And there are no prizes for guessing what my New Year's Resolution is going to be.

ACKNOWLEDGEMENTS

Writing this book has been an important undertaking. It has also been an opportunity to pay tribute to those faceless men and women in the front line of the war against rhino poaching, mostly battle-hardened rangers, who stand resolute while defending an island of wildlife in a sea of crisis. Penetrating the shroud of modesty and understatement to reveal the realities beneath the veneer of romanticism generally associated with this illustrious career has been a privilege. I have also made mention of people on the security front who have been integral to its compilation. To those colleagues and associates, too numerous to list individually here, and for fear of inadvertently leaving someone out, I use collective terms such as the Balule regional wardens and their field rangers, Protrack's anti-poaching units and the Black Mambas. To you all, I wish to convey my sincere gratitude.

The ability to track rhino poachers, who use every anti-tracking tactic known to escape detection, is undoubtedly one of the most useful skills we employ. Olifants' team of field rangers, in particular the unequalled, expert tracking ability of January Mahlaule, combined with Joachim Timani and Jabulaan Makhubedu's instincts, are singled out with accolades and sincere gratitude. Their ability to think like poachers has led to hundreds of disrupted forays and a number of dramatic arrests. Needless to say, as a result this team has been directly responsible for saving the lives of many rhino.

My sincere gratitude goes to Craig Spencer for his pragmatic approach and dedication to nature conservation. Besides his responsibilities as CEO of Transfrontier Africa, he steers the rudder at the helm of Balule's wardens' committee with a firm hand, wickedly quick wit and sense of humour. Craig also conceived and manages the now world-famous Black Mambas all-women anti-poaching team. And, biased as this may seem, he has earned my personal respect for his unconditional love of his three-legged Malinois named Shaya.

Thank you to the WWF's Dr Jacques Flamand for his faith in the Balule wardens' ability to conserve and manage some of the most threatened and beleaguered animals in the world. Monitoring Balule's rhino on a daily basis has been vital to their management and security. To this end, my grateful appreciation to Sinhle Mathebula, Leonie Hofstra, Lisa Trueman and Zala Hajdinjak, all of whom have endured the often difficult conditions associated with gathering data in the bush. Then to Melodie Ahlers, who compiles the data in informative monthly reports, thank you.

Thanks to Johan Grobbelaar and the late Jason Sherwood, who took on the arduous task of policing the most hostile regions with good effect. Also to Vincent Barkas and Shaene Tintinger of Protrack, who take charge of the autopsies associated with poaching incidents. Thank you for doing this unenviable but necessary task.

My grateful thanks to the wildlife vets we depend on, all of whom at very short notice, and often under trying circumstances, come to our calls for assistance. Namely: Dr Peter Rogers, his assistant Janelle Goodrich, Dr Gerrit Scheepers, Dr Sampie Ras and Dr Hein Müller.

A huge debt of gratitude for the quick response to our requests for airborne assistance by Big Game Heli's intrepid helicopter pilots: the late Benjamin Osmers (Bennie), Zander Osmers, Gerry McDonald and Marcus Philip. These machines in the hands of these men are key to our anti-poaching efforts and general wildlife conservation work. I dread to think what we'd do without them.

This is yet another opportunity to thank the Olifants River Game Reserve's board members and shareholders for placing their trust and resolute faith in my management of our field rangers to take care of their piece of Africa and all its wildlife.

ACKNOWLEDGEMENTS

I am encouraged by, and grateful for, the world's increasing awareness and abhorrence of the killing of its endangered wildlife. Not the least being the NGOs that raise funds to combat rhino poaching through exposure and awareness campaigns.

There is a sense of superiority bordering on extreme arrogance that prevails among some of the world's most populous and intelligent peoples, who paradoxically believe in the traditions and medicinal powers of rhino horn. Worse, it is perceived as their 'right' to acquire rhino horn, by whatever means, while fully cognisant of the dire consequences left in the wake to fulfil these spurious needs! I believe that in the near future those directly responsible for the extinction of a species will be called to an international court to account for their crimes: acts that may soon be viewed in the same light as genocide and war crimes are today. The more support we can muster the better.

To the little girl whose name I cannot recall, who sent $2 all the way from the USA to bolster our rhino anti-poaching fund! And not to forget those individuals who have made relatively large donations in difficult financial times. Thank you ... 'Little drops of water, little grains of sand ...'

In Italian culture it is all about *la famiglia*. And that's what the team at Jonathan Ball Publishers have become. My gratitude to all involved with this, my third publication. To publishing director Jeremy Boraine, whose guidance regarding the subject material for this book has been invaluable. Commissioning editor Sophy Kohler was emotionally moved by the importance of the content, which alone would have been enough to warm my heart. In addition, editor Frances Perryer later added that the manuscript had a 'very good feel'. Knowing how absorbed Frances became in editing the manuscript, it was the cherry on top for me. The layout and setting of the publication will be in the skilled hands of Ceri Prenter and Kevin Shenton, for which I am grateful.

And last, but by no means least, thanks to my tolerant family. To my children Eleana and Dino and my wife Meagan who have endured the countless hours of my burning midnight oil in its compilation ... and of course my beloved dog Saba, whose achievements have made me extremely proud.